Nelson Mathematics 4

Nelson Mathematics 4

Series Authors and Senior Consultants
Mary Lou Kestell • Marian Small

Senior Authors
Heather Kelleher • Kathy Kubota-Zarivnij • Pat Milot
Betty Morris • Doug Super

Authors
Carol Brydon • Andrea Dickson • Catharine Gilmour
Elizabeth Grill-Donovan • Jack Hope • Wendy Klassen • David Leach
Pat Margerm • Gail May • Scott Sincerbox • Debbie Sturgeon • Rosita Tseng Tam

Assessment Consultant
Damian Cooper

THOMSON
NELSON

Australia   Canada   Mexico   Singapore   Spain   United Kingdom   United States

THOMSON
NELSON

Nelson Mathematics 4

Series Authors and Senior Consultants
Mary Lou Kestell, Marian Small

Senior Authors
Heather Kelleher,
Kathy Kubota-Zarivnij, Pat Milot,
Betty Morris, Doug Super

Authors
Carol Brydon, Andrea Dickson,
Catharine Gilmour,
Elizabeth Grill-Donovan, Jack Hope,
Wendy Klassen, David Leach,
Pat Margerm, Gail May,
Scott Sincerbox, Debbie Sturgeon,
Rosita Tseng Tam

Assessment Consultant
Damian Cooper

Director of Publishing
David Steele

Publisher, Mathematics
Beverley Buxton

Senior Program Manager
Shirley Barrett

Program Manager
Colin Bisset

Developmental Editors
Brenda McLoughlin
Linda Nigro
Michael Tabor
Robert Templeton
Susan Woollam

Developmental Consultants
Jackie Williams
Mary Reeve

Editorial Assistants
Christi Davis
Darren McDonald
Matthew Sheehan

Executive Managing Editor, Development & Testing
Cheryl Turner

Executive Managing Editor, Production
Nicola Balfour

Senior Production Editor
Linh Vu

Copy Editor
Julia Cochrane

Senior Production Coordinator
Sharon Latta Paterson

Production Coordinator
Franca Mandarino

Creative Director
Angela Cluer

Art Director
Ken Phipps

Art Management
ArtPlus Ltd., Suzanne Peden

Illustrators
ArtPlus Ltd., Andrew Breithaupt,
Steven Corrigan, Deborah Crowle,
Vesna Krstanovic, Sharon Matthews

Interior and Cover Design
Suzanne Peden

Cover Image
Corbis/Magma

ArtPlus Ltd. Production Coordinator
Dana Lloyd

Composition
Valerie Bateman ArtPlus Ltd.

Photo Research and Permissions
Vicki Gould

Photo Shoot Coordinators
ArtPlus Ltd., Trent Photographics

Printer
Transcontinental Printing Inc.

National Library of Canada Cataloguing in Publication Data

Nelson mathematics 4 / Mary Lou Kestell ... [et al.].

Includes index.
For use in grade 4.
ISBN 0-17-625969-4

1. Mathematics—Textbooks.
I. Kestell, Mary Louise
II. Title: Nelson mathematics four.

QA135.6.N444 2003
510   C2003-902088-6

Advisory Panel

Senior Advisor

Doug Duff
Learning Supervisor
Thames Valley District School Board
London, Ontario

Advisors

Donna Anderson
Coal Tyee Elementary School
Nanaimo, British Columbia

Keith Chong
Principal
School District #41
Burnaby, British Columbia

Anne Cirillo
Consultant
Toronto Catholic District
School Board
Toronto, Ontario

Attila Csiszar
Math Helping Teacher
Surrey School District #36
Surrey, British Columbia

David P. Curto
Principal
Hamilton-Wentworth Catholic
District School Board
Hamilton, Ontario

Marg Curto
Principal of Programs, Elementary
Hamilton-Wentworth Catholic
District School Board
Hamilton, Ontario

Edna Dach
Director Instructional Services
Elk Island Public Schools

Wendy Dowling
Peel District School Board
Mississauga, Ontario

Lillian Forsythe, B.Ed., B.A., M.Ed.
Regina, Saskatchewan

Peggy Gerrard
Dr. Morris Gibson
Foothills School Division
Okotoks, Alberta

Mary Gervais
Durham Catholic District
School Board

C. Marie Hauk, Ph.D.
Consultant
Edmonton, Alberta

Rebecca Kozol
Maple Ridge School District #42
Maple Ridge, British Columbia

A. Craig Loewen, Ph.D.
Mathematics Education
University of Lethbridge
Lethbridge, Alberta

Frank Maggio
Mathematics Curriculum Consultant
Halton Catholic District
School Board
Burlington, Ontario

Moyra Martin
Principal
Msgr. O'Brien School
Calgary Catholic School District
Calgary, Alberta

Janet Millar Grant
Ontario

Meagan Mutchmor
Consultant
Winnipeg School District #1
Winnipeg, Manitoba

Mary Anne Nissen
Consultant
Elk Island Public Schools
Sherwood Park, Alberta

Darlene Peckford, B.Ed., M.A.
Principal
Taber, Alberta

Kathryn Perry
Peel District School Board
Brampton, Ontario

Susan Perry
Consultant
Durham Catholic District
School Board
Oshawa, Ontario

Bryan A. Quinn
Consultant
Edmonton Public District
School Board
Edmonton, Alberta

Ann Louise Revells
Vice-Principal/Teacher
Ottawa-Carleton Catholic
School Board
Ottawa, Ontario

Evelyn Sawicki
Mathematics Consultant
Calgary, Alberta

Lorraine Schroetter-LaPointe
Program Facilitator
Durham District School Board
Whitby, Ontario

Nathalie Sinclair, Ph.D.
Simon Fraser University
Faculty of Education

Susan Stuart
Professor
Nipissing University
North Bay, Ontario

Joyce Tonner
Learning Coordinator
Thames Valley District School
Board
London, Ontario

Stella Tossell
Mathematics Consultant
North Vancouver, British Columbia

Sandra Unrau
Principal
Calgary Board of Education
Calgary, Alberta

Gerry Varty
Math Coordinator
Wolf Creek School Division #72
Ponoka, Alberta

Michéle Wills
Calgary Board of Education
Calgary, Alberta

Reviewers

Mary Adams
Thames Valley District School Board

Michael L. Babcock
Limestone District School Board

Anne Boyd
Campbell River School District 72
British Columbia

James Brake
Peterborough, Victoria,
Northumberland, Clarington,
Catholic District School Board

Nancy Campbell
Rainbow Board of Education

Deborah Colvin-MacDormand
Edmonton Public District School
Board

Anna Dutfield
Toronto District School Board

Linda Edwards, B.A., B.Ed.
Toronto District School Board

Susan Gregson
Peel District School Board

Susannah Howick
North Vancouver School District

Julie Keough
Waterloo Catholic District
School Board

Wendy King
Avalon West School District

Joan McDuff
Faculty of Education
Queen's University

Ken Mendes
Ottawa, Ontario

Gillian Rudge
Richmond School District

Naomi Young, B.P.E., B.Ed., M.E.
Lewisporte Gander School
District #6
Newfoundland and Labrador

Rose Scaini

Aboriginal Content Reviewers

Brenda Davis
Education Consultant
Six Nations

Moneca Sinclaire, M.S.E., M.Sc.

Laura Smith
School District #34
Abbotsford, British Columbia

Perry Smith
District Teacher,
Aboriginal Education
School District #34
Abbotsford, British Columbia

Equity Reviewer

Arlene Campbell
Toronto District School Board
Educator
York University Doctoral Candidate

Literacy Reviewer

Dr. Roslyn Doctorow
Educational Consultant

*Thank you to the following
teachers for testing the
Chapter Tasks.*

Mary Lynne Alderdice
Niagara District School Board

Sonja Atwood
Central Okanagan School District 23

Rick Beetstra
Richmond School District 38

Kevin Corcoran
Peel District School Board

Anna Dutfield
Toronto District School Board

Lena Giorgio
Peel District School Board

Susan Gregson
Peel District School Board

Kelly Joel
Peel District School Board

Don Jones
Peel District School Board

Catherine Niven
Niagara District School Board

Kim Philip
Peel District School Board

Bryan Wood
Peel District School Board

Contents

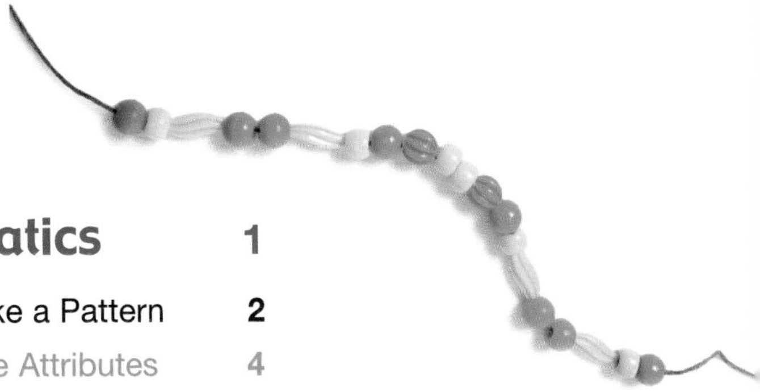

CHAPTER 1

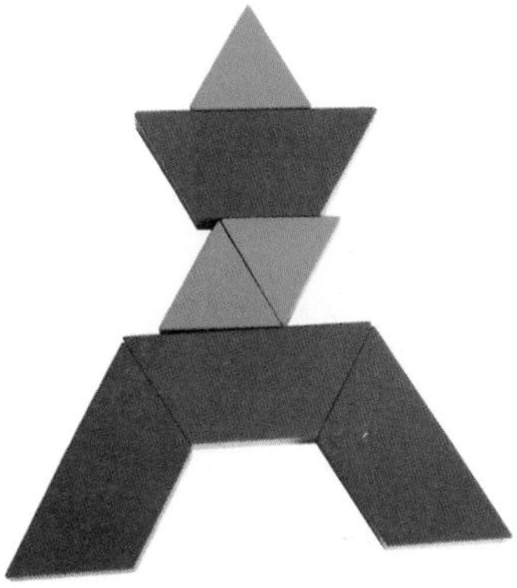

CHAPTER 2

- Guided Activity
- Direct Instruction
- Exploration

CHAPTER 3

Data Management   55

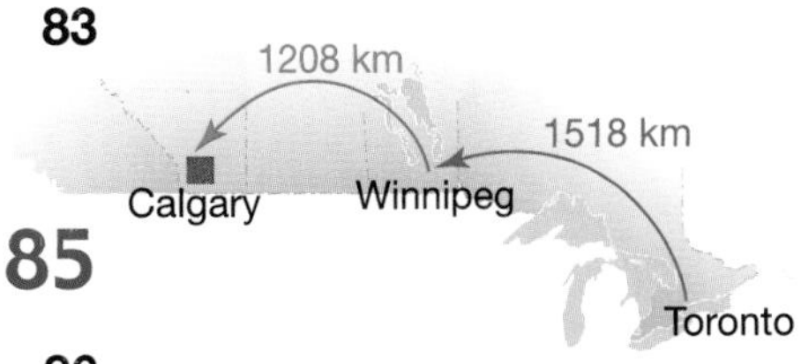

CHAPTER 4

Addition and Subtraction — 85

1208 km

1518 km

Calgary Winnipeg

Toronto

$37.67 $14.53

■ Guided Activity
■ Direct Instruction
■ Exploration

CHAPTER 5

Measuring Length and Time

CHAPTER 6

Multiplication and Division Facts

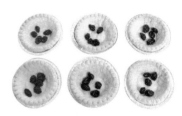

CHAPTER 7

2–D Geometry 179

■ Guided Activity
■ Direct Instruction
■ Exploration

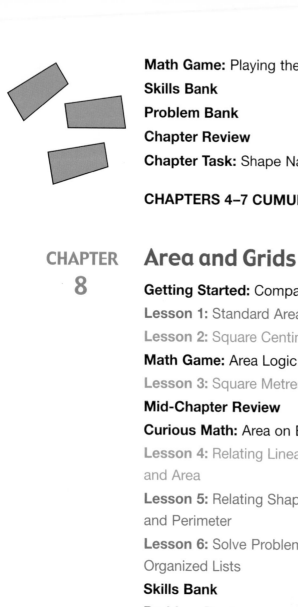

CHAPTER 8

Area and Grids   209

CHAPTER 9

Multiplying Greater Numbers   233

CHAPTER 10

Dividing Greater Numbers   261

■ Guided Activity
■ Direct Instruction
■ Exploration

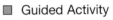

CHAPTER 11

3-D Geometry and 3-D Measurement   291

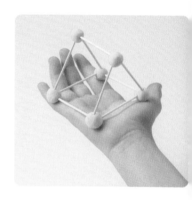

CHAPTER 12

Fractions and Decimals   321

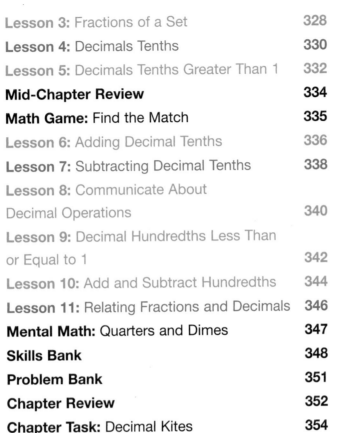

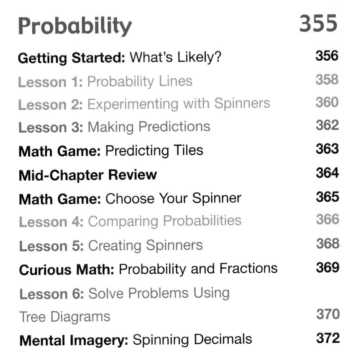

☐ Guided Activity
☐ Direct Instruction
☐ Exploration

CHAPTER
14

Patterns and Motion in Geometry 379

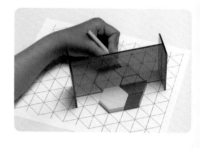

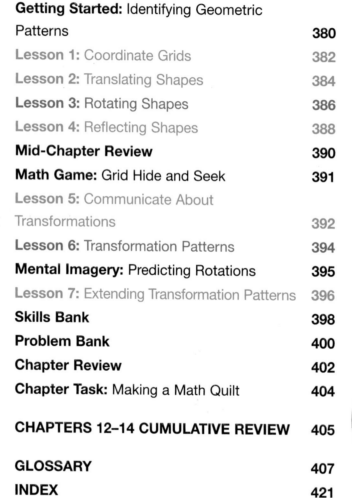

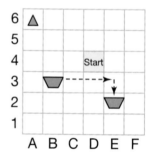

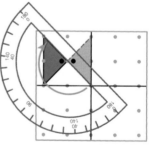

■ Guided Activity
■ Direct Instruction
■ Exploration

Patterns in Mathematics

Goals

You will be able to

- identify, extend, and create number and shape patterns

- describe how a pattern starts and how it can be extended

- create charts to identify and extend patterns

- look for patterns to solve problems

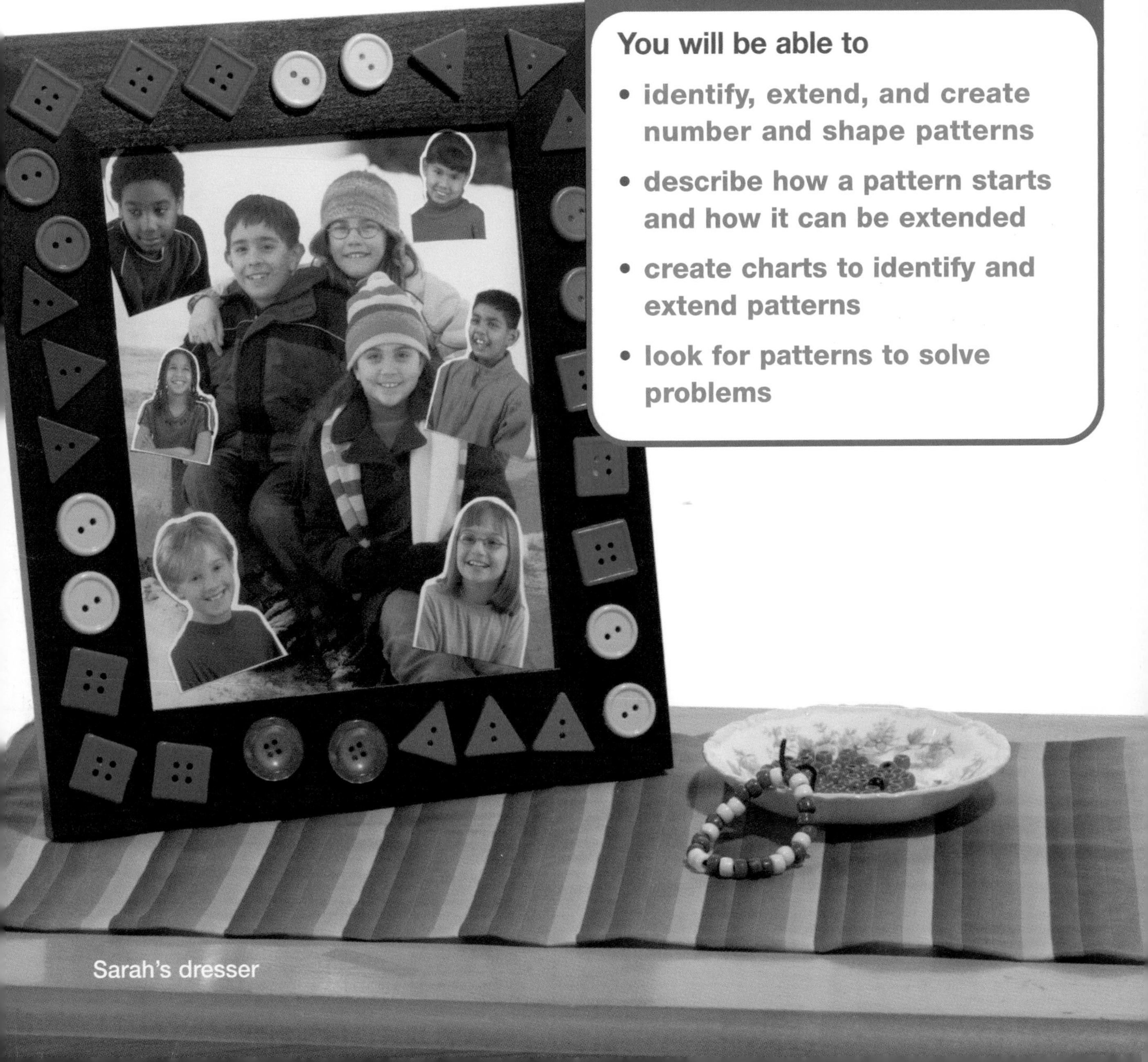

Sarah's dresser

Getting Started

Sorting to Make a Pattern

Sarah wants to make a bead necklace that shows a pattern.

You will need

- beads in different shapes, colours, sizes, and textures

- beading string

Sarah's Sorting

I sorted some of my beads into 4 groups. I used 2 **attributes**: colour and texture.

Now I can find the beads I need to make my necklace.

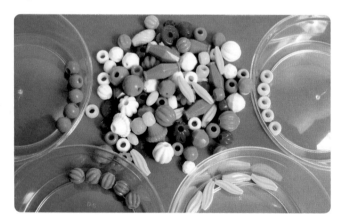

? **How would you sort the beads so you could make a pattern?**

A. List at least 4 attributes you could use to sort the beads.

B. Draw or describe a way to sort the beads using 2 or more attributes.
   Label your work with the attributes you used.

C. Sarah made this bead necklace.
Describe the pattern by telling
how each attribute changes.

D. Make your own necklace using a pattern
with 2 or more attributes.
Describe the pattern by telling how each
attribute changes.

Do You Remember?

1. Draw or describe the next 3 shapes in each pattern.

   a) ■ ◆ ■ ◆ ■ ◆

   b) ○ ○ △ ○ ○ ☆ ○ ○ △ ○ ○ ☆ ○ ○ △ ○ ○ ☆

   c)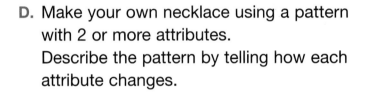

2. Write the next 3 numbers or letters in each pattern.
   a) 25, 50, 75, 100, 125, ■, ■, ■
   c) 100, 98, 96, 94, 92, ■, ■, ■
   b) 19, 28, 37, 46, 55, ■, ■, ■
   d) A, C, E, G, ■, ■, ■

3. Write the number 5.
   Add the number 2 and write the sum.
   Keep adding 2 to create a pattern with 6 numbers.

1 Patterns with Multiple Attributes

You will need
• pencil crayons
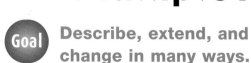

Goal Describe, extend, and create patterns that change in many ways.

Chris's Bracelet

I lost my favourite bead bracelet.

? **How can Chris describe his bracelet so someone can make a copy for him?**

A. Describe the pattern in Chris's bracelet by telling how the attributes of colour, shape, and size change.

B. Each type of bead in Chris's bracelet has been given a letter.
Complete the letter model to describe the pattern.
Repeat the pattern twice.

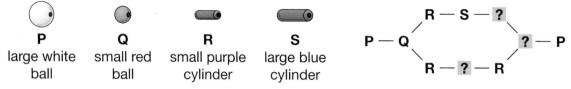

P	Q	R	S
large white ball	small red ball	small purple cylinder	large blue cylinder

$$P - Q \quad \begin{matrix} R - S - ? \\ \\ R - ? - R \end{matrix} \quad ? - P$$

C. Draw a different bracelet using the same 4 types of beads that were in Chris's bracelet.

D. Describe the pattern in your bracelet by telling how each attribute changes.

E. Describe your bead pattern using a letter model.
Repeat the pattern twice.

Reflecting

1. The bead pattern in Chris's bracelet is
   made up of smaller patterns.
   What does this mean?

2. How does the letter model describe the pattern?

Checking

3. a) Describe the pattern by telling how each
   attribute changes.

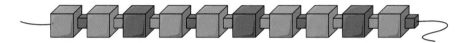

   b) Draw the next 3 beads.
   c) This letter model describes the pattern for the
   first 14 beads in part a).
   Describe the bead for each letter.

   A - B - C - D - E - F - A - B - C - D - E - F - A - B

Practising

4. Describe the pattern by telling how each
   attribute changes.
   Then draw the next 3 beads.

5. Create a letter model for this bead pattern.

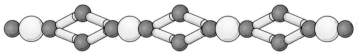

6. a) Draw your own bead pattern with 2 or more
   attributes that change.
   b) Describe the pattern by telling how each
   attribute changes.
   c) Describe your bead pattern using a letter model.

2 Number Patterns

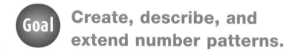

Goal Create, describe, and extend number patterns.

Pedro and 4 other students each created a number pattern. Then they described their number patterns.

Pattern A: 42, 46, 50, 54, 58, ...
Pattern B: 42, 24, 42, 24, 42, 24, ...
Pattern C: 45, 44, 41, 40, 37, 36, ...
Pattern D: 100, 95, 90, 85, 80, ...
Pattern E: 10, 12, 16, 22, 30, 40

? **Which student made each pattern?**

A. Match each student's pattern description with 1 of the number patterns above.
Then write the next 3 numbers in the pattern.

B. Create 5 new number patterns, 1 pattern for each of the student descriptions.
Include at least 5 numbers in each pattern.

Pedro's Pattern

The numbers decrease by the same amount each time.

Calvin's Pattern

The numbers decrease by different amounts.

Carmen's Pattern

The same 2 numbers repeat.

Josef's Pattern

The numbers increase by a different amount each time.

Mandy's Pattern

The numbers increase by the same amount each time.

Reflecting

1. a) Why is it possible to have more than
      1 pattern for each student description?
   b) How could you change each description so
      that only 1 pattern is possible?

Checking

2. a) Create a number pattern with at least 5 numbers.
   b) Describe your number pattern. Make sure only
      1 pattern is possible for your description.

Practising

3. Describe each pattern. Then write the next 3 numbers.
   a) 100, 98, 96, 94, 92, 90, ...   c) 3, 8, 13, 18, 23, ...
   b) 100, 99, 97, 94, 90, ...   d) 3, 6, 9, 3, 6, 9, 3, 6, 9, 3, ...

4. a) Create a number pattern that increases by a
      different amount each time.
   b) Explain why more than 1 pattern is possible
      for the description in part a).
   c) Change the description so that it describes only
      the pattern you created.

5. Terry has 8 pairs of socks.
   The pairs of socks made this pattern: 2, 4, 6, 8, ...
   a) Write the next 3 numbers in Terry's pattern.
   b) Describe Terry's pattern.

6. Zola is watching this clock.
   She sees this pattern in the hours: 2, 4, 6, 8, ...
   a) Write the next 3 numbers in Zola's pattern.
   b) Describe Zola's pattern.
   c) Compare Zola's pattern and Terry's pattern from
      Question 5. How are the patterns the same?
      How are they different?

3 Patterns in T-Charts

Goal Use t-charts to identify and extend patterns.

An inukshuk is a marker or signpost made of rocks built in the shape of a person.
The plural of inukshuk is inukshuit.
Manitok collected 15 small rocks and 26 large rocks.

? **Does Manitok have enough small rocks to make 6 inukshuit like this one?**

Manitok's Inukshuk Project

Step 1 I made models of the inukshuk using pattern blocks.
I used green blocks for the small rocks.

Step 2 I created a **t-chart** to record how many green blocks I used in each model.

Step 3 After making 3 inukshuit, I found a pattern in the t-chart: 3, 6, 9, ...

Step 4 I extended the pattern to complete the t-chart.

For 6 inukshuit, I need 18 small rocks. I only have 15 small rocks, so I don't have enough.

Inukshuk	Total number of green blocks
1	3
2	6
3	9
4	12
5	15
6	18

Reflecting

1. Explain how the t-chart helped Manitok solve the problem.

2. Describe another strategy Manitok could have used to solve the problem.

Checking

3. a) Manitok has 26 large rocks. Does he have enough large rocks to make 6 inukshuit? Use this t-chart to solve the problem.

   b) Look at the numbers in the 2nd column of your t-chart. Describe the pattern.

Inukshuk	Total number of large rocks
1	
2	
3	

Practising

4. There is an inukshuk on the Nunavut flag.

   a) Create a t-chart to find the total number of rocks needed to make 7 of these inukshuit.

Inukshuk	Total number of rocks
1	
2	
3	

   b) Describe the pattern.

5. a) Build your own inukshuk model. Use 2 sizes of blocks. Use a different number of each size.

   b) How many blocks of each type do you need to make 7 inukshuit? Use t-charts.

   c) How many inukshuit can you make if you have 30 small blocks and 15 large blocks? Explain your thinking.

4 Measurement Patterns

Goal Extend time patterns in t-charts.

You spend about 195 days in school each year.

? **How many days will you spend in school by the end of grade 4?**

Jon's Calculator Pattern

In kindergarten, I spent 195 days in school.
In grade 1, I spent another 195 days
in school, so I add:

$195 \boxed{+} 195 \boxed{=} 390 \boxed{=} \boxed{=} \boxed{=}$

I use the constant feature of the calculator
to extend the pattern.

Grade	Total number of school days
K	195
1	390
2	
3	
4	

A. What is the **pattern rule** for the numbers in the 2nd column?

B. Complete Jon's t-chart.

C. How many days will Jon spend in school by the end of grade 4?

D. Look at the digits in the 2nd column of the t-chart. Describe the pattern.

E. Predict the number of school days by the end of grade 5 and by the end of grade 6. Use a calculator to check your predictions.

pattern rule

A description of how a pattern starts and how it can be extended

Reflecting

1. Explain how the pattern in the digits helped you to predict the number of days you spent in school by the end of grades 5 and 6.

2. Could 1456 ever appear in the 2nd column of Jon's t-chart? Explain your thinking.

Checking

3. There are about 19 holidays in a school year.
   a) How many holidays are there by the end of grade 4? Use the t-chart.
   b) Write the pattern rule.
   c) Describe any patterns you see in the digits in the 2nd column of the t-chart.
   d) Predict the number of holidays by the end of grade 6. Then check your prediction.

Grade	Total number of holidays
K	19
1	38
2	
3	

Practising

4. Complete 7 rows of each t-chart.

a)

Days	Total number of hours
1	
2	
3	

b)

Years	Total number of months
1	
2	
3	

5. Look at the 2nd column of each t-chart in Question 4. Write the pattern rule for each t-chart.

6. How old are you in months? Show your work.

7. Chantal has 45 minutes of computer time each day at home. How much computer time does she have in 1 week? Use a t-chart.

Mid-Chapter Review

1 1. a) Describe the pattern by telling how each attribute changes.

   b) Draw or describe the next 3 shapes in the pattern.
   c) Describe the pattern using a letter model.

2 2. Write the next 3 numbers in each pattern.
   a) 6, 12, 18, 24, ...   c) 5, 15, 25, 35, ...
   b) 49, 42, 35, 28, ...   d) 1, 3, 5, 1, 3, 5, 1, 3, 5, 1, ...

3. Describe each pattern. Write the next 3 numbers.
   a) 25, 27, 29, 31, ...
   b) 0, 1, 3, 4, 6, 7, 9, ...
   c) 22, 19, 16, 13, ...
   d) 0, 15, 30, 45, 0, 15, 30, 45, 0, 15, 30, 45, ...

4. A pattern starts at 60 and then decreases by 1, then 2, then 3, and so on.
   What is the 10th number in the pattern?
   Show your work.

4 5. The library gets 16 new books each month.
   a) Complete the t-chart to show how the number of new books grows over 1 year.
   b) Write a rule for the pattern in the 2nd column of the t-chart.
   c) Describe any patterns in the digits. Predict the next 3 numbers.

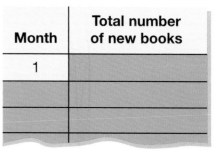

Month	Total number of new books
1	

6. It takes Suki about 45 minutes to make a bracelet.
   Make a t-chart that shows how many bracelets she can complete in 4 hours.

Calculator Patterns

Number of players: 2

How to play: Player 1 enters a secret pattern into a calculator.
Player 2 tries to figure out how the numbers in the pattern change.

Step 1 Enter a 3-digit start number.
Press ⊞.
Enter a change number.

Step 2 Press ⊟.
Give the calculator to your partner.

Step 3 Your partner presses ⊟ and tries to figure out how the numbers are changing.
After your partner figures out how the numbers change, it is your turn to figure out a secret pattern.

Josef's Secret Pattern

start number	change number	
134	⊞ 4	⊟ 138

Sarah's Solution

I pressed ⊟ twice.
138 ⊟ 142 ⊟ 146
I think the change is ⊞ 4.

Other ways to play:

• Use ⊟ instead of ⊞.
• Figure out the start number of the pattern.

5

Solve Problems Using a Patterning Strategy

You will need

• a 100 chart

1	2	3	4
11	12	13	14
21	22	23	24
31	32	33	34

 Goal Look for a pattern to solve a problem.

Here comes a parade of 100 clowns!
Every 2nd clown has a red nose.
Every 3rd clown wears glasses.

? **How many clowns have a red nose *and* glasses?**

 Miki's Solution

Understand

I need a way to count every 2nd and 3rd clown in a line of 100 clowns. That way I can see how many clowns have red noses *and* glasses.

Make a Plan

I can mark every 2nd and 3rd number on a 100 chart.
Then I'll count the marks.

Carry Out the Plan

In the first 3 rows of the chart, I mark every 2nd number with \ and every 3rd number with / .

I see a pattern! Every 6th number has both marks.
I can now circle every 6th number and then count.

16 clowns have a red nose and glasses.

1	2	3	4	5	6	7	8	9	10
11	12	13	14	15	16	17	18	19	20
21	22	23	24	25	26	27	28	29	30
31	32	33	34	35	36	37	38	39	40
41	42	43	44	45	46	47	48	49	50
51	52	53	54	55	56	57	58	59	60
61	62	63	64	65	66	67	68	69	70
71	72	73	74	75	76	77	78	79	80
81	82	83	84	85	86	87	88	89	90
91	92	93	94	95	96	97	98	99	100

Reflecting

1. How did looking for a pattern make the problem easier to solve?

Checking

2. Every 5th clown in the parade of 100 clowns wears a hat.
   Every 2nd clown has a red nose.
   How many clowns have a hat *and* a red nose?

Practising

3. a) Every 3rd clown in the parade of 100 clowns wears glasses. How many clowns have a hat *and* glasses?

   b) How many clowns have a hat, glasses, *and* a red nose?

4. a) Describe a pattern in the digits of the badge numbers.

   b) Make a badge with a 7-digit number that has the same pattern.

5. Britney's family went skating together on a Tuesday. After that, Britney and her brother Liam skated every 2nd day. Their mom skated every 3rd day and their dad skated every 4th day.
   On what day of the week did Britney's family skate together again?

6. Look for a pattern in the numbers to find the answer.

   $20 - 19 + 18 - 17 + 16 - 15 + 14 - 13 + 12 - 11 + 10 - 9 + 8 - 7 + 6 - 5 + 4 - 3 + 2 - 1$

7. Create and solve a problem that can be solved by looking for a pattern.

6 Multiple Number Patterns

Goal Extend and describe special number patterns.

Allison made a number chain.

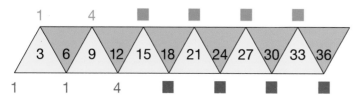

? What are the missing numbers in Allison's number chain?

Allison's Number Chain

I wrote a number pattern inside the triangles.

On the corners of each triangle, I wrote numbers that add up to the number inside.

A. Explain how to find the missing number for the 12 triangle.

B. Complete Allison's number chain.

C. Write the number pattern for
   a) the red corner numbers above the chain: 1, 4, ...
   b) the numbers inside the chain: 3, 6, 9, 12, ...
   c) the blue corner numbers below the chain: 1, 1, 4, ...
   d) the zig-zagging blue and red numbers: 1, 1, 1, 4, 4, ...

D. Predict the next number in each pattern in part C.
   Extend the number chain for 2 more triangles to check.

E. Describe each number pattern in part C.

Reflecting

1. Compare the 4 number patterns in the chain.
   How are the patterns the same?
   How are they different?

Checking

2. a) Complete the number chain by adding corner numbers to get the sums inside the triangles.

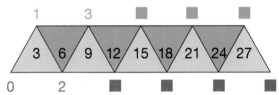

   b) Write each number pattern in the chain.
   c) Predict the next number in each pattern.
      Then extend the number chain by 2 more triangles to check.
   d) Describe each number pattern in part b).

Practising

3. a) Complete the number chain and then extend it by 6 more triangles.

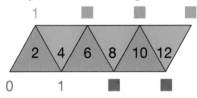

   b) Describe each number pattern in the chain.

4. These are zig-zag number chain patterns.
   Write the next 3 numbers for each pattern.
   a) 1, 1, 2, 4, 4, 5, 7, 7, 8, ■, ■, ■
   b) 2, 3, 5, 7, 8, 10, 12, 13, 15, 17, ■, ■, ■

7 Finding Missing Terms

You will need

- base ten blocks

Goal Find the missing number in a pattern and in an equation.

You can find a missing number in a pattern if you know how the numbers in the pattern change.

❓ What is the missing number in this pattern?
15, 21, 27, 33, ■, 45, ...

Natalie and Rami figured out that the numbers in the pattern change by 6 each time.
Then they each wrote an **equation** with a missing number to find ■.

equation

A number sentence with an equal sign to show that the left side is equal to the right side

4 + 2 = 6
4 = 6 − 2

Natalie's Addition Equation

$$+6$$
15, 21, 27, 33, ■, 45, ...
■ + 6 = 45

To find ■, I started at 45 on a number line.

Then I thought, "Where on the number line would I have started, if I added 6 and ended up at 45?"

So I subtracted 6 to find out.

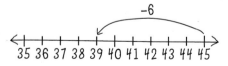

The missing number, ■, is 39.

Rami's Subtraction Equation

$$-6$$
15, 21, 27, 33, ■, 45, ...
■ − 6 = 33

To find ■, I modelled 33 with blocks.

Then I thought, "What would I have started with, if I took away 6 and had 33 left?"

So I added 6 to find out.

39 − 6 = 33

The missing number, ■, is 39.

18

Reflecting

1. Explain how you would use a number line to find ■ in the equation ■ − 6 = 33.

2. Explain how you would use blocks to find ■ in the equation ■ + 6 = 45.

3. Explain how you might use guess and test and mental math to find ■ in the equations ■ − 6 = 33 and ■ + 6 = 45.

Checking

4. What is the missing number in this pattern?

   6, 11, ■, 21, 26, 31, …

   Use ■ + 5 = 21.

5. What is the missing number in this pattern?

   27, 23, 19, 15, ■, 7, …

   Use ■ − 4 = 7.

Practising

6. Use the equation to find the missing number in each pattern.
   a) 16, 25, 34, 43, ■, 61, …   ■ + 9 = 61
   b) 31, ■, 25, 22, 19, 16, …   ■ + 3 = 31
   c) ■, 77, 73, 69, 65, 61, 57, … ■ − 4 = 77

7. Write the pattern rule for each pattern in Question 6.

8. Find ■ in each equation.
   a) ■ + 7 = 16   d) ■ + 12 = 19   g) 15 + ■ = 44
   b) 21 − ■ = 5   e) 27 − ■ = 11   h) ■ − 14 = 17
   c) ■ − 9 = 35   f) 36 + ■ = 52   i) 74 − ■ = 39

8 Equivalent Equations

(Goal) **Use patterns to create equations.**

Each shape in the equation ■ + ▲ = 11 + 4 represents a number.

? **How many different number pairs can you find for the 2 shapes?**

A. Use counters to find 1 pair of numbers. Draw a picture of the counters.

B. Replace the shapes in the equation ■ + ▲ = 11 + 4 with the number pair from part A.

C. Find another number pair. Record the equation.

D. Complete the t-chart to show different number pairs.

E. Look for patterns in the t-chart. If you do not see a pattern, try rearranging the rows in another t-chart. Describe the patterns you see.

F. Find 5 or more number pairs for the shapes in the equation 15 + 8 = ■ + ▲. Record an equation for each number pair.

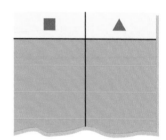

Reflecting

1. Did you find all possible number pairs in part D? How do you know?

2. Explain how you can use patterns to find different number pairs for the equation 17 + 9 = ■ + ▲.

3. How is finding number pairs for the equation ■ − ▲ = 15 − 9 different?

Adding with 5s

Think of two 5s when you want to add a number ending in 5.

15 + 7 = 15 + 5 + 2
          20 + 2 = 22

A. Why is it easy to add 2 numbers ending in 5?

Try These

1. a) 15 + 8   b) 25 + 6   c) 45 + 9   d) 95 + 7

2. a) 5 + 18   b) 69 + 5   c) 38 + 45   d) 36 + 6

Pascal's Triangle

In 1653, Blaise Pascal used this triangular pattern of numbers to solve a problem.

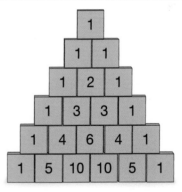

1 Choose any number inside the triangle. Look at the 2 numbers above it. How did Pascal make his triangle?

2 Write the next row of numbers in Pascal's triangle.

Skills Bank

1 1. Describe each pattern by telling how each attribute changes.
Then draw the next 3 shapes or symbols.

a) ♣ ♦ ♠ ♥ ♣ ♦ ♠ ♥ ♣ ♦ ♠ ♥

e) ↑ → ↓ ← ↑ → ↓ ← ↑ → ↓ ←

b) ▼ ▽ ● ○ ▼ ▽ ● ○ ▼ ▽ ● ○

f) ☺ ☺ ☺ ☺ ☺ ☺ ☺ ☺ ☺ ☺ ☺ ☺

c) ■ ▲ ■ ▲ ■ ▲ ■ ▲ ■

g) ▲▼◆ ◆▼▲ ▲▼◆ ◆▼▲ ▲▼◆ ◆▼▲

d) □ ◆ ▲ ▽ ■ ◆ △ ▽ ■ ◇ ▲ ▼

h) ▲■★■▲■★■▲■★■▲■★■▲■

2 2. Describe each pattern. Then write the next 3 numbers.

a) 99, 96, 93, 90, 87, …

e) 98, 91, 84, 77, 70, …

b) 4, 9, 14, 19, 24, …

f) 100, 98, 94, 88, 80, 70, …

c) 5, 10, 15, 5, 10, 15, 5, 10, 15, …

g) 4, 9, 5, 10, 6, 11, 7, 12, 8, …

d) 1, 2, 3, 5, 6, 7, 9, 10, 11, 13, …

h) 13, 20, 28, 37, 47, 58, …

3 3. There is a maple leaf on the Canadian flag.

a) Create a t-chart to find the total number of points on 6 maple leaves.

b) Describe the pattern in the 2nd column of the t-chart.

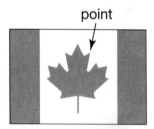

point

Number of leaves	Total number of points
1	11
2	
3	

4. Create a t-chart to find the total number of vertices on 7 octagons.

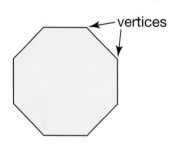

vertices

5. Complete 7 rows of each t-chart. Use a calculator.
Write a pattern rule for the pattern in the 2nd column of the t-chart.

a)

Years	Total number of weeks
1	52
2	
3	

b)

Weeks	Total number of hours
1	168
2	
3	

6. Complete each number chain.
Then extend each chain by adding 6 more triangles.

a)
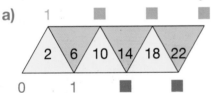

b)
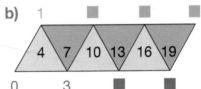

7. Write the next 3 numbers for each pattern.
a) 0, 1, 2, 2, 3, 4, 4, 5, 6, 6, 7, 8, …
b) 0, 1, 3, 4, 5, 7, 8, 9, 11, 12, …
c) 0, 1, 4, 5, 6, 9, 10, 11, 14, 15, 16, …
d) 0, 1, 2, 6, 7, 8, 12, 13, 14, 18, 19, 20, …

8. Use the equation to find the missing number in each pattern.
a) 8, 15, 22, ■, 36, 43, …   ■ − 7 = 22
b) ■, 65, 59, 53, 47, 41, …   ■ − 6 = 65
c) 17, ■, 23, 26, 29, 32, …   3 + ■ = 23

9. Find ■ in each equation.
a) 11 + ■ = 36   c) 73 − ■ = 49   e) 23 + ■ = 42
b) ■ + 26 = 54   d) ■ − 12 = 56   f) ■ − 8 = 76

10. Find 3 different pairs of numbers for the shapes in each equation.
a) 11 + 3 = ■ + ▲   d) 19 + 2 = ■ + ▲   g) ■ + ▲ = 9 + 18
b) ■ + ▲ = 10 + 6   e) 16 − 12 = ■ − ▲   h) 21 + 8 = ■ + ▲
c) 9 − 4 = ■ − ▲   f) ■ + ▲ = 13 + 4   i) 23 − 9 = ■ − ▲

Problem Bank

LESSON

5

1. Jennifer put markers along a running track.
   She put the first marker at 100 m.
   Then she put a marker at every 50 m.
   How many markers does she need to reach 400 m?

2. Kelly ran a 10 km race.
   She ran the 1st kilometre in 5 minutes.
   She then slowed down, and each kilometre after that
   took 1 minute longer to run than the kilometre before.
   How long did it take Kelly to run the race?

3. Corey walks past doors 1 to 12
   and opens every 2nd door.
   On his 2nd trip past the doors,
   he stops at every 3rd door.
   If the door is closed, he
   opens it. If the door is open,
   he closes it. Which doors are
   open after Corey's 2nd trip?

4. Brian just had his 5th birthday.
   He gets a new haircut every 8 months.
   How many haircuts has Brian had in his life?

6

5. Anil is helping his aunt around the house for 5 days.
   He can choose between these 2 ways to be paid:
   - $10 each day
   - $1 for the first day and, on each day after that,
     double the amount of the day before
   a) Which payment method should Anil choose? Why?
   b) Would your answer change if he worked for 1 week?
      Explain your thinking.

8

6. Find at least 5 different ways to complete the equation
   $13 + \blacksquare = \blacktriangle - 17$. What do you notice?

Chapter Review

LESSON

1. Describe the pattern by telling how each attribute changes.
Draw or describe the next 3 shapes.

a)  •••

b) •••

2. Write the next 3 numbers in each pattern.

a) 7, 11, 15, 19, ... b) 24, 21, 18, 15, ...

3. A pattern starts at 51 and decreases by 8.
Write 6 numbers in this pattern.

4. Complete each t-chart and describe the pattern rule.

a)

Hours	Total number of minutes
1	60
2	120
3	180
4	
5	
6	
7	

b)

Cats	Total number of claws
1	18
2	36
3	54
4	
5	
6	
7	

5. Create a problem that could be solved using 1 of
the t-charts in Question 4.

6. a) Create 2 different patterns that start with 1, 3, ...
  b) Write the pattern rule for each of your patterns.
  c) Compare your patterns. How are they the same?
    How are they different?

7. Find ■ in each equation.

a) ■ + 13 = 21 b) 5 + ■ = 34 c) 100 − ■ = 91 d) ■ − 22 = 66

8. Use numbers for ■ and ▲ to write 3 equations for each part.

a) ■ + ▲ = 19 + 8 b) ■ + ▲ = 15 + 6 c) 25 + 8 = ■ + ▲

Chapter Task

Finding Number Patterns in Shape Patterns

Pedro created this shape pattern using pattern blocks.

? **What number patterns can you see in the shape pattern?**

shape 1 shape 2 shape 3 shape 4

1 block

4 blocks

9 blocks

?

Part 1

A. Draw or make a model of shape 4. Describe the shape pattern in words.

B. Complete a t-chart to show the number pattern for Pedro's shape pattern.

C. Extend the t-chart to find out how many blocks would be in shape 5 and shape 6.

D. Write a rule for the number pattern.

Shape	Total number of blocks
1	1
2	4
3	9
4	
5	

Part 2

E. Create your own shape pattern using pattern blocks. Draw and describe your shape pattern.

F. Describe a number pattern in your shape pattern.

G. How is your pattern and Pedro's pattern the same?
How are the patterns different?

Task Checklist

☑ Did you include a diagram?

☑ Did you use t-charts to show number patterns?

☑ Did you describe the number patterns by writing pattern rules?

Numeration

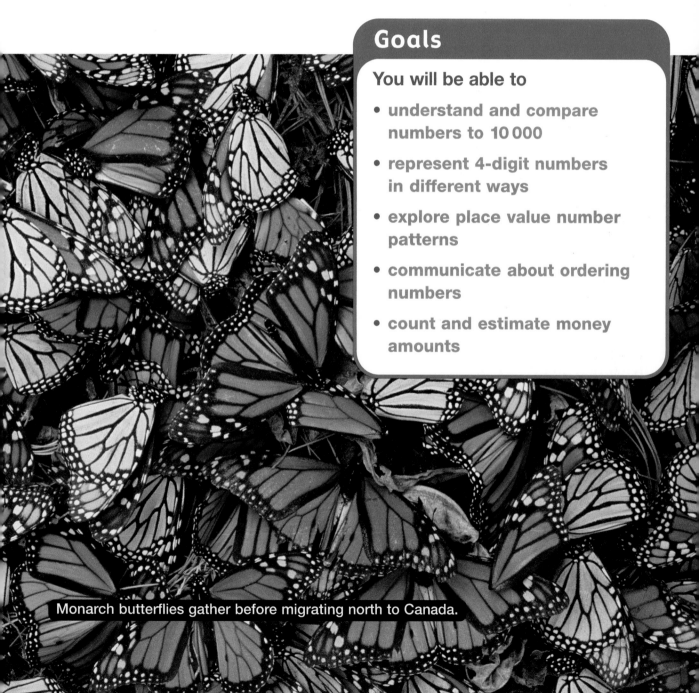

Goals

You will be able to

- understand and compare numbers to 10 000

- represent 4-digit numbers in different ways

- explore place value number patterns

- communicate about ordering numbers

- count and estimate money amounts

Monarch butterflies gather before migrating north to Canada.

Getting Started

Modelling Numbers

You will need

- base ten blocks

- play money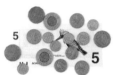

A man in India has learned how to mimic the calls of 326 animals and birds.

Here is 1 way to represent 326 using base ten blocks.

11 blocks were used.

A. How do you know that 326 is between 300 and 400?

B. How could you model 326 if you had no tens blocks?

C. How could you model 326 using exactly 20 blocks?

For each task below, choose 11 blocks.
You may choose different blocks each time, but you must always have at least 1 hundreds block, 1 tens block, and 1 ones block.

D. What is the greatest number you can make with the 11 blocks you chose?
How do you know that this number is the greatest number?

E. What is the least number you can make with the 11 blocks you chose?

F. Use 11 blocks to make 2 numbers that are close to 300. Make 1 number that is less than 300 and 1 number that is greater than 300.

Do You Remember?

1. Represent each number using base ten blocks.
   Write each number as ■ hundreds + ■ tens + ■ ones.
   a) 169   b) 961   c) 320   d) 507

2. Which number in each pair is greater?
   a) 639 or 714   b) 495 or 475   c) 306 or 360

3. Write each set of numbers in order from least to greatest.
   a) 384, 389, 364, 368   b) 870, 780, 817, 728

4. Describe 2 ways to make each amount of money using coins.
   a) $4.50   b) $9.75

1 Place Value

You will need

• base ten blocks

Goal Model numbers up to 10 000.

Chantal is studying spiders.
She has found a spider that can lay 1200 eggs.

? **How can Chantal model 1200 with the least number of base ten blocks possible?**

Chantal's Model

I can model 1200 with 1200 ones blocks.

If the ones blocks are regrouped as tens blocks, I only need 120 blocks to model 1200.

A. If the tens blocks are regrouped as hundreds blocks, how many blocks will there be? Make the new model.

B. 10 hundreds blocks can be regrouped as a thousands block. Regroup the hundreds blocks. How many blocks are there now?

Reflecting

1. a) Which model uses the least number of blocks?

   b) How is this model related to the digits in a place value chart?

Thousands	Hundreds	Tens	Ones

2. How is building a thousands block from hundreds blocks the same as building a hundreds block from tens blocks?

Checking

3. 3 spiders laid a total of 2065 eggs.
   a) Model 2065 with hundreds, tens, and ones blocks.
   b) Model 2065 using the least number of blocks possible. You can use thousands, hundreds, tens, and ones blocks.
   c) Did you need all 4 types of blocks in part b)? Explain why or why not.

Practising

4. A monarch butterfly migrated 3256 km.
   Find 3 ways to model 3256.
   Draw each model.

5. Write the number.
   a)

   b)

6. If you used only 1 type of block to model each number, how many hundreds blocks would you need? How many thousands blocks would you need?
   a) 2000   b) 5000   c) 9000

7. A fast-food restaurant has a sign that reads 4562 hamburgers sold.
   Each week for the next 5 weeks, the restaurant sells 100 more hamburgers.
   a) Model 4562 using the least number of blocks.
   b) Add blocks to your model to include the additional 100 hamburgers sold each week. Regroup blocks so the model uses the least number of blocks.
   c) What should the sign read at the end of 5 weeks?
   d) Which blocks changed in your model? Why?

2 Expanded Form

You will need

- base ten blocks

- a place value chart

Thousands	Hundreds	Tens	Ones

Goal Write numbers up to 10 000 in expanded form.

A professional baseball player played 3562 games in his career.

? In what ways can 3562 be represented?

Shani's Ways

I can model 3562 using base ten blocks in a place value chart.

Thousands	Hundreds	Tens	Ones
3	5	6	2

I can say 3562 as
3 thousands, 5 hundreds, 6 tens, 2 ones.

I can read 3562 as
three thousand five hundred sixty-two.

When I write the number as 3562, it is in **standard form**.

I can also show a number in **expanded form**.
3562 in expanded form using words is
3 thousands + 5 hundreds + 6 tens + 2 ones.

3562 in expanded form using numerals is
3000 + 500 + 60 + 2.

standard form
The usual way in which we write numbers

expanded form
A way to write a number that shows the value of each digit

Reflecting

1. When writing in expanded form, why is 3000 + 500 + 60 + 2 better than 500 + 3000 + 2 + 60?

2. How would writing numbers like 3062, 3502, or 3560 in expanded form be different than writing 3562?

3. Why are numbers usually written in standard form rather than expanded form?

Checking

4. Pele of Brazil scored 1281 goals as a professional soccer player.
   a) Write 1281 in a place value chart.
   b) Write 1281 as ■ thousands, ■ hundreds, ■ tens, ■ ones.
   c) How would you read this number?
   d) Write 1281 in expanded form using numerals.

Practising

5. Rob Peterson holds the record for good tennis serves in a row.
   The number of serves in expanded form is 8000 + 10 + 7.
   a) Write this number in expanded form using words.
   b) Write this number in standard form.

6. Write in expanded form using a place value chart, numerals, and words.
   a) 7845   c) 9999   e) 8050
   b) 4309   d) 6006   f) 7700

3 Comparing and Ordering Numbers

Goal Compare and order numbers up to 10 000.

Thousands	Hundreds	Tens	Ones

In a Tour de France bicycle race, the cyclists rode 1368 km of mountain terrain and 1982 km of flat terrain.

? **Which distance is longer, the mountain terrain or the flat terrain?**

Chris's Solution

I record the digits in place value charts.
Then I model the numbers with base ten blocks.

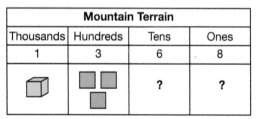

Mountain Terrain			
Thousands	Hundreds	Tens	Ones
1	3	6	8
		?	?

Flat Terrain			
Thousands	Hundreds	Tens	Ones
1	9	8	2
	?	?	?

A. Finish modelling the numbers.

B. Compare the numbers to find which distance is longer.

C. When comparing numbers, you can use the symbols **<** and **>**.
Show how the numbers compare by replacing ■ with <, =, or >.

1368 ■ 1982   1982 ■ 1368

< and >
The symbol > means the 1st number is greater than the 2nd number.
The symbol < means the 1st number is less than the 2nd number.

8 > 5   5 < 8

Reflecting

1. Write a number between 1368 and 1982. What digits can be in the thousands place and hundreds place?

2. When you compare numbers like 1368 and 1982, you look at each number from left to right. Explain what you do when you get to the 1st place value with a different digit.

Checking

3. Look at the 2 headlines.
   Use < or > to show which race has the greater distance. Explain how you know.

   > Dogsleds cover 1795 km in Arctic race

   > Cyclists ride 3350 km in Tour de France

4. Use the digits 3, 3, 5, 0 to make 4 new distances. Order the distances from shortest to longest.

Practising

5. Ashley lives in Vancouver. She made a table showing the distances between 6 Canadian cities and Vancouver.

   Distances from Vancouver

City	Distance (km)
Whitehorse, Yukon	2700
Toronto, Ontario	4500
Montreal, Quebec	4800
Moncton, New Brunswick	5825
Calgary, Alberta	1050
St John's, Newfoundland	7675

   a) Which city is closest to Vancouver? Explain.
   b) Which city is farthest from Vancouver? Explain.
   c) Which cities are between 3000 km and 6000 km away from Vancouver?
   d) Rewrite Ashley's table so the cities are in order from farthest from Vancouver to closest to Vancouver.

6. Complete by using >, =, or <. Explain your thinking.
   a) 9981 ■ 654   b) 6772 ■ 7276   c) 2365 ■ 7942

4 Exploring 10 000

You will need
- base ten blocks

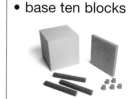

Goal Explore place value patterns to 10 000.

Josef's Place Value Patterns

I made place value puzzles using number patterns. Each pattern has 4 numbers in it.

Pattern 3 starts with 10 ones blocks. Replace all of the ones with tens. Continue replacing blocks with the next bigger size block.

Pattern 1 starts with 9 thousands + 9 hundreds + 7 tens. The number of tens blocks increases by 1 for each number.

Pattern 2 starts with 9 thousands + 9 hundreds + 9 tens + 1 ones. The number of ones blocks increases by 3 for each number.

Pattern 4 starts with 4 thousands blocks. The number of thousands blocks increases by 2 for each number.

? **How are Josef's patterns alike?**

A. Use base ten blocks to model the 4 patterns.

B. What do you notice about the 4th number in each pattern?

C. Create an increasing number pattern with the same 4th number. Write a description for your pattern.

Reflecting

1. Draw or describe a base ten block model for the 4th number in Josef's patterns.

Adding Tens, Hundreds, and Thousands

Natalie and Manitok played Spin to Win.
Natalie spun 3000 and 5000.
Manitok spun 4000 and 2000.

? **Who wins the point?**

Natalie's Solution

I know 3 + 5 = 8, so I can add
3000 + 5000 in my head.

3	3000	3 thousand
+ 5	+ 5000	+ 5 thousand
8	8000	8 thousand

Spin to Win
How to play:

Step 1 Spin twice.

Step 2 Add your spins to get a score.

Step 3 The person with the greatest score wins 1 point.

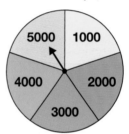

A. How does knowing 3 + 5 = 8 help Natalie calculate her score?

B. What score did Manitok get? Who wins the point?

Try These

1. Use 3 + 2 = 5 to find each sum.
   a) 30 + 20   b) 300 + 200   c) 3000 + 2000

2. Use 7 − 4 = 3 to find each difference.
   a) 70 − 40   b) 700 − 400   c) 7000 − 4000

3. Find 4 different scores you can get with 2 spins.

4. What is the best score you can get with 2 spins?
   Explain how you found the answer.

5 Multiplying by 10, 100, and 1000

Goal Multiply by 10, 100, and 1000.

Jon can multiply by 10, 100, and 1000.
He has found a pattern that helps him to multiply.

? **What pattern did Jon use to multiply by 10, 100, and 1000?**

Jon's Pattern

I made a table to help me see the patterns.

I started by multiplying numbers by 10.

2×10 is like making 2 groups of 10.

There are 2 tens and 0 ones, so the value is 20.

Multiplication by 10	Standard form of the number
2×10	20
3×10	30

A. Choose 4 numbers. Use base ten blocks to multiply each number by 10. Write your results in the table.

B. Look for a pattern in the products.

C. Create a new table for multiplying by 100.
Multiply 4 numbers by 100.
Look for a pattern in the products.

D. Create another table to find a pattern for multiplying by 1000.

Reflecting

1. What pattern do you see when you multiply by each number?
   a) 10   b) 100   c) 1000

2. Why does it make sense that there will be 0 ones when you multiply a number by 10, 100, or 1000?

Checking

3. Use the patterns you found to multiply.
   a) 14×10 b) 61×100 c) 2×1000

4. What is the missing number?
   a) $2500 = \blacksquare \times 100$ b) $2500 = \blacksquare \times 10$

Practising

5. Multiply.
   a) 99×10 c) 1000×10 e) 15×100
   b) 5×1000 d) 10×1000 f) 100×100

6. For 10 years, Darren's parents have made him a photo album for his birthday.
   Each photo album has 144 photographs.
   How many photographs does Darren have in total?

7. What is the missing number?
   a) $5000 = \blacksquare \times 1000$ d) $8000 = \blacksquare \times 100$
   b) $5000 = \blacksquare \times 100$ e) $10\,000 = \blacksquare \times 1000$
   c) $8000 = \blacksquare \times 1000$ f) $10\,000 = \blacksquare \times 100$

8. What is the missing number?
   a) $2090 = \blacksquare \times 10$ c) $5000 = \blacksquare \times 10$
   b) $1100 = \blacksquare \times 10$ d) $4780 = \blacksquare \times 10$

9. Keiko's family bought a used car with 45 one-hundred dollar bills. How much did the car cost?

Mid–Chapter Review

1 1. A blue whale ate 3750 kg of plankton in 1 day.
Model 3750 with the least number of blocks possible.
Draw the model.

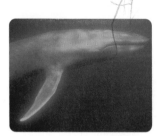

2 2. There are 4809 species of jumping spiders in the world.
Write 4809 in expanded form using words and then
using numerals.

3. Write each number in standard form.
a) $2000 + 80 + 5$ b) 6 thousands + 2 hundreds + 5 tens + 6 ones

3 4. Use words to write the number that is 100 less than 566.

5. Use numerals to write the number that is three
thousand greater than one thousand twenty-nine.
Show your work.

6. Complete each number sentence by using <, =, or >.
Explain your thinking.
a) 654 ■ 7843
b) 9823 ■ 9832
c) 5478 ■ 8962

7. This table shows the number of dogs of
different breeds owned by Canadians.
Order the numbers from least to greatest.

Dog	Number
poodle	2817
Yorkshire terrier	2185
boxer	1444
golden retriever	6047
German shepherd	4576

4 8. Complete these number patterns.
a) 5, ■, 500, 5000
b) 8 ones, 8 tens, ■, 8 thousands
c) 4281, 4381, 4481, ■
d) 1, 10, ■, 1000, ■

5 9. What is the missing number?
a) $2000 = ■ \times 100$ c) $5600 = ■ \times 100$ e) $10\,000 = ■ \times 100$
b) $2000 = ■ \times 10$ d) $5600 = ■ \times 10$ f) $10\,000 = ■ \times 10$

Getting to 10 000

Number of players: 2 or more
How to play: Get as close as you can to 10 000, but don't go over!

Step 1 Roll a die and record the number rolled on your game sheet.

Step 2 Decide if you will multiply the number rolled by 1, 10, 100, or 1000. Record your decision on your game sheet.

Step 3 Multiply and then record the product.

Step 4 Use a calculator to add the product to your previous running total. Record the new running total on your game sheet.

After every player has had 10 rolls, the player closest to, but not over, 10 000 wins.

You will need

- a die

- game sheet

  Getting to 10 000

Turn	Number rolled

- a calculator

Sarah's Game

On my first 3 turns, I rolled a 5, a 6, and another 5.

Getting to 10 000

Turn	Number rolled	× 1, × 10, × 100, or × 1000	Product	Running total
1	5	x 1000	5000	5000
2	6	x 100	600	5600
3	5	x 100	500	6100

Rounding to the Nearest 10, 100, or 1000

 Goal Round numbers to the nearest 10, 100, or 1000.

Allison, Calvin, and Pedro report on school sports for the local newspaper.
2943 spectators came to a track and field meet.
They decide to round the number of spectators for the headline in the newspaper.

? **How can Allison, Calvin, and Pedro round the number 2943?**

Allison's Rounding

I'll round 2943 to the nearest thousand.

2943 is between 2000 and 3000.

It is closer to 3000, so 2943 rounds to 3000.

2943

2000 ———————————— 3000

3000 spectators attend track meet

Calvin's Rounding

I'll round 2943 to the nearest hundred.

2943 is between 2900 and 3000.

It is closer to 2900, so 2943 rounds to 2900.

2943

2900 ———————————— 3000

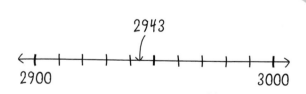
2900 spectators attend track meet

Pedro's Rounding

I'll round 2943 to the nearest ten.

2943 is between 2940 and 2950.

It is closer to 2940,
so 2943 rounds to 2940.

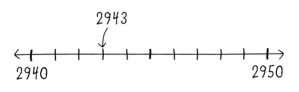

2940 spectators attend track meet

Reflecting

1. Which of the 3 rounded numbers do you think is best for the newspaper headline? Why?

2. In a 4-digit number like 1729, how is rounding to the nearest thousand different from rounding to the nearest hundred?

Checking

3. There were 4365 spectators at a provincial softball championship. Round 4365 to the nearest thousand, the nearest hundred, and the nearest ten.

Practising

4. a) Draw a number line to show how you would round the population of Fergus to the nearest thousand.

   b) What is the population of Pelee rounded to the nearest hundred? What is Pelee's population rounded to the nearest ten?

   c) What community has about 3000 people?

   d) Explain why the populations of Mount Forest, Petrolia, and Gananoque are all about 5000 when rounded to the nearest thousand.

Place	Population
Fergus	8884
Pelee	283
Kincardine	2954
Mount Forest	4580
Petrolia	4908
Gananoque	5210

7 Communicate About Ordering Numbers

 Goal Explain how to order a set of numbers in a complete, clear, and organized way.

Miki organized a computer-game contest for her sister's friends.

When she awarded 1st, 2nd, 3rd, and 4th prizes, the players asked how she ordered the scores.

Top Scores	
909	9009
9909	999

? **How can Miki explain the steps she followed to order the numbers?**

 Miki's Rough Copy

I wrote the numbers with 4 digits first.

I wrote the numbers with 3 digits last.

I compared the digits to put them in order.

 Miki's Good Copy

The winning scores were 909, 9009, 999, and 9909.

I wrote the numbers with 4 digits first.

Then I wrote the numbers with 3 digits, because 4-digit numbers are greater than 3-digit numbers.

9009   9909   909   999

I compared the hundreds digits in the 4-digit numbers to see which number was greater.

9909   9009   909   999

I compared the tens digits in the 3-digit numbers to see which number was greater.

9909   9009   999   909

Reflecting

1. Find and describe differences between Miki's rough copy and her good copy.
   Use the Communication Checklist.

Checking

2. Rami was asked to put these game scores in order from greatest to least.
   865   1876   1540   86   1000
   Here is the rough copy explaining his steps.
   Use the Communication Checklist to write a good copy.

Rami's Rough Copy

I wrote 1000 in the middle.

I wrote the 4-digit numbers first.

I wrote the numbers less than 1000 last.

| 1876 | 1540 | 1000 | 86 | 865 |

They were all in order except 86 and 865, so I switched them.

| 1876 | 1540 | 1000 | 865 | 86 |

Practising

3. a) Order these numbers from greatest to least.
      3867   3869   392   473   450
   b) Write an explanation of how you did the ordering. This is your rough copy.
   c) Use the Communication Checklist to find ways to improve your rough copy. Then write a good copy.

8 Counting Money Collections

Goal Estimate, count, and write money amounts up to $50.00.

The class is fund-raising for a camping trip.
Paulette is the class treasurer.
She records how much money is collected each day.

Day 1	Day 2	Day 3	Day 4
3 five-dollar bills	1 toonie	1 five-dollar bill	1 five-dollar bill
5 loonies	2 quarters	2 toonies	1 toonie
3 quarters	10 dimes	4 quarters	5 loonies
5 dimes	3 nickels	5 dimes	18 nickels
2 nickels	10 pennies	2 nickels	50 pennies
5 pennies		80 pennies	

? **How much money has Paulette's class collected?**

Paulette's Estimate

First, I will estimate the total for each day.
When I write number values, the number before the decimal tells how many dollars.
The number after the decimal tells how many cents.

Day	Estimate
1	$21.00
2	$4.00
3	$11.00
4	$13.00

A. Add the estimates for each day together to estimate the total amount collected.

B. Calculate the actual total.

Reflecting

1. Compare your estimate with your actual total. Is your actual total reasonable?

2. Share your method for finding the actual total with others. Why were some methods different?

Checking

3. On day 5 of fund-raising, Paulette's class collected this amount.
   a) Estimate how much money the class raised.
   b) Calculate the actual total for day 5.

4. Use bills and coins to make $10.00 in 3 different ways.

Practising

5. Estimate each total. Calculate the actual total.
   a) 2 twenty-dollar bills, 1 quarter, 2 dimes, 4 nickels, 4 pennies
   b) 1 five-dollar bill, 2 toonies, 1 loonie, 5 pennies
   c) 4 ten-dollar bills, 4 loonies, 4 quarters, 4 dimes, 4 nickels, 4 pennies

6. How would you make each amount using the fewest bills and coins possible?
   a) $20.75   b) $32.30

7. Jeff has 25 quarters, 10 dimes, 5 nickels, and 1 penny in his piggy bank. How much money does Jeff have?

LESSON

Skills Bank

1

1. Write the number.

a)

c)

b)

d)

2. Model each number using the least number of blocks.
   Draw each model.
   - a) 1873
   - b) 3604
   - c) 6037
   - d) 2080
   - e) 4000
   - f) 1004
   - g) 621
   - h) 9999

3. Suppose you used only hundreds blocks to model
   each number. How many blocks would you need
   for each of these numbers?
   - a) 1000
   - b) 6000
   - c) 7500
   - d) 8300

2

4. Write each number in expanded form using numerals.
   - a) 9803
   - b) 7007
   - c) 1030
   - d) 9999
   - e) 7777
   - f) 9876
   - g) 573
   - h) 7500

5. Write each number in expanded form using words.
   - a) 6791
   - b) 893
   - c) 1023
   - d) 1100

6. Write each number in standard form.
   - a) one thousand six hundred fifteen
   - b) 7 thousands, 8 hundreds, 3 ones
   - c) 8000 + 300 + 50 + 4
   - d) 5000 + 200 + 7

7. Complete each number sentence by using <, =, or >.
   a) 986 ■ 953
   b) 2234 ■ 2432
   c) 7629 ■ 983
   d) 10 000 ■ 1000
   e) 9909 ■ 9990
   f) 7685 ■ 7658
   g) 559 ■ 5590
   h) 1342 ■ 1351
   i) 3980 ■ 4995

8. Order each set of numbers from least to greatest.
   a) 8561, 7982, 8642, 693
   b) 9805, 3248, 653, 3379, 3241
   c) 7982, 7984, 7992, 7899
   d) 543, 5672, 9870, 5070, 9930

9. Use each set of digits to write four 4-digit numbers.
   Order the numbers from least to greatest.
   a) 7, 9, 9, 0
   b) 2, 4, 4, 8
   c) 1, 3, 5, 0

10. The table shows the number of people in
    Ottawa-Hull who speak each language as
    their first language.
    a) Which language is spoken by the greatest
       number of people?
    b) Which language is spoken by the least
       number of people?
    c) Write the numbers from greatest to least.

First language	Number of people
Dutch	3055
German	7455
Greek	2325
Polish	6495
Portuguese	6345
Spanish	9020

11. Complete each number pattern.
    a) 7, ■, 700, 7000
    b) 4997, 4998, 4999, ■, ■
    c) 8719, 8723, 8727, ■, ■
    d) 4682, 5682, 6682, ■, ■
    e) 683, 783, 883, ■, ■
    f) 8970, 8980, 8990, ■, ■

12. Write an increasing number pattern with 4 numbers
    in each pattern.
    a) starts at 4098 and increases by 1 each time
    b) starts at 3286 and increases by 10 each time
    c) starts at 5709 and increases by 100 each time

13. Find each product.
    a) 12×100
    b) 25×100
    c) 6×100
    d) 8×1000
    e) 3×1000
    f) 4×1000
    g) 10×10
    h) 10×100

5 **14.** Gabe's family bought an entertainment system with 14 one-hundred dollar bills. How much did the system cost? Show your work.

15. Amit's mom bought a digital camera with 50 ten-dollar bills. How much did the camera cost? Show your work.

6 **16.** Round each number to the nearest thousand.
a) 8245   c) 789   e) 3333   g) 2954
b) 9079   d) 6378   f) 7690   h) 6193

17. Round each number in Question 16 to the nearest hundred.

18. Round each number in Question 16 to the nearest ten.

8 **19.** Estimate each total. Then calculate the actual total.

a)

c)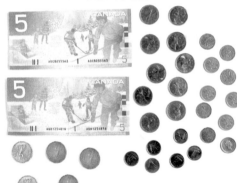

b)

d)

20. How would you make each amount using the fewest bills and coins possible?
a) $16.00   c) $18.52   e) $5.75   g) $24.98
b) $24.90   d) $46.63   f) $49.99   h) $35.79

Problem Bank

1

1. Ravi wants to build a model of 2232.
He has these blocks. Can Ravi build the model?
Use pictures, numbers, and words to explain
your answer.

2. A number is represented by 10 hundreds blocks and
some tens blocks. What could the number be?

3

3. Write the number in standard form that is 100 less
than the least 5-digit number.

4. Write 2 numbers that match this description.
The 1st number is less than the 2nd number.
The 1st number has a 4 in the thousands place.
The 2nd number has a 4 in the hundreds place.

5. a) Write as many different 4-digit numbers as you
can using the digits 7, 9, 7, and 0.
   b) Which of your 4-digit numbers is the greatest?
Which of your numbers is the least?

5

6. There are 100 holes in a ceiling tile.
How many tiles would you need to make a total
of 1000 holes?

6

7. 3 towns each have a population that rounds to 8000.
Use the digits 2, 3, 7, and 8 to create possible
populations for the 3 towns.

8

8. Lily has $42.60 in her pocket.
She has 2 bills and 8 coins.
What bills and coins could she have?

9. a) Predict which is worth more, 160 quarters,
480 dimes, or 3999 pennies.
   b) Use a calculator to find the answer.

Chapter Review

2

1. There are 2230 organic farms in Canada.
   a) Model 2230 using the least number of blocks. Draw the blocks.
   b) Use words to write 2230.
   c) Write 2230 in expanded form using numerals and then using words.

2. Write each number in standard form.
   a) 1000 + 90 + 6
   b) 4 thousands + 2 hundreds + 6 ones
   c) six thousand one hundred twenty-nine

3

3. What number is two hundred less than nine thousand one hundred twenty-four? Write the number in standard form.

4. Use words to write the number that is 300 greater than 649.

5. Complete each number sentence by using >, =, or <. Explain your thinking.
   a) 1082 ■ 9781
   b) 9891 ■ 9981
   c) 1683 ■ 1683

6. Find 3 ways to make this number sentence true. Explain your thinking.
   ■295 > 15■4

7. This table lists the number of performances for some Broadway shows.
   a) Which shows had between 2000 and 4000 performances?
   b) List the shows in order from the least number of performances to the greatest number of performances.

Broadway show	Number of performances
Chicago	1891
Grease	3388
Cats	7485
Beauty and the Beast	2887
The Phantom of the Opera	5566

8. Extend each pattern.

a) 2, 20, 200, ■   b) 5481, 6481, 7481, ■   c) 9920, 9940, 9960, ■

9. Mark's family bought a boat with 25 one-hundred dollar bills. How much did the boat cost?

10. A 14 g bag of raisins contains 40 raisins. How many raisins would you expect to find in a 140 g bag? Explain your thinking.

11. Multiply.

a) 10 × 10   b) 25 × 10   c) 65 × 100

12. What is the missing number?

a) 6000 = ■ × 100   c) 4700 = ■ × 100   e) 9900 = ■ × 100

b) 6000 = ■ × 10   d) 4700 = ■ × 10   f) 9900 = ■ × 10

13. In 1 year there were 6478 earthquakes throughout the world. What is the number of earthquakes rounded to the nearest thousand?

14. A giant squid weighed 2946 kg. How much did it weigh to the nearest thousand kilograms, nearest hundred kilograms, and nearest ten kilograms?

15. What is 895 rounded to the nearest hundred? Write the number in words.

16. Draw or describe how you would make each amount using the fewest number of bills and coins possible.

a) $6.50   b) $12.75   c) $45.30   d) $36.65

17. Estimate how much money is shown. Then calculate the actual total.

a)    b)

Chapter Task

Creating a Puzzle

Roundtree

Carmen has created a population puzzle.
She created 6 make-believe towns.

- All of the towns have 4-digit populations.
- Each population can be modelled using
  exactly 16 base ten blocks.

? **What is the population of each town?**

A. Use Carmen's clues to figure out the population
of each town. Explain your thinking for
each answer.

Everytown

The population is made
using the same number
of each type of block.

Centuria

The population is
made using only
hundreds blocks.

Littleville

The population is
the least number
you can make.

Roundtree

The population rounds down to
8000 and is made using only
thousands and tens blocks.

Middletown

The population is between 1200 and
1300 and is made using only hundreds
and tens blocks.

Hugo

The population is the greatest number
you can make less than 10000.

B. List the populations of the towns
in order. Explain how you ordered
the populations.

Task Checklist

☑ Did you explain how you figured
out each population?

☑ Did you show all your steps
when you explained your order?

Data Management

Goals

You will be able to

- collect and organize data

- make pictographs and bar graphs by hand

- make bar graphs and circle graphs using a computer

- read and interpret tables, charts, and graphs

- explain how people use data

Planning a playground

Getting Started

Graphing Treasures of the Sea

You will need

• a sorting chart

Category	Number of objects

• grid paper

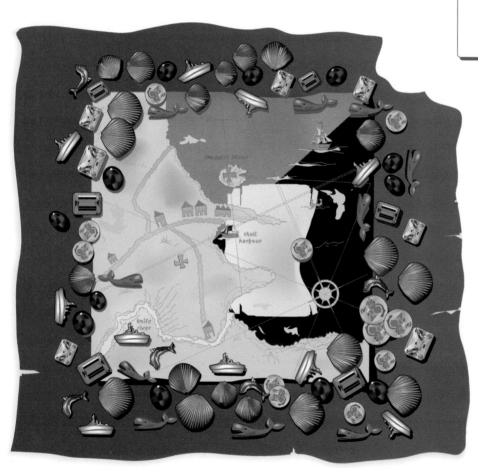

? **How can you make a graph to represent the objects in the picture?**

A. List categories you can use to sort the objects in the picture.

B. Make a **tally chart** to show how many objects there are for each category.

C. Use the **data** in your tally chart to make a **bar graph**. Number the **axis** by 2s or 5s.

D. Which bar or bars on your graph don't end exactly on a line? Explain how you decided where to end each bar.

E. Can you use your graph to find the total number of objects in the picture? Explain your answer.

Do You Remember?

1. Write 2 things you can tell from each data display.

a) bar graph

Favourite Ice Cream Toppings

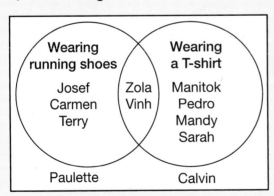

c) chart

How Many Pets Do You Have?

Name	Pets
Carmen	5
Manitok	2
Vinh	1
Sarah	7
Zola	0
Terry	2

b) Venn diagram

Wearing running shoes: Josef, Carmen, Terry

Zola, Vinh

Wearing a T-shirt: Manitok, Pedro, Mandy, Sarah

Paulette   Calvin

d) pictograph

How Old Are You?

7 ☺ ☺ ☺ ☺
8 ☺ ☺ ☺ ☺ ☺ ☺ ☺ ☺
9 ☺ ☺ ☺ ☺ ☺ ☺ ☺
10 ☺ ☺ ☺

Each ☺ means 5 people.

1 Constructing a Pictograph

Goal Construct and interpret pictographs.

Gotta Find a Footprint

Gotta find a footprint, a bone, or a tooth
To grab yourself a piece of dinosaur truth.
All the dino knowledge that we've ever known
Comes from a footprint, a tooth, or a bone.

JEFF MOSS

Pedro's Data

I asked people which dinosaur they like best. I will make a pictograph to display the data I collected.

Which Dinosaur Do You Like Best?

Dinosaur	Number of people
tyrannosaurus rex	60
triceratops	45
brachiosaurus	25
velociraptor	50
other	20

? How should Pedro display his data in a pictograph?

NEL

Pedro's Pictograph

I chose a footprint symbol to represent the number of people who like each dinosaur.

My **scale** is "Each 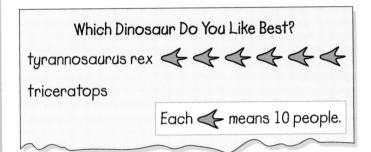 means 10 people."

I drew 6 footprints for tyrannosaurus rex, but I don't know how many to draw for triceratops.

Which Dinosaur Do You Like Best?

tyrannosaurus rex

triceratops

Each means 10 people.

A. How many symbols should triceratops have? Explain.

B. Is a footprint the best symbol to use or would a bone, a tooth, or another symbol be better? Explain.

C. Make a pictograph to show the dinosaur data.
Use a different scale than Pedro.
Write the title and show the scale you used.

Reflecting

1. What scale did you use for your pictograph? Explain your thinking.

2. How many symbols did you use for brachiosaurus? Why?

3. What do you need to know about the data before you can choose a scale for a pictograph?

Checking

4. The chart shows some data for you to display in a pictograph.
   a) What symbol will you use to represent the number of visitors? Why?
   b) How many people will 1 symbol represent on your pictograph? Explain your choice of scale.
   c) Make the pictograph. Include the title and the scale.

Visitors to the Dinosaur Show

Day	Number of visitors
Monday	150
Tuesday	300
Wednesday	200
Thursday	225
Friday	450

Practising

5. Dinosaur bones were found at many sites. Use this pictograph to answer the questions.

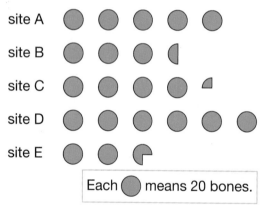

Number of Dinosaur Bones Found

Each ● means 20 bones.

   a) Which site had the greatest number of bones? Which site had the least number of bones?
   b) Make a chart to show how many bones were found at each site.
   c) How many bones were found at site E? Explain how you know.
   d) Why do you think the person who made this graph used a circle symbol instead of a bone?
   e) Make a new pictograph of the data that uses a different scale.

Dot-Paper Diagrams

The sides of this rectangle touch 6 dots.
There are 0 dots inside.

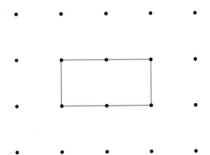

A. What other rectangles can you make
with 0 dots inside?

B. What triangle can you make with sides that
touch 6 dots and with 0 dots inside?

Try These

1. Draw each shape on dot paper.
   a) The sides of a rectangle touch 6 dots.
      There are 2 dots inside.
   b) The sides of a square touch 4 dots.
      There is 1 dot inside.
   c) The sides of a square touch 4 dots.
      There are 4 dots inside.

2. Find as many shapes as you can where the sides of
   the shape touch 4 dots and there is 1 dot inside.

2 Choosing a Scale for a Bar Graph

Goal Explain how to choose a graph and a scale that are appropriate for the data.

Mandy's Experiment

When I play board games, it seems like somebody rolls a 5 on almost every turn.

To see if this is true, I'm going to roll 3 dice and see if I get a 5 on at least 1 die.

I'll do 50 sets of rolls.

? **How can Mandy use an appropriate graph to display the results of her experiment?**

A. Try Mandy's experiment.
Make a tally chart to keep track of how many rolls have a 5. Roll 50 times.
Make only 1 tally mark for each roll, even if you roll more than one 5.

B. This bar graph shows Mandy's results.
About how many times did she roll at least one 5?

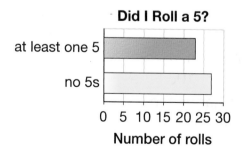

Did I Roll a 5?

at least one 5

no 5s

0 5 10 15 20 25 30
Number of rolls

C. Make a bar graph to show the results of your experiment. Use the same scale as Mandy.

D. What does your graph show about how often you rolled a 5 compared to how often you didn't? Explain your answer.

E. Make a chart with the combined results for your whole class. Show the results in a bar graph. Use a different scale than Mandy.

Reflecting

1. What scale did you use for the class graph? Why did you use this scale?

2. How did you decide where to graph numbers that were between the scale marks? Describe what you did using an example.

Checking

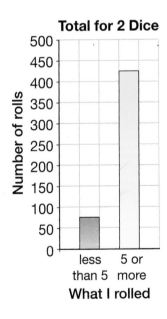

Total for 2 Dice

3. Rami did an experiment with 2 dice. On each roll, he added the 2 dice to find the total. He rolled 500 times and graphed the results.
   a) Tell how many rolls each bar could represent.
   b) Why is there more than 1 possible answer for part a)?
   c) If you add the numbers that the bars represent, what should the sum be? Why?

Practising

4. a) Try an experiment like Rami's. Roll 2 dice and tally whether the sum is "less than 5" or "5 or more." Repeat 100 times.
   b) Make a bar graph to show what happened. Choose a scale that is appropriate for the data.
   c) Explain how you chose your scale.

3 Collecting Data

Goal Predict results, collect and organize data, and find the range.

You will need
- paper clips

- a clock

? How many paper clips can you link in 2 minutes?

A. Predict how many paper clips you can link in 2 minutes. Record your prediction.

B. Make a paper-clip chain while your partner times 2 minutes.

C. Count and record the number of paper clips in your chain. Compare the number with your prediction. Now it's your partner's turn to make a chain.

D. Make a chart that shows all the class chains. What is the *least* number of paper clips in a chain? What is the *greatest* number of paper clips in a chain?

Person	Number of paper clips in chain
1	
2	

E. What is the **range** for the chains made by your class?

F. How can you organize the numbers in groups to make the data easier to understand? Work with a partner to make a table to record the groups. Show every number in its appropriate group. Record every number, including those that came up more than once.

range

The difference between the greatest number and the least number in a set of data

If the least number is 14 and the greatest number is 46, then the range is 46 − 14, or 32.

Reflecting

1. What groups did you use to organize the numbers in your table? Explain your thinking.

2. What information is easier to see in the organized numbers than it was in the original chart?

Stem-and-Leaf Plots

You will need
- chart of class chains from Lesson 3
- grid paper

Josef's Data Displays

Allison and I organized our data from the paper-clip chains by making this table.

My brother showed us how to display the same data on a **stem-and-leaf plot**.

Tens	Ones
40s	43
30s	30 31 31 33 35 35 36 38
20s	21 22 22 23 24 26 26 28 28 28
10s	12 12 14 16 17 17 19

Stem	Leaves
4	3
3	0 1 1 3 5 5 6 8
2	1 2 2 3 4 6 6 8 8 8
1	2 2 4 6 7 7 9

1 Look at Josef and Allison's stem-and-leaf plot.
- **a)** How many people linked 31 paper clips?
- **b)** Which value occurs most often? How many times does this value occur?

stem-and-leaf plot
A way to organize data in groups. The stem shows the beginning of the number and the leaf shows the rest.

2 Make a stem-and-leaf plot to show the lengths of the chains your class made.
- **a)** Which stem has the most leaves? What does this tell you about the chains?
- **b)** How is this type of data display the same as graphs you know about? How is it different?

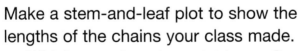

4 Constructing a Bar Graph with Intervals

Goal Construct a bar graph using appropriate intervals for the range of data.

? How can you make a bar graph to show how many paper clips can be linked in 2 minutes?

Natalie's Bar Graph

Our class made a list of everybody's paper-clip chain lengths.

A graph with a bar for every number would have 18 bars! That's too many.

I decided to group the numbers in **intervals** so my graph would have only 3 or 4 bars.

The **range** of the numbers is about 30. An interval of 2 will mean about 15 bars. An interval of 5 will mean about 6 bars. I will use an interval of 10 to get about 3 bars.

My bars are from 12–21, 22–31, and 32–41.

I had to add a 4th bar for 42–51 because somebody got 43.

How Many Paper Clips Can We Link in 2 Minutes?

12	12	14	16	17	17	19	21	22	22	23
24	26	26	28	28	28	30	31	31	33	35
35	36	38	43							

Number of paper clips	Number of people
12–21	8
22–31	12
32–41	5
42–51	1

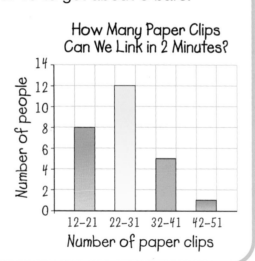

How Many Paper Clips Can We Link in 2 Minutes?

interval

The distance between 2 endpoints on a graph scale. Intervals on a graph should be equal.

12–21 and 22–31 are intervals of 10.

Reflecting

1. Which bar on Natalie's graph includes all the people who linked 28 paper clips? Explain how you know.

2. How did Natalie use the range of chain lengths to help her make the bar graph?

3. Write a question you could answer using Natalie's bar graph. Find the answer to your question. Explain how you found the answer.

Checking

4. This list shows how many small paper clips some students were able to hang from a big paper clip in 2 minutes.
   a) What is the range of the data?
   b) Choose intervals and organize the data in a table.
   c) Explain how you chose the intervals for your table.

Number of Paper Clips Attached

16	18	19	20	21
21	22	24	24	24
25	26	26	26	27
28	29	29	30	32
32	35	36	36	37

Practising

5. This list shows how many elastics some students were able to tie together in a chain in 4 minutes.
   a) Make a table and a bar graph with appropriate intervals.
   b) Explain how you chose the intervals for your graph. Use the word *range* in your explanation.
   c) Explain how you chose the scale for the axis that shows the number of people.

Number of Elastics Tied Together

31	32	32	33	35
36	36	36	37	37
37	39	39	41	41
41	42	42	42	42
43	43	44	44	45
45	45	47	48	48
49	49	49	50	50

5 Reading and Interpreting Graphs

Goal Read and interpret graphs and identify their features.

Manitok's Data

I collected these data about favourite lunchtime activities at my school.

Favourite Lunchtime Activities

Activity	Number of students
chess	40
floor hockey	75
volleyball	20
craft club	60
choir	25

These 3 graphs are supposed to show Manitok's data.

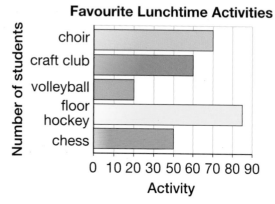

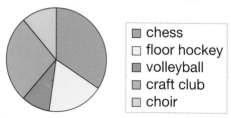

? What mistakes can you find in each graph?

A. Describe the mistakes you found on each graph. Use words such as *title*, *axis*, *label*, *scale*, and **legend**.

legend
A feature on a graph that explains what colours or symbols mean

Reflecting

1. What would a correct bar graph show about the students' favourite lunchtime activities?

2. Explain how each type of graph helps you to compare data.

3. How might Manitok use the data he collected?

Checking

4. What mistakes can you find in each graph?

   a) **Games Won by Each Floor Hockey Team**

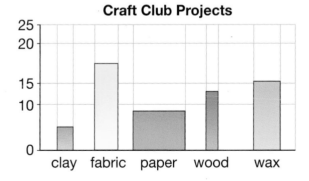

   b)

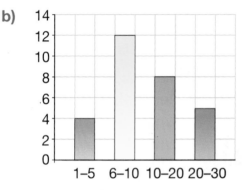

Practising

5. What's wrong with this bar graph?

   Craft Club Projects

6. These 2 graphs are supposed to show the same information about how many games a floor hockey team has won and lost. Do the graphs show the same information? Explain your thinking.

Mid-Chapter Review

1

1. The pictograph shows data about what students chose to read in the library.

   a) How many students chose comics?

   b) Draw a new pictograph of the data. Use a different scale.

   c) Explain your choice of scale.

What Students Are Reading

books   📖 📖 📖 📖 📖 📖

newspapers 📖 📖

magazines 📖 📖 📖

comics   📖 📖 📖 📖 📖

Each 📖 means 8 students.

2

2. The Sub Shop kept track of sales for 1 week to find out which sandwiches are most popular.

Sandwich	turkey	vegetarian	roast beef	tuna	meatball
Number sold	168	137	206	155	124

   a) Make a bar graph to show the data. Remember to include the title and labels for the axes.

   b) What scale did you use on the Number sold axis? Why did you choose this scale?

   c) Which sandwich is most popular? Which sandwich is least popular?

3

3. Chris made a table to show the numbers of pets owned by 10 people. The range is 6. What might the total number of pets be? Explain.

5

4. a) List 3 things the graph shows about students' hot dog orders.

   b) Which bar includes students who ordered 18 hot dogs?

   c) About how many students ordered hot dogs this year? Explain how you know.

5. Write a question you can answer using the hot dog graph. Write the answer for your question.

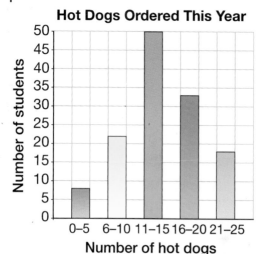

Hot Dogs Ordered This Year

Number of students

0–5 6–10 11–15 16–20 21–25
Number of hot dogs

6 Graphing with Technology

You will need

• coloured candies

• spreadsheet software
• a computer

Goal Use spreadsheet software to organize and display data.

? **What colour will you find most often in a package of coloured candies?**

A. Predict the colour you will find most often.

B. Open a package of candies.
Sort the candies by colour.
Enter the results into a spreadsheet.

C. Use the graphing function in your spreadsheet to make a bar graph of your data.

D. Change the data in your spreadsheet by doubling the number of candies for 1 colour.
What happened to the graph?
Explain your answer.

	A	B	C
1	blue	5	
2	brown	12	
3	green	4	
4	orange	5	
5	pink	8	
6	purple	6	
7	red	7	
8	yellow	9	
9			

A9

Sheet1 / Sheet2 / Sheet3

E. Make a circle graph of your data.
Why is it important to include a legend?

Reflecting

1. What are some of the advantages of using software to make a graph?
What are some of the disadvantages?

7 Communicate About Collecting Data

Goal Describe the steps for collecting data in a clear and organized way.

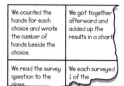

Miki's Survey

Our group surveyed four grade 4 classes to find out about their favourite activities during indoor recess.

We made cards to show the steps we used to collect our data, but the cards got all mixed up.

Survey Question

What is your favourite activity during indoor recess?

• playing board and card games
• playing sports in the gym
• reading in the library
• other

? **How can Miki put the steps in order?**

We counted the hands for each choice and wrote the number of hands beside the choice.	We got together afterward and added up the results in a chart.	We wrote a survey question with 3 choices and "other."	We read the question again and asked students to raise their hands for their choice.
We read the survey question to the class.	We each surveyed 1 of the 4 classrooms.	My friend Chris picked sports because he likes basketball.	We told the students to raise their hands only once.

A. Which step do you think Miki's group did first? Which step did they do next?

B. Arrange the rest of the steps in order.

C. Read the Communication Checklist.
How would Miki's group answer the 3rd question?

D. Compare your order of the steps with another group's order. Were there any differences?
If so, what were the differences?

Reflecting

1. How did you decide on the order of the steps?

Communication Checklist
☑ Did you show all the steps?
☑ Did you put the steps in order?
☑ Did you include only necessary information?

Checking

2. Allison's group collected data about favourite board and card games. Put their steps in order.

We made a survey form for each person. We put our survey question on the form.	We went to each class and gave each person a survey form.	We asked everyone to write an answer on the survey form.	We wrote our survey question, "What is your favourite board or card game?"	We sorted the survey forms to see how many people liked each game.

Practising

3. Sarah's group collected data about favourite sports.
   a) Put their steps in order.
   b) Which step is not necessary?
   Explain your thinking.

We asked the people who like sports to put a cube in one of 3 pails. We had 1 pail for each sport.	We decided to ask, "Which sport do you like best – basketball, floor hockey, or volleyball?"	The cubes were all the same colour.	We went to each class and asked the people who like sports to raise their hands.	We counted the cubes in each pail to see which sport was the favourite.

8 Conducting a Survey

You will need

• grid paper

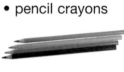

• pencil crayons

Goal Conduct a survey and make a graph to display the data.

? How can you conduct a survey and display the data you collected?

A. Make a plan for collecting the data.
   • What do you want to find out?
   • Who will you ask?
   • Where and when will you do your **survey**?

B. Create the question you will ask in your survey.

C. What answers do you think you will get most often? What answers do you think you won't get very often? Give reasons for your predictions.

D. Conduct your survey. Record your data on a tally chart.

E. Make a graph to show the data you collected. Choose the type of graph to display your data. Decide whether you will use a spreadsheet or draw your graph by hand. Explain your choices.

Reflecting

1. How well does your finished graph help you answer the question for your survey?
   Did you get the answers you expected?
   Why or why not?

2. How could you use the data you collected?

3. Create 2 questions about the data in your graph. Tell how you would answer each question.

Race to the Top

Number of players: 2

How to play: Find the sum of your cards and place a tile on the appropriate bar in the graph.
Try to fill a bar of the graph.

Step 1 Shuffle the cards and deal 2 cards to each player. Place the other cards face down in a pile.

Step 2 Find the sum of your 2 cards.

Step 3 Decide whether you will take one more card from the pile.
If you do, add the new card to your sum.

Step 4 Put a tile on the appropriate bar to show your sum. The dealer plays first.

Step 5 Switch dealers and deal again.

The person who fills the last square in any bar wins.

You will need

- Race to the Top bar graph

  0–4 5–9 10–14 15
  Race to the Top

- 4 sets of number cards (1 to 10)

- tiles

Calvin's Turn

I was dealt 2 and 6.
I drew 9.
My sum is 2 + 6 + 9 = 17.
I put a tile on the 15−19 bar.

LESSON

Skills Bank

1 1. This pictograph shows the number of students that ride each bus.

Students Who Ride the Bus

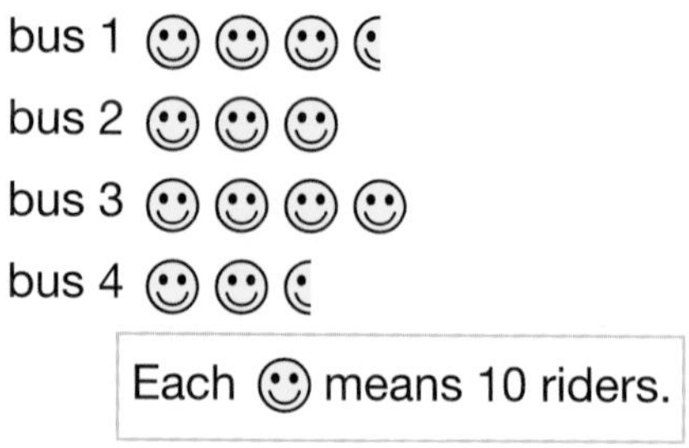

bus 1 ☺ ☺ ☺ ◖

bus 2 ☺ ☺ ☺

bus 3 ☺ ☺ ☺ ☺

bus 4 ☺ ☺ ◖

Each ☺ means 10 riders.

a) Which bus has the most students? Which bus has the fewest students?

b) Make a chart to show how many students ride each bus.

c) Make a new chart to show how many students will be on each bus after these changes:

- 1 student from bus 4 moves to bus 1.
- 2 students from bus 2 move to bus 3.

d) Make a new pictograph to show the data from part c). Use a different scale.

2 2. This table shows the cost of some food items at a restaurant in 1950.

a) Make a bar graph to show the data. Choose an appropriate scale.

b) Write 3 things the graph shows about the cost of the foods.

Cost of Some Foods in 1950

Food item	Cost
hamburger	45¢
soup	25¢
milk	15¢
cheese sandwich	40¢
banana split	60¢
apple pie	30¢

3 3. Find each value using the pictograph in Question 1.

a) the least number of students in a bus

b) the greatest number of students in a bus

c) the range of students riding the buses

4. Find the least price, the greatest price, and the range of prices for the data in the table in Question 2.

4 **5.** This list shows the ages of 48 customers at a restaurant.

a) What is the range of the data?

b) Organize the data in a table like this.

Customer Ages

2	5	6	7	7	8
11	15	16	16	16	19
20	21	21	21	21	23
24	27	28	29	29	30
31	32	32	35	36	36
37	37	37	38	41	45
46	48	50	51	51	52
54	56	60	62	73	81

Age of customer	Number of customers
1–10	
11–20	
21–30	
31–40	
41–50	
51–60	
61–70	
71–80	
81–90	

c) Make a bar graph to show the data from your table.

d) Write at least 1 question you could answer using your graph from part c).

5 **6.** Describe the mistakes on each graph.
Use words such as title, axis, label, scale, and legend.

a)

apple			
orange			
grape			
fruit punch			

Each ◯ means 20 bottles.

b)

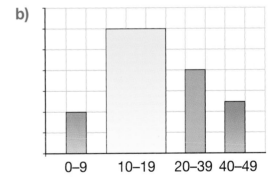

0–9   10–19   20–39 40–49

7. Match each feature of a graph with its purpose.

a) title   V. tells what the colours or symbols mean

b) axis   W. tells what the graph is about

c) scale   X. tells the value of each pictograph symbol

d) legend   Y. tells what each bar represents

e) label   Z. where you show the scale on a bar graph

Problem Bank

1 **1.** The pictograph shows the number of milk cartons some grade 4 students bought at the school in October.
The students bought 84 cartons altogether.
How many cartons does each ⬜ represent?
Explain your answer.

Milk Sales in October

Tim 🥛 🥛 🥛 🥛 🥛 🥛 🥛 🥛 🥛

Rosie 🥛 🥛 🥛

Aputik 🥛 🥛 🥛 🥛 🥛

Kelvin 🥛 🥛 🥛 🥛

Each 🥛 means ■ cartons.

2 **2.** Use the graph to solve the problem.
The temperature in one city was 7°C warmer than in another city.
Which were the 2 cities?
Explain your thinking.

High Temperature on a Day in October

3. 12 more families shop at store E than at store D.
How many families shop at store A?
Explain how you know.

Where We Shop

4. Greg surveyed 50 students to see how many CDs they owned. There were twice as many students who owned between 11 and 15 CDs as students who owned fewer than 6 CDs. How many students owned fewer than 6 CDs? Explain your thinking.

Number of CDs	Number of students
fewer than 6	
6–10	8
11–15	
more than 15	18

5. There are 45 fish in Casey's tank. There are twice as many black mollies as neon tetras. There are 15 goldfish in the tank. How many of each kind of fish are in Casey's tank? Explain your thinking.

Casey's Fish Tank

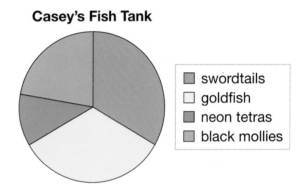

☐ swordtails
☐ goldfish
☐ neon tetras
☐ black mollies

6. Create a problem with addition, subtraction, or both operations that someone could solve using the graph about favourite seasons.
Write the answer to your problem.
Show the steps you would use to solve your problem.

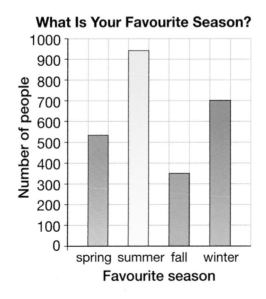

What Is Your Favourite Season?

Chapter Review

1. 1. Use the pictograph to answer these questions.

Goals Scored by Hockey Teams

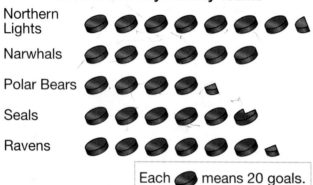

Each ⬤ means 20 goals.

a) Is a hockey puck a good symbol to use for this pictograph? Explain your answer.

b) Is "Each ⬤ means 20 goals" a good scale to use for this pictograph?
What other scales could have been used?
Explain your answer.

c) Make a table of data to show the number of goals scored by each team.
Find the range of the data.

2. 2. Use the bar graph to answer these questions.

a) About how many more people prefer browsing to games?

b) About how many people in total are represented on the graph?

c) What scale was used to make the graph?

d) What are some of the advantages and disadvantages of this scale?
Would another scale be better?
Explain your answer.

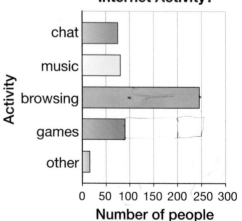

What Is Your Favourite Internet Activity?

3. These data show how long some grade 4 students were able to stand on 1 foot.

Seconds on 1 Foot

12 19 20 21 21 21
22 28 29 32 34 36
37 37 37 41 41 42
43 45 46 48 50 51
57 58 59 60 63 64
65 67 70 72 78 80

Seconds	Number of students
1–10	
11–20	
21–30	
31–40	
41–50	
51–60	
61–70	
71–80	

a) Complete the table.
b) Make a bar graph with intervals to display the data.

4. The pictograph is supposed to show the data from the Read-a-Thon table. What mistakes can you find?

Pages Read in the Read-a-Thon

Miki   📖 📖 📖 📖 📖 📖 📖

Vinh   📖 📖 📖 📖 📖 📖 📖 📖 📖 📖 📖

Zola   📖 📖 📖 📖 📖 📖 📖 📖 📖 📖 📖 📖 📖

Allison 📖 📖 📖 📖 📖 📖

Jon   📖 📖 📖 📖 📖 📖 📖 📖 📖

Books Read for the Read-a-Thon

Name	Number of books
Miki	13
Vinh	21
Allison	25
Zola	11
Jon	18

5. Describe a survey you could conduct to find out how many families bake cookies at home.
a) Write a survey question.
b) Where, when, and how would you conduct your survey?
c) How would you organize the survey information? Explain with words and a drawing.
d) Predict what the survey results might show. Explain your predictions.

Chapter Task

Planning a Playground

Lakeview School will buy 4 new pieces of playground equipment. Lakeview students conducted a survey of all the students to find out what they think the school should buy.

What I Want Most for the Playground (Kindergarten to Grade 2)

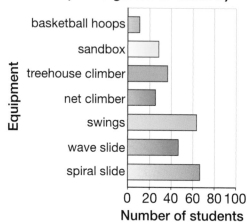

? **What 4 pieces of playground equipment should the school buy?**

Part 1

Justin saw the results of the survey. He said the school should buy the spiral slide, the wave slide, the swings, and the treehouse climber.

A. Do you think Justin was looking at the graph or the table? Explain.

B. Why do you think the most popular suggestions are different in the graph and in the table?

C. Make a bar graph to show the data in the table. Explain how you chose your scale.

Part 2

D. What 4 pieces of playground equipment do you think the school should buy? Justify your decision.

What I Want Most for the Playground (Grades 3 to 6)

Equipment	Number of students
basketball hoops	58
sandbox	2
treehouse climber	34
net climber	15
swings	51
wave slide	16
spiral slide	37

Task Checklist

☑ Did you use math language?

☑ Did you explain your thinking?

Cumulative Review

Cross-Strand Multiple Choice

Cars	Wheels
1	4
2	8
3	12
4	16
5	20

1. Which rule describes the number pattern in the Wheels column?
   A. start at 4 and multiply by 2 each time
   B. start at 4 and multiply by 4 each time
   C. start at 4 and add 1 each time
   D. start at 4 and add 4 each time

2. Extend this pattern:
   $2 + 6 - 5, 3 + 7 - 5, 4 + 8 - 5,$ ■
   E. $5 + 9 - 5$
   F. $5 + 8 - 7$
   G. $5 + 9 - 7$
   H. $5 + 8 - 5$

3. Which set of numbers is in order from least to greatest?
   A. 3508, 5081, 7125, 7095, 9091
   B. 9109, 9108, 9107, 9105, 9103
   C. 8236, 8335, 8434, 8533, 8632
   D. 3919, 3818, 3717, 3616, 3515

4. Which is the expanded form of 8205?
   E. $8200 + 200 + 5$
   F. $8000 + 20 + 5$
   G. $8000 + 200 + 5$
   H. $8200 + 5$

5. Which part of the bar graph tells about the range of the data?
   A. title
   B. Number of objects scale
   C. height of bars
   D. Number of wheels on object intervals

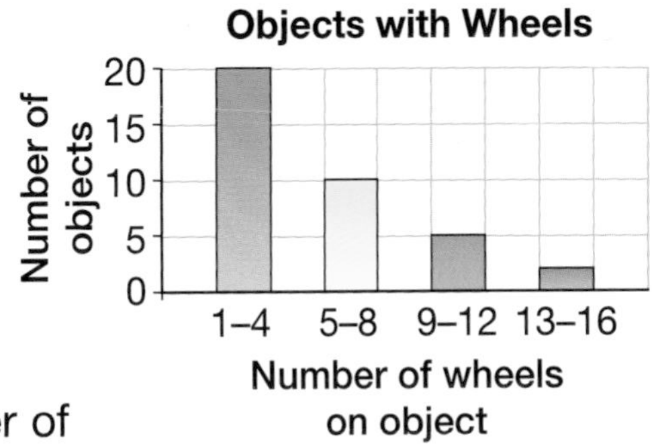

6. What is the difference between the number of objects that have fewer than 5 wheels and the number of objects that have more than 12 wheels?

Cross-Strand Investigation

Wheels in Our Lives

7. Some students picked their favourite toy with wheels.
   a) Create a bar graph of the data.
   b) How do you think the data were collected?
   c) Describe the data. Use math words.
   d) Bicycle wheels can have solid centres or spokes. Here is a pattern of wheels in a bicycle store.

Favourite Toy with Wheels

Favourite toy	Number of students
skateboard	30
bicycle	25
inline skates	15
scooter	20
other	15

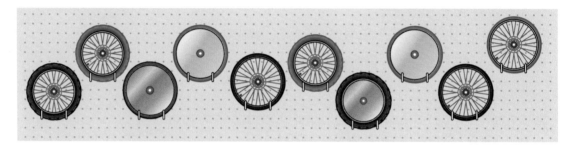

   i) What attributes change in the pattern?
   ii) Describe how each attribute changes.
   e) Make a different wheel pattern.
   i) List attributes that could change in your pattern.
   ii) Make a pattern that has 2 or more changing attributes.
   iii) Describe your pattern.

8. Vehicles are parked in a garage.
   a) Describe the number patterns in the chart.
   b) How is the number pattern for Vehicles related to the number pattern for Number of wheels?
   c) What will be the number of wheels on level 2? Show your work.
   d) Describe the patterning strategy you used in part c).

Level	Vehicles	Number of wheels
7	130	520
6	170	680
5	210	840

Addition and Subtraction

Goals

You will be able to

- **estimate sums and differences**
- **add and subtract with 4-digit numbers**
- **add and subtract numbers mentally**
- **create and solve addition and subtraction problems**

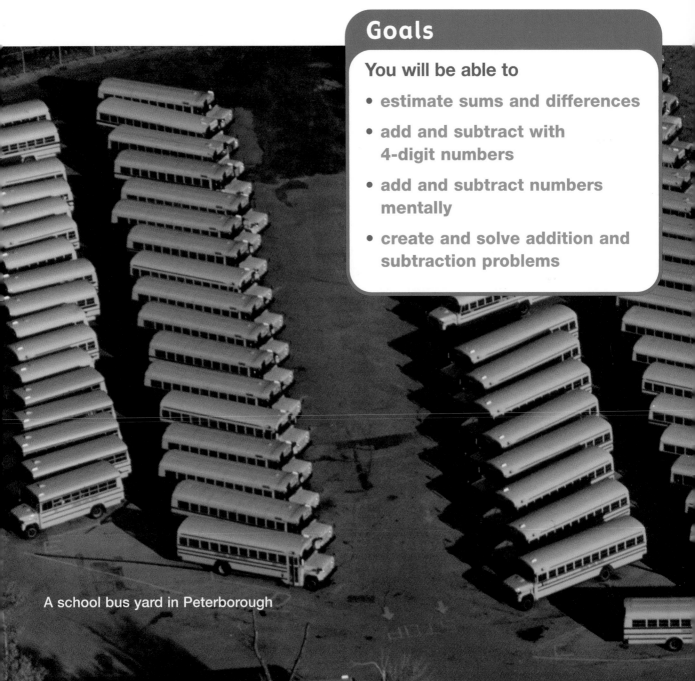

A school bus yard in Peterborough

Getting Started

Counting Students

Number of Elementary
School Students

North
School

185
students

Lakeview
School

205
students

South
School

The circle graph shows the numbers of students
who go to 3 different schools.

? **About how many students go to the 3 schools?**

A. What is the total number of students who go to North and South schools? Explain how you know.

B. Estimate the number of students who go to Lakeview School. Explain how you estimated.

C. Estimate the total number of students who go to the 3 schools.

Do You Remember?

1. Explain how to use one **equation** to complete the other equation.
   a) Use $18 + 20 = 38$ to find $18 + 19 = \blacksquare$.
   b) Use $11 + 19 = 30$ to find $30 - 19 = \blacksquare$.

2. Estimate by **rounding**.
   Show your rounded numbers.
   a) $185 + 188$ b) $435 + 75$ c) $811 - 378$ d) $456 - 378$

3. Calculate each **sum** or **difference**.
   Show your thinking.
   a) $150 + 150$ b) $456 - 200$ c) $418 + 99$ d) $456 - 66$

4. a) Find the total cost of the 2 caps.
   b) Describe or draw the coins and bills you would use to pay the exact amount for each cap.

$4.04

$6.96

1 Adding Mentally

Goal Use mental math strategies to add 2-digit numbers.

There are 28 people in the top section of an arena.
There are 22 people in the bottom section of the arena.

? **What is the total number of people in the arena?**

Mandy's Method

I imagine rows of 10 people.

When I think of moving people to other rows, it's easier to see how many people there are.

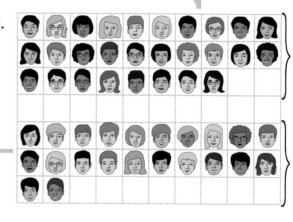

28 people in the top section

22 people in the bottom section

A. Which people might Mandy think of moving? Why?

B. What is the total number of people in the arena? Show your calculations.

Vinh's Method

I used a different method to add 28 and 22.
I drew a number line and used mental math to find the sum.

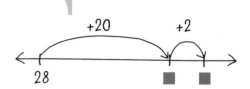

C. What numbers are missing from Vinh's number line?

D. Explain how Vinh used a number line and mental math to add 28 and 22.

Reflecting

1. Use Mandy's method and Vinh's method to add 47 and 23. Show your thinking.

2. What names would you give to Mandy's method and Vinh's method? Explain your thinking.

Checking

3. In an arena, there are 49 people in the top section and 21 people in the bottom section.
Show 2 ways to use mental math to find the total number of people in the arena.

Practising

4. Use mental math to calculate the total number of people in each arena.
Choose a method that fits each situation.
Explain what you did.

a)
Top section	Bottom section
18	42

c)
Top section	Bottom section
37	23

b)
Top section	Bottom section
49	39

d)
Top section	Bottom section
25	45

5. How can 40 + 40 = 80 be used to calculate each sum?
Show your work.
   a) 39 + 41   c) 39 + 39
   b) 38 + 42   d) 45 + 45

2 Estimating Sums

Goal Estimate sums by rounding.

1869 km

Winnipeg

Vancouver

1518 km

Toronto

? How far is it from Vancouver to Toronto?

Manitok's Number Line

I used a calculator to calculate the distance from Vancouver to Toronto.

Sketching a number line can help me figure out if 4387 km is a reasonable answer.

4387.

0 km
Vancouver

2000 km
Winnipeg

Toronto

A. Why did Manitok round 1869 km to 2000 km instead of 1000 km?

B. What rounded number could Manitok use to estimate the distance from Winnipeg to Toronto?

C. Estimate the total distance from Vancouver to Toronto. Use rounded numbers.

D. Does Manitok's calculator show a reasonable answer? Explain your thinking.

E. Use a calculator to find the distance from Vancouver to Toronto.

Reflecting

1. How did the number line help Manitok estimate?

2. When you estimate, can you tell if your estimate will be greater or less than the answer from a calculator?
   Explain your answer using examples.

Checking

3. Estimate these total flight distances.
   Show your rounded numbers.

   a)

   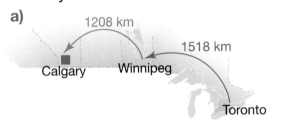

   b)

   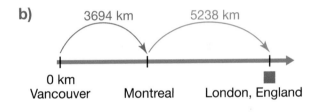

Practising

4. Estimate. Show your rounded numbers.
   a) 1567 + 813   b) 2611 + 1489   c) 4156 + 1722

5. Choose a trip you can make that combines at least 2 flights. Estimate the total distance.
   Show your work.

Trip	Flight distance
Toronto ➤ St. John's	2112 km
St. John's ➤ London, England	3774 km
London, England ➤ Cairo, Egypt	3530 km
Cairo, Egypt ➤ Athens, Greece	1130 km
Athens, Greece ➤ St. John's	6106 km

6. Josef estimates that 1437 + 1498 is about 2000.
   Allison thinks that the sum is close to 3000.
   Are the 2 estimates reasonable? Explain.

3 Communicate About Number Concepts and Procedures

You will need

• a calculator

Goal Explain your thinking when estimating a sum.

The local arena has 9000 seats for a hockey game.
3488 tickets for blue seats and 4834 tickets for green seats were sold.

Rey's Sum

I used a calculator to find out how many tickets were sold altogether.
I pressed 3488 ⊞ 4834 ⊟ and got 8322.

? **Is Rey's answer reasonable? Explain how you know.**

Rami's Explanation

There are 9000 seats, so 8322 tickets seems reasonable.

I'll estimate to check. I'll use rounding because rounded numbers are easy to add.

3488 is about 3000 because it's closer to 3000 than 4000.

4834 is close to 5000.

I'll start at 3000 and add on 5 jumps of 1000.

+1000 +1000 +1000 +1000 +1000

```
      3000  4000  5000  6000  7000  8000
```

The answer should be close to 8000, so I think 8322 is reasonable.

Allison's Explanation

I'll use rounded numbers, because they're easy to work with.

3488 rounds to 3000 and 4834 rounds to 5000.

The sum should be close to 3000 + 5000.

I know 3 + 5 = 8, so I can add the thousands.

8322 is close to 8000, so it's a reasonable answer.

$$\begin{array}{r} 3 \text{ thousand} \\ + 5 \text{ thousand} \\ \hline 8 \text{ thousand} \end{array}$$

Reflecting

1. Read the Communication Checklist.
   How would Rami and Allison answer each question?
   Give evidence from each person's work.

2. How does Rami's number line help you understand what he is thinking?

Communication Checklist

- ☑ Did you show the right amount of detail?
- ☑ Did you explain your thinking?

Checking

3. The arena has 6000 seats for the circus.
   1631 adult tickets and 3712 children's tickets were sold. How many tickets were sold altogether? Use a calculator. Explain why your answer is reasonable.

Practising

4. The arena has 7500 seats for a basketball game.
   2815 tickets for blue seats and 3947 tickets for green seats were sold. How many tickets were sold altogether? Use a calculator.
   Explain why your answer is reasonable.

5. Is the sum reasonable? Explain how you know.

$$\begin{array}{r} 4829 \\ + 2301 \\ \hline 6130 \end{array}$$

4 Adding 4-Digit Numbers

Goal Solve addition problems using regrouping.

? **What is the total number of Girl Guides in the Central and Niagara areas?**

Girl Guide Membership

Area	Number of Girl Guides
Central	2539
Hamilton	1172
Niagara	1509
Ottawa	1728
Toronto	2621

Natalie's Addition

There are 2539 Girl Guides in the Central area.

There are 1509 Girl Guides in the Niagara area.

2539 is between 2000 and 3000.

1509 is between 1000 and 2000.

That means there must be between 3000 and 5000 Girl Guides altogether.

$$
\begin{array}{ccccc}
2000 & \longleftarrow & 2539 & \longrightarrow & 3000 \\
+\,1000 & \longleftarrow & +\,1509 & \longrightarrow & +\,2000 \\
\hline
3000 & & & & 5000
\end{array}
$$

I can find the actual number of Girl Guides by adding on a place value chart.

Step 1 I added the ones and regrouped them.

9 ones + 9 ones = 18 ones
18 ones = 1 ten and 8 ones

$$
\begin{array}{r}
1 \\
2539 \\
+\,1509 \\
\hline
8
\end{array}
$$

Thousands	Hundreds	Tens	Ones
			1
2	5	3	9
1	5	0	9
			8

Step 2 I added the tens.

1 ten + 3 tens + 0 tens = 4 tens

```
    1
  2539
+ 1509
    48
```

Thousands	Hundreds	Tens	Ones
		1	
2	5	3	9
1	5	0	9
		4	8

Step 3 I added the hundreds and regrouped them.

5 hundreds + 5 hundreds = 10 hundreds

10 hundreds = 1 thousand + 0 hundreds

```
  1 1
  2539
+ 1509
   048
```

Thousands	Hundreds	Tens	Ones
1		1	
2	5	3	9
1	5	0	9
	0	4	8

Step 4 I added the thousands.

1 thousand + 2 thousands + 1 thousand = 4 thousands

```
  1 1
  2539
+ 1509
  4048
```

Thousands	Hundreds	Tens	Ones
1		1	
2	5	3	9
1	5	0	9
4	0	4	8

There are 4048 Girl Guides in the Central and Niagara areas.
My estimate was between 3000 and 5000 Girl Guides, so 4048 seems reasonable.

Reflecting

1. In Step 1, why did Natalie **regroup** 18 ones as 1 ten and 8 ones?

2. Is it possible to add two 4-digit numbers without regrouping? Give an example to support your answer.

regroup
Trade 10 smaller units for 1 larger unit, or 1 larger unit for 10 smaller units

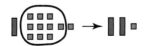

Checking

3. **a)** There are 2539 Girl Guides in the Central area and 1172 Girl Guides in the Hamilton area. What is the total number of Girl Guides in the Central and Hamilton areas?

   b) Explain how you know your answer is reasonable.

Practising

4. There are 2867 Wolf Cubs in the Greater Toronto area and 3301 Wolf Cubs in the Voyageur area. Estimate and then calculate the total number of Wolf Cubs in the Greater Toronto and Voyageur areas.

5. Estimate. Complete the calculation if the estimated sum of the numbers is between 4000 and 6000. Show your rounded numbers.

   a) 2987
       + 2145

   b) 3254
       + 162

   c) 2311
       + 2499

   d) 1300
          2253
       + 1701

6. Is the answer reasonable? Explain how you know.
   a) 4566 + 2869 = 9435
   b) 1859 + 2899 = 3758
   c) 3532 + 4499 = 8031

7. Create your own addition problem about the Girl Guide data. Show how to solve your problem.

8. Write two 4-digit numbers with a sum that is just less than 10 000. Show your work.

9. Would you calculate each sum using mental math, pencil and paper, or a calculator? Give a reason for each choice.
   a) 26 + 24   **b)** 3456 + 239   **c)** 18 264 + 11 495

10. Calculate each sum in Question 9 using your chosen method. Show your work.

Race to 150

Number of players: 2
How to play: Cross out numbers and find the total.

Step 1 Copy this array of numbers.

5	10	15	20	25	30
5	10	15	20	25	30
5	10	15	20	25	30
5	10	15	20	25	30

Step 2 Player 1 crosses out a number.

Step 3 Player 2 crosses out another number and adds to find the total of the crossed out numbers.

Step 4 Take turns crossing out and totalling all the numbers.

The player who reaches a total of exactly 150 wins.

Chris's Turn

Shani and I have crossed out a total of 120 so far.
I can win if I cross out a 30!

5	1̶0̶	15	20	25	3̶0̶
5	1̶0̶	1̶5̶	20	25	30
5	10	15	20	2̶5̶	3̶0̶
5	10	15	20	25	30

Mid–Chapter Review

1. Use mental math to add.
Explain your steps for 2 of the questions.
   a) 46 + 18   **d)** 19 + 46
   b) 38 + 22   **e)** 39 + 56
   c) 29 + 31   **f)** 75 + 25

2. Estimate. Explain your steps for 2 of the estimates.
   a) 6455 + 2876   **c)** 3658 + 4444
   b) 999 + 1786   **d)** 5110 + 3459

3. Is each answer reasonable?
Explain your thinking.
   a) 4579 + 518 = 5097
   b) 2367 + 2710 = 6077
   c) 5145 + 4145 = 9290
   d) 4821 + 2197 = 6018

4. Estimate and then add.
   a) 4217 + 3572   **c)** 3169 + 825   **e)** 3876 + 5678
   b) 746 + 615   **d)** 7394 + 2527   **f)** 1750 + 5250

5. On the same day, a plane flew 5456 km to one city and then flew 3567 km to another city. Calculate how far the plane flew that day. Explain how you know that your answer is reasonable.

6. Pedro estimates that the sum of 2 numbers is close to 5000. One of the numbers is 2878. What might the other number be? Explain how you know that your answer is reasonable.

Subtract by Adding On

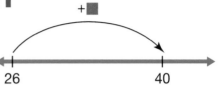

You can subtract by thinking about adding on.
To subtract 26 from 40, think $26 + \blacksquare = 40$.

Chantal's Method

I jumped $4 + 10$.

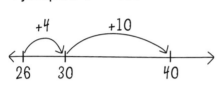

Carmen's Method

I jumped $10 + 4$.

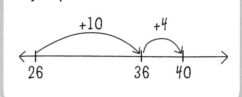

A. How much is $40 - 26$?
   Explain how you know.

B. How would you use your answer from
   part A to find $40 - 27$?

C. Write another pair of numbers you could
   subtract by adding on.
   Draw a number line to show the jumps
   you would use to find the answer.

Try These

1. Subtract by adding on.
   Use a number line to show your steps.

   a) $30 - 12$
   b) $30 - 11$
   c) $50 - 12$
   d) $80 - 45$
   e) $30 - 19$
   f) $45 - 15$
   g) $40 - 25$
   h) $55 - 35$

5 Subtracting Mentally

 Goal Develop mental math strategies for subtracting 2-digit numbers.

Pedro's brother is 19 and his father is 45.

❓ **How much older is Pedro's father than Pedro's brother?**

 ## Pedro's Solution

I can show the problem on a number line.

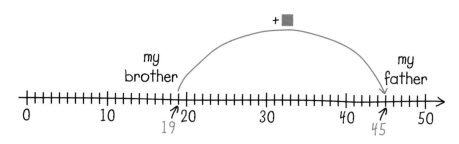

If I add 1 year to each age, the difference between the ages will still be the same, but the numbers will be easier to subtract.

Then 45 − 19 = ■ becomes 46 − 20 = ■.

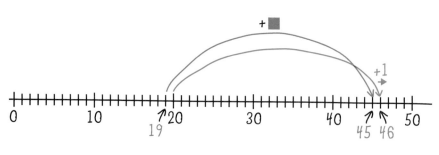

A. How much older is Pedro's father than Pedro's brother? Explain how you know.

B. Did you subtract by taking away or by adding on? Explain your method.

Reflecting

1. Explain why the red arrow and the blue arrow show the same size of jump on the number line.

2. Why is 46 − 20 easy to solve mentally?

Checking

3. Sarah's sister is 28 years old and Sarah's mother is 51 years old.
   How much older is Sarah's mother than Sarah's sister?
   Use mental math to find the answer.
   Explain your steps.

Practising

4. Use mental math to find each age difference.
   Use a different strategy to check your answers.
   a) 28 years and 53 years
   b) 49 years and 81 years

5. Use mental math to subtract.
   Explain your steps.
   a) 33 − 19   c) 67 − 29
   b) 66 − 18   d) 81 − 69

6. Write 2 different ages between 20 and 100.
   Show how to use mental math to find the difference between the ages.

6 Estimating Differences

Goal Estimate differences by rounding.

The height of Ishpatina Ridge
in Ontario is 693 m.
The height of Cypress Hills
in Saskatchewan is
1468 m.

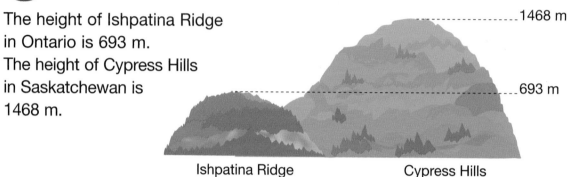

Ishpatina Ridge   Cypress Hills

1468 m

693 m

**? How can you estimate the height difference
between Cypress Hills and Ishpatina Ridge?**

A. How can you use rounding to estimate?
   Show 2 different ways.

B. How can you use the drawing to estimate?

C. How else could you estimate?
   Show at least 2 ways.

Reflecting

1. Carmen said she estimated the height
   difference by subtracting 1468 − 693 and
   rounding the result to the nearest thousand.
   Is this a good way to estimate? Explain.

2. Manitok said he estimated by counting on
   by 100s from 700 to 1400.
   Is this a good way to estimate? Explain.

3. Find the range of the estimates for your class.
   Why are many different estimates possible?

River Crossing

You will need

- 2 dice

- River Crossing game sheet

Number of players: team of 2
How to play: Try to get the greatest total in your river crossing.

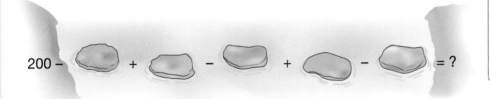

$$200 - \bigcirc + \bigcirc - \bigcirc + \bigcirc - \bigcirc = ?$$

Step 1 Player 1 rolls both dice to make a 2-digit number. The player writes this number on the 1st stepping stone.

Step 2 Take turns rolling the dice and writing numbers on the stones until you have crossed the river.

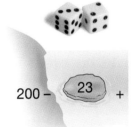

$$200 - \boxed{23} +$$

Step 3 Once you have crossed the river, use subtraction and addition to calculate your score.
Use the ranges below to see how you did.

0 to 50	51 to 100	101 to 150	151 to 200	201 to 250	251 to 300
Watch out for the alligators!	I hope you brought some dry clothes!	Nice work! You made it all the way across without falling in!	Hey, you're pretty good! Let's see you do that again!	Didn't I see you doing stunts in that white-water rafting movie?	Would you like a job as a nature tour guide?

7 Subtracting from 4-Digit Numbers

Goal Use a pencil and paper method to subtract from a 4-digit number.

A video store has 1257 DVDs.
848 DVDs have already been rented.

? How many DVDs are left at the video store?

Jon's Subtraction

I think 1257 − 848 must be about 400 because

12 hundreds − 8 hundreds = 4 hundreds.

I can subtract to find the actual difference.

Step 1 I compare the numbers column by column.
I need more hundreds and more ones before I can
subtract 8 **hundreds**,
4 **tens**, 8 **ones**.

$$\begin{array}{r} 1257 \\ -\ 848 \end{array}$$

Thousands	Hundreds	Tens	Ones

Step 2 If I regroup 1 thousand as 10 hundreds,
I'll have 12 hundreds altogether.
But I still need more
ones before I can
subtract.

$$\begin{array}{r} 0\,12 \\ \cancel{1}257 \\ -\ 848 \end{array}$$

Thousands	Hundreds	Tens	Ones

NEL

Step 3 I'll regroup 1 **ten** as 10 **ones**.
Now I have 0 thousands,
12 hundreds, 4 **tens**,
17 **ones**.

012417
~~1257~~
– 848

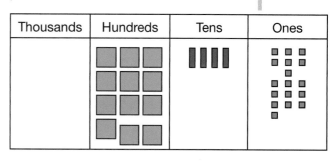

Thousands	Hundreds	Tens	Ones

Step 4 Now I have enough
in each place value
column to subtract.

012 417
~~1257~~
– 848
409

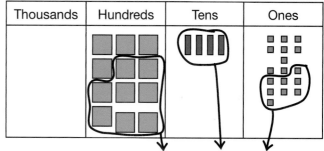

Thousands	Hundreds	Tens	Ones

There are 409 DVDs left at the video store.

This answer seems reasonable because
it's pretty close to my estimate of 400.

Reflecting

1. In Step 1, how did Jon know he would need
   more hundreds and more ones before he
   could subtract?

2. How does Step 4 show that 1257 was regrouped
   as 1200 + 40 + 17?

3. Explain how Jon could use addition to make
   sure he subtracted correctly.

Checking

4. On Saturday, 788 of the 1257 DVDs are rented.
   a) How many DVDs are left at the video store?
   b) Show how to add to check your answer.

Practising

5. The video store was giving away tickets for a
   lucky prize draw.
   By Wednesday, 571 of the 4325 lucky
   prize tickets had been given away.
   How many lucky prize tickets were left?

6. Estimate each subtraction.
   Complete the subtraction if the estimated difference
   is greater than 2000.
   a) 2348 − 999   b) 3649 − 682   c) 4567 − 768

7. Estimate and then subtract.
   Show your work.

   a)   1234   b)   5045   c)   8129   d)   1000
       − 621   − 347   − 518   − 235

8. Is the answer reasonable?
   Explain how you know.
   a) 6434 − 178 = 6256   c) 4533 − 751 = 3782
   b) 2257 − 388 = 1689   d) 5624 − 591 = 6215

9. Use a 3-digit number and a 4-digit number
   to create a subtraction problem about renting
   DVDs from a video store.
   Solve your problem. Show your work.

10. What is the greatest difference you can get when you
    subtract a 3-digit number from a 4-digit number?
    Explain how you know.

Hidden Digits

Someone spilled ink on Paulette's notebook.
Can you help her figure out the hidden digits?

When you replace the ink spots, the addition or
subtraction should be correct.

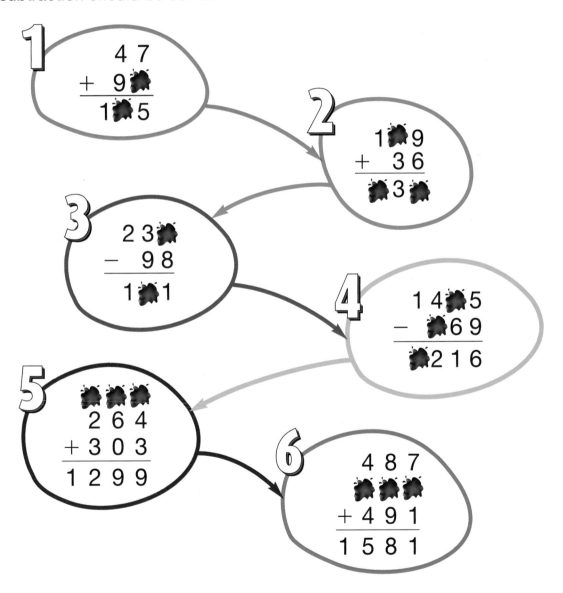

8 Subtracting in a Different Way

Goal Use regrouping to make subtraction easier.

A recent survey showed that 1000 nine-year-olds and 855 four-year-olds live in Sault Ste. Marie.

? **How many more 9-year-olds than 4-year-olds live in Sault Ste. Marie?**

Paulette's Subtraction

The answer must be between 100 and 200 because 855 is between 800 and 900. I know $1000 - 800 = 200$ and $1000 - 900 = 100$.

I will regroup the 1000 so it's easier to subtract 8 hundreds, 5 tens, and 5 ones.

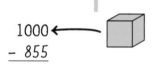

Step 1 If I think of 1000 as $999 + 1$, then I can do all the regrouping in 1 step.

$$\begin{array}{r} 999 + 1 \\ \cancel{1000} \\ - \ 855 \end{array}$$

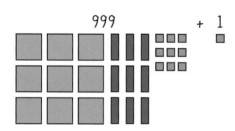

Step 2 Now I subtract 855.

$$\begin{array}{r} 999 + 1 \\ \cancel{1000} \\ - \ 855 \\ \hline 144 + 1 = 145 \end{array}$$

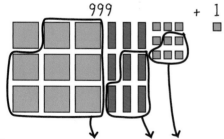

There are 145 more 9-year-olds than 4-year-olds.

My answer seems reasonable because my estimate was between 100 and 200.

Reflecting

1. Why did Paulette add 1 to 144 in Step 2?

2. Would you use Paulette's method to solve these subtractions? Explain your thinking.
   a) 6588 − 699   b) 5000 − 467

3. How is Paulette's method like Jon's method in Lesson 7? How is it different?

Checking

4. In a town of 2000 people, 598 are children.
   How many adults live in this town?
   Show your work.
   Use addition to check your answer.

Practising

5. In a town of 3000 people, 965 are children.
   How many adults live in this town?
   Show your work.
   Use addition to check your answer.

6. Estimate and then subtract.
   Use addition to check your answer.

   a)   1000
       − 435

   c)   3000
       − 278

   b)   2000
       − 849

   d)   6000
       − 332

7. Why don't you have to regroup 4467 to subtract 235?

8. Show 2 different ways to calculate 1000 − 250.
   Which way was easier for you?
   Explain your thinking.

9 Making Change

Goal Make purchases and change for money amounts.

Calvin has a $20.00 bill. He plans to buy the skateboard at the yard sale.

❓ How much change will Calvin get?

$19.98
$11.27
$25.25
$18.35
$21.99
$0.75 each
$7.75
$26.98

Calvin's Solution

My change should be less than $2.00 because $18.00 + $2.00 = $20.00.

I can count on from $18.35 to $20.00 to figure out the actual amount.

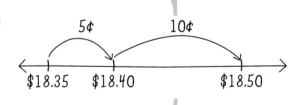

5¢   10¢

$18.35 $18.40 $18.50

A. Use a number line to show how Calvin might continue counting.

B. Use your number line to find out how much change Calvin will get from $20.00. Explain how you know.

Reflecting

1. Draw a different number line to show how Calvin could count his change. Start with a $1.00 jump.

2. Show a 3rd way Calvin could have calculated his change.

3. Some people say counting on is addition and others say it is subtraction. What do you think? Explain your thinking.

Checking

4. Tamika wants to use  to buy  .

   a) Estimate how much change she will get. Show your work.
   b) Calculate the amount of change she will receive.

Practising

5. Estimate and then calculate the change.

   a)

   b)

   c)

   d)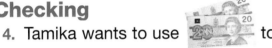

6. You have  to spend at the yard sale.
   Choose an item you could buy.
   Which bill or bills would you use to pay for the item?
   Show how to calculate your change.

7. Describe 2 different ways to calculate change.
   Give an example for each way.

10 Adding and Subtracting Money

Goal Use different methods to add and subtract money.

The class raised $50.00 for a retirement gift for the principal. Terry and Shani will buy the gift. Terry wants to buy a plaque that costs $24.99. Shani wants to buy a plant that costs $14.99. They decide to buy both.

Thank you for 40 years!

? **How much change will they get from $50.00?**

Terry used mental addition to find the answer.
Shani used the pencil and paper method.

Terry's Method

I will add 1¢ to each price to make it easier to add.

$25.00 + $15.00 = $40.00

Then I will take away 2¢ from the answer so the sum will be correct.

$40.00 − 2¢ = $39.98

The total cost of the gift is $39.98.

Shani's Method

I will add $24.99 + $14.99.

$$
\begin{array}{r}
11 \\
\$\ 24.99 \\
+14.99 \\
\hline
\$\ 39.98
\end{array}
$$

The answer is in dollars and cents, so I need to write a dollar sign and a decimal point.

The total cost of the gift is $39.98.

A. Describe how Terry used mental math to add.

B. Describe a different mental math strategy Terry could have used.

C. Finish the solution by calculating the change from $50. Show your work.

D. Show how to calculate the change in a different way.

Reflecting

1. **a)** Give an example of a money addition problem that is easier to solve using mental math than with paper and pencil. Explain why.
   b) Give an example of a money addition problem that you think would be easier to solve using pencil and paper.

Checking

2. You have  to spend at this yard sale.
   a) Choose 2 items you could buy.
   Calculate the total cost. Show your work.
   b) Calculate the amount of money you will have left. Show your work.

$21.50
$9.99
$11.99
$8.75
$18.98

Practising

3. A shirt in Ontario costs $9.95 plus $1.49 in tax. What is the total cost of the shirt? Show your work.

4. Add or subtract. Show your work.
   a) $10.99 + $5.67
   b) $42.08 − $3.99
   c) $35.00 − $17.03
   d) $23.97 + $11.03 + $6.50

5. Would you calculate each sum using mental math, pencil and paper, or a calculator?
   Give a reason for each choice.
   a) $17.66 + $4.59
   b) $2.40 + $2.99
   c) $235.97 + $145.88 + $4.56

6. Calculate each sum in Question 5 using your chosen method. Show your work.

Skills Bank

LESSON

1 1. Use mental math.
   a) 73 + 21   c) 71 + 29   e) 54 + 19   g) 43 + 27
   b) 32 + 28   d) 49 + 33   f) 39 + 49   h) 67 + 14

2. Use 20 + 20 = 40 to calculate each sum.
   a) 19 + 21   b) 19 + 19   c) 22 + 21   d) 19 + 23

3. There are 59 students in grade 3.
   There are 36 students in grade 4.
   Use mental math to calculate the total number of
   students in both grades.

2 4. Estimate. Show your rounded numbers.
   a) 2035 + 915   c) 1392 + 1429   e) 3436+ 2602
   b) 3942 + 495   d) 2688 + 1975   f) 3725 + 4983

5. Estimate the total distance from Vancouver
   to Montreal. Show your work.

Trip	Flight distance
Vancouver → Regina	1722 km
Regina → Montreal	3320 km

4 6. Estimate. Then calculate the sum.
   a)   1651   c)   2627   e)   4488   g)   6450
        + 1237   + 3148   + 2369   + 1762

   b)   2453   d)   4255   f)   1876   h)   4139
        + 1832   + 3694   + 3547   + 5367

7. There are 3301 Wolf Cubs in the Voyageur area.
   There are 3048 Wolf Cubs in the White Pine area.
   What is the total number of Wolf Cubs in the
   Voyageur and White Pine areas? Show your work.

8. Use mental math to subtract.

a) $23 - 9$ c) $75 - 45$ e) $67 - 25$ g) $93 - 47$

b) $40 - 18$ d) $58 - 29$ f) $92 - 39$ h) $86 - 78$

9. Rashad's brother is 22 years old.
Rashad's mother is 51 years old.
Use mental math to find the age difference
between Rashad's mother and brother.

10. Estimate. Show your rounded numbers.

a) $1597 - 483$ c) $4788 - 826$ e) $2678 - 413$

b) $2037 - 545$ d) $3615 - 389$ f) $5092 - 478$

11. Use the chart to estimate each height difference.
Show your work.

a) between Mount Carleton and Fairweather Mountain

b) between Cypress Hills and Fairweather Mountain

c) between Cypress Hills and Mount Carleton

Mountain	Province	Height or highest point
Fairweather Mountain	British Columbia	4663 m
Mount Carleton	New Brunswick	817 m
Cypress Hills	Saskatchewan	1468 m

12. Estimate. Then calculate each difference.

a) $\begin{array}{r} 4376 \\ -\ 254 \\ \hline \end{array}$ c) $\begin{array}{r} 2371 \\ -\ 640 \\ \hline \end{array}$ e) $\begin{array}{r} 7256 \\ -\ 431 \\ \hline \end{array}$ g) $\begin{array}{r} 6223 \\ -\ 475 \\ \hline \end{array}$

b) $\begin{array}{r} 1687 \\ -\ 536 \\ \hline \end{array}$ d) $\begin{array}{r} 3695 \\ -\ 287 \\ \hline \end{array}$ f) $\begin{array}{r} 8170 \\ -\ 962 \\ \hline \end{array}$ h) $\begin{array}{r} 5018 \\ -\ 766 \\ \hline \end{array}$

13. A store has 2416 DVDs. 508 of the DVDs are rented.
How many DVDs are left at the store?
Show your work.

14. Subtract. Use addition to check your answer.

a) 1000
   − 145

b) 5000
   − 275

c) 4000
   − 817

d) 2000
   − 458

e) 6000
   − 695

f) 9000
   − 918

g) 8000
   − 999

h) 3000
   − 699

15. In a town of 7000 people, 914 of the people
are 6 years old or younger.
How many people are older than 6 years old?
Show your work.

16. Estimate and then calculate the change.

a) A flashlight costs $7.60.
   You pay with a $10 bill.

b) A skateboard costs $28.75.
   You pay with two $20 bills.

c) A book costs $14.98.
   You pay with a $20 bill.

d) A backpack costs $32.69
   You pay with a $50 bill.

17. Add or subtract. Show your work.

a) $12.50 + $26.25
b) $17.99 + $25.99
c) $27.35 + $30.90

d) $16.42 + $23.39
e) $36.50 − $4.30
f) $42.05 − $24.95

g) $42.00 − $39.98
h) $38.55 − $17.95
i) $75.99 − $50.98

18. Calculate the total cost. Then find the change.

a)

b)

116

Problem Bank

1 1. Keenan had 48¢. Rami had 29¢.
Use mental math to answer each question.
   a) How much more money did Keenan have than Rami?
   b) How much money did they have altogether?

2. Find the least number that can be used to
make this sentence true.

   $53 + \blacksquare$ is greater than 100.

   Use mental math. Explain your reasoning.

2 3. Show 2 different ways to make this equation true.
   $\blacksquare 500 + \bullet 500 = 8000$

4. Rey estimated a sum by rounding 2 numbers
up to the nearest thousand.
His estimate was 7000.
What could the numbers have been?
Find more than 1 answer.

6 5. Find numbers that fit each riddle.
Look for more than 1 answer.
   a) There are two 2-digit numbers.
      One number is greater than 50 and ends in 0.
      When you subtract one number from the other
      number, the difference is 29.
   b) There are 2 numbers with no 0s.
      When you subtract the numbers, the
      difference is close to 3000.

8 6. A truck carrying 2 crates has a total
mass of 8341 kg.
The 1st crate has a mass of 1499 kg.
The truck has a mass of 5443 kg.
What is the mass of the 2nd crate?

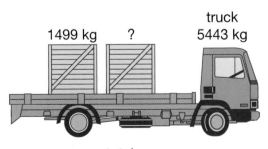

1499 kg   ?   truck 5443 kg

total mass
8341 kg

9 7. Zola used 3 bills to pay for a calculator.

Zola's Change

Adding 75¢ makes $19.00 and another $1.00 makes $20.00.

a) How much did the calculator cost?
b) How much change did Zola receive?
c) What bills did Zola use to pay for the calculator?

8. Miki's lunch cost $5.56. She paid with  .
   a) How much change did Miki receive?
   b) Why might Miki have decided to pay this way
      instead of just paying [5] ?

10 9. Change 1 digit in each price so the total cost is
   exactly $50.00. Look for more than 1 solution.
   Show your work.

$37.67 $14.53

10. 2 TV sets cost $1000 altogether.
    1 TV set cost $280 more than the other TV set.
    What is the price of each TV set?

11. Use mental math or a calculator to find each sum.
    a) $9 + 99 = \blacksquare$ b) $9 + 99 + 999 = \blacksquare$ c) $9 + 99 + 999 + 9999 = \blacksquare$

12. Predict the sum.
    $9 + 99 + 999 + 9999 + 99\,999 + 999\,999 + 9\,999\,999 = \blacksquare$

Chapter Review

1 1. Find all pairs of these numbers that add to 100.

64, 72, 18, 9, 91, 36, 51, 82, 28

3 2. Mandy added 6524 + 1208 and got 7732.
Explain how you can tell if her answer is reasonable.

6 3. Estimate each sum or difference. Which answers are
greater than 3000? Show your work.

A.	1868	B.	1276	C.	5000	D.	4000
	+ 2487		+ 1367		− 2675		− 264

4. Estimate to see which answer is closest to 6000.
Show your work.

A.	1756	B.	5200	C.	7000	D.	3599
	+ 2855		− 857		− 845		+ 2001

7 5. Explain why you can use addition to check
subtraction answers. Give an example.

8 6. An online store sold 3435 books on Saturday and
3675 books on Sunday.
a) Explain how you know the store sold more than
7000 books in total.
b) Exactly how many books were sold?
Show your work.
c) The store also sold 745 DVDs on Saturday.
How many more books than DVDs were sold
on Saturday?

10 7. You have 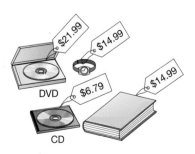 .
a) What 2 items could you buy at the sale?
b) What coins and bills would you use to
pay for the 2 items?
c) How much change would you receive?

DVD $21.99 $14.99 $6.79 $14.99

CD

Chapter Task

On the Move

Every 3 weeks, about 7500 people move into Ontario.

People Who Moved in During Winter

- week 3
- week 2
- week 1

People Who Moved in During Spring

- week 3
- week 2
- week 1

? **What are some possible numbers of people who moved in each week?**

Part 1

A. For each graph, determine some possible numbers for weeks 1, 2, and 3. Show your work. Explain your thinking.

Part 2

B. Draw another bar graph for 3 weeks in a different season. Show the possible numbers of people that move into Ontario each week.

C. Explain how you created your graph.

Task Checklist

- ☑ Did you add and subtract correctly?
- ☑ Did you verify that your numbers fit with the given information?
- ☑ Did you show all your steps?
- ☑ Did you explain your thinking?

Measuring Length and Time

Goals

You will be able to

- use a variety of length units and describe how they are related

- use a variety of time units and describe how they are related

- relate the perimeter of a rectangle to its length and width

- measure length and time with appropriate precision

- solve length problems using diagrams

Measuring Zola's height

Getting Started

Surrounding Shapes

Carmen is making a tray by gluing together pieces of coloured glass.

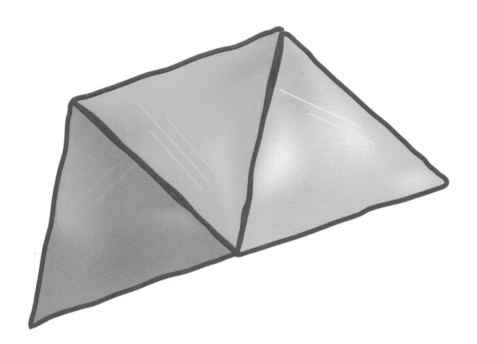

? **How can you draw a shape with the same perimeter as one of Carmen's triangles?**

A. Estimate the length of the strip of glue around 1 triangle of glass. Explain how you estimated.

B. Why do you think this length is called the **perimeter** of the triangle?

C. Measure to find the perimeter of the triangle.

D. Use string to make a different triangle with the same perimeter as the original triangle.
Draw or describe your new triangle.

E. Create a 4-sided shape that has the same perimeter as the original triangle.
Draw or describe your new shape.

F. Do you think every student created the same shapes for parts D and E? Explain your thinking.

Do You Remember?

1. Arrange these length units in order from shortest to longest.

   kilometre   metre   centimetre

2. Match each unit with its symbol.
   a) 1 centimetre   **X.** 1 m
   b) 1 metre   **Y.** 1 km
   c) 1 kilometre   **Z.** 1 cm

3. Suppose you see these times on the clock at your school.

   A   B

   a) What time is shown on each clock?
   b) Is the time shown on each clock in a.m. or p.m.?
   How do you know?

4. What year will it be 5 years from now?
   Show your work.

1 Measuring with Decimetres

Goal Measure with decimetres and relate decimetres to centimetres and metres.

Human hair grows about 10 cm each year.
10 cm is also called 1 **decimetre**, or 1 dm.

? **How long will your hair be in 5 years, if you don't cut it?**

A. Look at a metre stick.
   How many decimetres are in a metre?

B. Cut a piece of string to a length of 1 dm.

C. Use a 30 cm ruler and your 1 dm string to answer these questions.
   a) How many centimetres are in a decimetre?
   b) How many decimetres are in a 30 cm ruler?

D. a) How long is your hair in centimetres?
   b) Is it possible to measure the exact length of your hair in decimetres?
      Explain why or why not.
   c) What is the length of your hair to the nearest whole decimetre?

E. Cut a piece of string to model the length of your hair in 5 years.
   How long is the string?

decimetre
A unit of length that is longer than a centimetre and shorter than a metre

1 dm = 10 cm
10 dm = 1 m

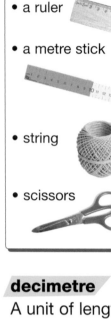

124

Reflecting

1. What does it mean to measure something to the nearest whole decimetre?

2. a) When might you use decimetres rather than metres?
   b) When might you use decimetres rather than centimetres?

Checking

3. Find an object of each length in your classroom. Then measure the object in centimetres.
   a) shorter than 1 dm
   b) between 1 dm and 2 dm
   c) longer than 2 dm

Practising

4. Find an object of each length. Then measure the object to the nearest whole decimetre.
   a) about 3 dm
   b) longer than 5 dm
   c) between 10 dm and 20 dm

5. Draw a line that is 2 dm long.
   a) How long is the line in centimetres? How do you know?
   b) Which number is greater, the decimetre measurement or the centimetre measurement? Explain how you could have predicted this.

6. About how many years would it take you to grow your hair to each length below? How do you know?
   a) 2 m   b) 25 cm

2 Measuring with Millimetres

You will need
- printer paper
- construction paper
- a ruler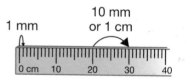

Goal Use millimetres to measure with precision.

Chantal wanted to know whether printer paper or construction paper is thicker.

Chantal's Measurement

I made a stack of 50 sheets of white printer paper.

I made another stack of 50 sheets of construction paper.

I measured to find out how much thicker the stack of construction paper is.

The white paper is about 1 cm thick.

The construction paper is between 1 cm and 2 cm thick.

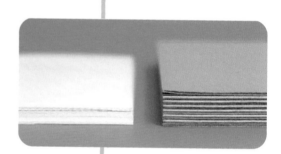

? **How can Chantal make a more precise measurement to compare the stacks?**

A. Use a ruler marked with **millimetres** to answer these questions.

a) How many millimetres fit between 50 mm and 70 mm?

b) How many centimetres fit between 50 mm and 70 mm?

c) The length of an object is about halfway between 2 cm and 3 cm.
How long could the object be in millimetres?

d) How many millimetres are in 1 dm?
Explain how you know.

millimetre

A unit of length that is shorter than a centimetre

10 mm = 1 cm

The space between the small markings is 1 mm.

The space from 20 mm to 30 mm is 10 mm, or 1 cm.

B. Make 2 stacks of paper like Chantal's.

C. Measure and record the thickness of each stack of paper in millimetres.

D. How much thicker is the stack of construction paper?

Reflecting

1. How many millimetres are in 1 m?
   Explain how you know.

2. Why are long distances not measured in millimetres?

3. Why is it possible to be more precise when measuring in millimetres rather than centimetres?

Checking

4. Compare 25 sheets of construction paper with 25 sheets of white paper.
   How much thicker is the stack of construction paper?

Practising

5. Estimate in millimetres.
   Measure the object to check your estimate.
   a) the thickness of a CD case
   b) the length of a paper clip
   c) the width of your thumb
   d) the thickness of your shirt

6. Look at this line.

   ―――――――――――

   a) Estimate how many millimetres you would have to add to make the line 1 dm long.
   b) Measure to check your estimate.
      How close were you?

3 Record Measures Using Multiple Units

Goal Measure and record using a combination of units.

Pedro and Manitok competed in the long jump.
Both boys jumped a distance between 3 m and 4 m.
Manitok won by 3 cm.

Miki and Allison raced their snails.
Both snails travelled about 10 cm.
Allison's snail won by 3 mm.

You will need

- a metre stick

- a ruler

- string

- scissors

? **How could you record each winner's results?**

A. Cut 2 lengths of string to represent 2 distances that Pedro and Manitok could have jumped.
Each string should be between 3 m and 4 m long.
1 of the strings should be 3 cm longer.

B. Measure the string for the winning long-jump distance.
   a) Use both metres and centimetres: ■ m ■ cm
   b) Use only centimetres: ■ cm

C. Draw 2 lines to represent 2 distances Miki's and Allison's snails could have travelled.
Each line should be about 10 cm long.
1 of the lines should be 3 mm longer.

D. Measure the line for the winning snail's distance.
   a) Use both centimetres and millimetres: ■ cm ■ mm
   b) Use only millimetres: ■ mm

Reflecting

1. Why might someone record a measurement like 304 cm as 3 m 4 cm?

2. How could you make a measurement like 3 m 4 cm more precise?

Checking

3. Which measurement is more precise?
   a) 3 m or 2 m 25 cm   b) 121 mm or 12 cm

4. Complete each measurement.
   a) 316 cm = 3 m ■ cm   d) 3 m 15 cm = ■ cm
   b) 56 mm = ■ cm 6 mm   e) 6 cm 3 mm = ■ mm
   c) 175 mm = 17 cm ■ mm   f) 14 cm 8 mm = ■ mm

Practising

5. a) Measure the total length of this line using both centimetres and millimetres: ■ cm ■ mm
   b) Measure the line using only millimetres: ■ mm

6. Complete each measurement.
   a) 37 mm = ■ cm 7 mm   c) 217 cm = ■ m ■ cm
   b) 4 m 8 cm = ■ cm   d) 15 cm 6 mm = ■ mm

7. Estimate each length.
   Work with a partner to measure the length as precisely as you can.
   a) your arm length
   b) your hand span

arm length

hand span

8. Describe a situation in which you would use more than 1 unit to measure length. Tell why.

4 Solve Problems by Drawing Diagrams

Goal Use diagrams to solve problems.

Paulette's team is playing in a soccer tournament near her home.
Her home is also near this sign.
Paulette and her mom must pick up some players in Madoc and Norwood to bring them to the tournament.

NORWOOD 27 km   MADOC 18 km

? **How far will Paulette travel?**

Paulette's Solution

Understand

My trip has 4 parts.

① from home to Madoc

② from Madoc to home

③ from home to Norwood

④ from Norwood to the tournament

Make a Plan

I will draw a diagram to show the parts of my trip.

Then I will add the distances to get the total distance that I will travel.

Carry Out the Plan

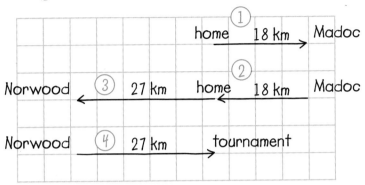

$18\ km + 18\ km + 27\ km + 27\ km = 90\ km$

I will travel 90 km altogether.

Reflecting

1. How did Paulette's diagram help her to describe the problem?

2. Was drawing a diagram the only way to solve the problem? Explain your thinking.

Checking

3. Bobby sees this sign in a parking lot.
   How far will he have to hike to get drinking water,
   see the waterfall, and then return to the parking lot?

Practising

4. Maria lives 27 km east of Jeff.
   Zack lives 18 km east of Jeff.
   How far apart do Maria and Zack live?

5. Write a problem that can be solved using a diagram.
   Show your solution.

Mid-Chapter Review

2

1. What unit would you use for each measurement?
   Explain your thinking.
   a) the width of a tack
   b) the length of a finger
   c) the width of a large picture frame

2. a) The length of a piece of paper is 3 dm.
   What is the length of the paper in centimetres?
   b) The width of a recipe card is 8 cm.
   What is the width of the card in millimetres?

3

3. Estimate whether the perimeter of your desk
   or table is shorter or longer than 20 dm.
   Measure to check your estimate.

4. Five 9-year-olds measured and recorded
   their heights. Which of these height
   measurements are probably wrong?
   Explain your thinking.

Lisa	123 m
Michael	1 m 3 cm
Yuka	132 cm
Angie	182 cm
Carlos	1 m 28 mm

5. Complete each measurement.
   a) A room that is 487 cm long is ■ m ■ cm long.
   b) A window that is 39 cm wide is ■ dm ■ cm wide.
   c) A pencil that is 89 mm long is ■ cm ■ mm long.
   d) A table that is 503 mm wide is ■ cm ■ mm wide.

6. Measure each item as precisely as you can.
   a) a pen   b) a pencil case

4

7. Emma has a purse that is 15 cm long and 10 cm wide.
   a) Can a pencil that is 120 mm long lie flat inside
   her purse? Explain your thinking.
   b) Can a bookmark that is 1 dm 90 mm long lie flat
   inside her purse? Explain your thinking.

Cutting and Measuring

You will need

- ribbon

- scissors

1

A ribbon is 100 cm, or 1 m, long.
If you fold the ribbon in half and
make 1 cut at the fold,
you get 2 pieces.
Each piece is 50 cm long.

If you fold the metre of ribbon in
half and make 1 cut through
the middle, you get 3 pieces.
1 piece is 50 cm long and
2 pieces are 25 cm long.

How many pieces could you get if you folded the
metre of ribbon twice and then made 1 straight cut?
How long would each piece be? Explain your thinking.

2

Some units are
even smaller than
millimetres.
Do some research
to find out about
nanometres.
What types of
things are measured
in nanometres?

3

You may have heard length
measurements given in units
of feet. 3 feet is about 1 m.
About how many metres is
each length?

a) 6 feet   c) 30 feet
b) 15 feet   d) 10 feet

5 Perimeter of Rectangles

Goal Use the length and width of a rectangle to find its perimeter.

You will need
- a geoboard
- elastics

Shani is trimming a rectangular bulletin board.
The bulletin board is 1 m high and 2 m wide.

? **How can Shani figure out the length of trim she needs?**

A. On a geoboard, create rectangles using the lengths and widths in the table.
Find the perimeter for each rectangle.
All measurements are in geoboard units.

Length	Width	Sum of length and width	Perimeter
3	2		
4	2		
5	2		
3	3		
4	3		
5	3		

B. As the length increases by 1, how does the perimeter change?

C. As the width increases by 1, how does the perimeter change?

D. How does the sum of the length and the width relate to the perimeter?

E. What length of trim will Shani need for the perimeter of the bulletin board? How do you know?

Reflecting

1. Tell how the perimeter of a shape increases when either the length or the width increases.

2. How does knowing the length and the width of a rectangle help you to find its perimeter?

Checking

3. Use the length and width measurements to calculate the perimeter of each rectangle. Measure to check.

a)

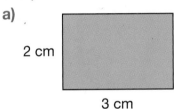

2 cm

3 cm

b)

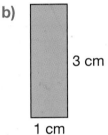

3 cm

1 cm

Practising

4. Calculate the perimeter of each rectangle.
   a) 5 m long and 6 m wide
   b) 21 cm long and 13 cm wide
   c) 14 cm long and 8 cm wide

5. A rectangle is 5 cm wide and 8 cm long. What would happen to its perimeter if each change happened?
   a) the width increased by 1 cm
   b) the length increased by 1 cm
   c) both the width and the length increased by 1 cm
   d) the width increased by 1 cm and the length decreased by 1 cm

6. How many sides of a square do you need to measure to find its perimeter?
   Explain your answer.

6 Decades, Centuries, and Millenniums

You will need
- base ten blocks

- metre sticks

Goal Relate decades, centuries, and millenniums.

? **How can you use length to make a model of years, decades, centuries, and millenniums?**

A. What is the current year?
Use base ten blocks to model the number.

B. Draw a 10 cm long line to represent the age of a 10-year-old person.
This length represents 1 **decade**.
How does 1 decade compare to your age?

decade
10 years

C. The Internet became popular about 1 decade ago.
What year was it 1 decade ago?

century
100 years

D. Use a metre stick to represent the age of a 100-year-old person.
This length represents 1 **century**.
How many decades are in 1 century?

millennium
1000 years

E. The ice cream cone was invented about 1 century ago.
What year was it 1 century ago?

F. Use a line of 10 metre sticks to represent 1000 years.
This length represents 1 **millennium**.
How many centuries are in 1 millennium?
How many decades is that?

G. Playing cards were invented about 1 millennium ago.
What year was it 1 millennium ago?

H. Use a time line like the one below. Estimate how long ago each event happened. Write the letter of each event where it belongs on the time line.

a) Vikings settle in Newfoundland
b) first salmon cannery in B.C.
c) snowboarding becomes popular
d) first glass windows appear
e) the zipper becomes popular
f) wearing seat belts becomes law

1 millennium ago   1 century ago   1 decade ago   today

Reflecting

1. a) What things were different a decade ago? What things were the same?
   b) What things were different a century ago? What things were the same?
   c) What things were different a millennium ago? What things were the same?

Mental Imagery

Estimating Length

This line is 40 mm long and 1 mm thick.

You will need
• a ruler

Try These

1. Estimate the length and thickness of each line. Test your estimates by measuring.

a) ▬▬▬▬▬
b) ▬▬▬▬▬▬▬▬▬▬
c) ▬▬▬▬▬▬▬▬
d) ▬▬▬▬▬▬▬▬▬
e) ▬▬▬▬

7 Time in Minutes

Goal Find out how long an event takes.

Terry and Calvin are going to see a movie.

? How many minutes long is the movie?

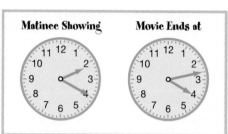

Matinee Showing   Movie Ends at

Terry's Method

I will count from 2:20 to 4:13.

From 2:20 to 3:20 is   From 3:20 to 4:00   From 4:00 to 4:13
1 hour, or 60 minutes.   is 40 minutes.   is 13 minutes.

60 minutes + 40 minutes + 13 minutes = 113 minutes

The movie is 113 minutes long.

Calvin's Method

I will count up in hours and then subtract.

There are 2 hours from 2:20 to 4:20.

That's 60 + 60 = 120 minutes.

But the movie ends at 4:13, not 4:20, so I subtract 7 minutes.

The movie is 113 minutes long.

Reflecting

1. Whose method do you prefer? Explain why.

2. Would you have used Calvin's method if the movie had ended at 3:45? Explain why or why not.

3. a) About how many hours is 113 minutes?
   b) When might you want to be precise about the length of a movie to the nearest minute?
   c) When might you only need an estimate to the nearest hour?

Checking

4. Vanessa is playing hockey in the backyard with her friends.
   The clocks show the times when she left the house and when she came in.
   a) What time did she leave?
   b) What time did she come in?
   c) How long was she playing?

left house

came in

Practising

5. How long does each event take?
   a) walking your dog

   b) talking on the phone

start   end

start   end

6. Make up your own problem about length of time in minutes. Give your problem to a partner to solve.

LESSON

Skills Bank

1

1. How long is each measurement in centimetres?
   a) 3 dm   c) 7 dm   e) 12 dm   g) 20 dm
   b) 5 dm   d) 10 dm   f) 15 dm   h) 25 dm

2. You hair grows about 1 dm in 1 year. About how many
   years would it take to grow your hair to each length?
   a) 20 cm   c) 1 m   e) 3 m   g) 35 cm
   b) 30 cm   d) 60 cm   f) 4 m   h) 45 cm

2

3. Give an estimate in millimetres.
   Then measure to check your estimate.
   a) the thickness of a calculator   d) the width of your pinkie finger
   b) the thickness of an empty pencil case   e) the length of your pinkie finger
   c) the thickness of an eraser   f) the length of a CD case

4. A line is 63 mm long. How many millimetres would you
   have to add to the line to make a line of each length?
   a) 7 cm   b) 1 dm   c) 12 cm

3

5. Measure each total length using centimetres and
   millimetres.
   a)

   ■ cm ■ mm

   c)

   ■ cm ■ mm

   b)

   ■ cm ■ mm

   d)

   ■ cm ■ mm

6. Complete each measurement.
   a) 32 mm = ■ cm 2 mm   e) 318 cm = ■ m ■ cm
   b) 47 mm = ■ cm 7 mm   f) 167 cm = ■ m ■ cm
   c) 3 m 5 cm = ■ cm   g) 16 cm 15 mm = ■ mm
   d) 4 m 38 cm = ■ cm   h) 21 cm 12 mm = ■ mm

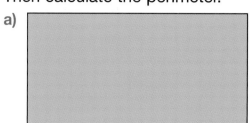

5 **7.** Measure the length and width of each rectangle.
Then calculate the perimeter.

a)
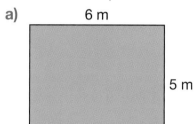

b)

8. Calculate the perimeter of each rectangle.

a)   6 m

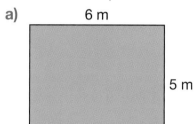

5 m

d)   19 cm

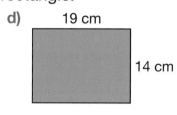

14 cm

b) 14 m long and 1 m wide   e) 7 cm long and 9 cm wide
c) 8 m long and 3 m wide   f) 11 cm long and 10 cm wide

6 **9.** For each year, write the year 1 decade before it.

a) 2050   b) 2000   c) 1995   d) 1967

10. For each year in Question 9, write the year 1 century
before it.

11. Complete.

a) 7 decades = ■ years   c) 3 centuries = ■ years
b) 2 millenniums = ■ years   d) 20 decades = ■ centuries

7 **12.** How long does each event take?

a) seeing a play   b) playing soccer

start   end   start   end

Problem Bank

1　**1.** A plant grows about 1 dm every 2 years.
About how long does the plant take to grow 32 cm?

2　**2.** Your hair grows about 1 dm each year.
   a) About how long does it take your hair to grow 1 cm?
   b) About how long does it take your hair to grow 1 mm?

3　**3.** A regular hexagon has 6 sides of equal length.
Each side of this hexagon is 2 m 6 cm long.
Suppose you rounded each side length to 2 m to find
its perimeter. How far off would your estimate be?

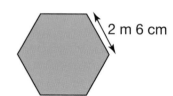
2 m 6 cm

4. A shape with 6 sides has a perimeter of 82 mm.
Draw 2 possible shapes that fit this description.
Mark all of the side measurements on your shape.

4　**5.** Kingston is 260 km east of Toronto.
Belleville is 70 km west of Kingston.
Kitchener-Waterloo is 105 km west of Toronto.
How far is it from Belleville to Kitchener-Waterloo?

6　**6.** What is today's date?
What would the date be at each of these times?
   a) 2 decades ago　　　**c)** 3 centuries ago
   b) 2 decades from now　　**d)** 3 centuries from now

7　**7.** Ravi takes 25 minutes to read 17 pages of a book.
About how long will it take him to read 100 pages?

8. Suppose we measured time in decidays and
centidays instead of in hours and minutes.
There would be 10 decidays in a day and
100 centidays in a day.
   a) About how many hours would a deciday be?
   b) About how many minutes would a centiday be?

Chapter Review

2

1. Name an object that might be about each length.
   a) 50 cm   b) 12 mm   c) 3 m

3

2. a) Draw a line that is 2 dm 1 cm long.
   b) Draw a line that is 47 mm long.

3. Complete each measurement.
   a) 165 mm = ■ cm ■ mm
   b) 4 m 82 cm = ■ cm

4. Lee walked to the store. She said she walked 3 km. Do you think this was an exact measurement or an estimate? Explain your answer.

5

5. Victoria wants to measure her bed to find out what size comforter she needs. What measurement unit or units should she use? Explain your answer.

6. A rectangular picture is in a metal frame that is 92 cm long. List 2 possible pairs of lengths and widths for the frame.

7. a) All the sides of this shape are equal in length. Estimate the perimeter of this shape.
   b) Draw and label another shape with the same perimeter.

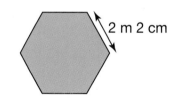

2 m 2 cm

6

8. How many more years are in 2 millenniums than in 2 centuries?

7

9. Amit decided to read one evening. He noticed the time when he started reading and the time when he finished reading. How much time did he spend reading?

start reading

finish reading

Chapter Task

Suncatchers

Beth wants to glue ribbon all around the edges of these 2 suncatchers. She also wants to hang each one by a loop that is 10 cm long. She has a piece of red ribbon that is 80 cm long.

? **Does Beth have enough ribbon for both suncatchers?**

Understand

A. What do you need to work out to solve the problem?

Make a Plan

B. What strategy will you use to solve the problem?

Carry Out the Plan

C. Measure as precisely as you can. Record your measurements.

D. Make the necessary calculations.

Look Back

E. Check that your solution fits the original problem.

Communicate

F. Explain why you need to measure precisely.

Task Checklist
☑ Did you check your measurements carefully?
☑ Did you check your calculations?
☑ Did you show all the steps?
☑ Did you use math language?

Multiplication and Division Facts

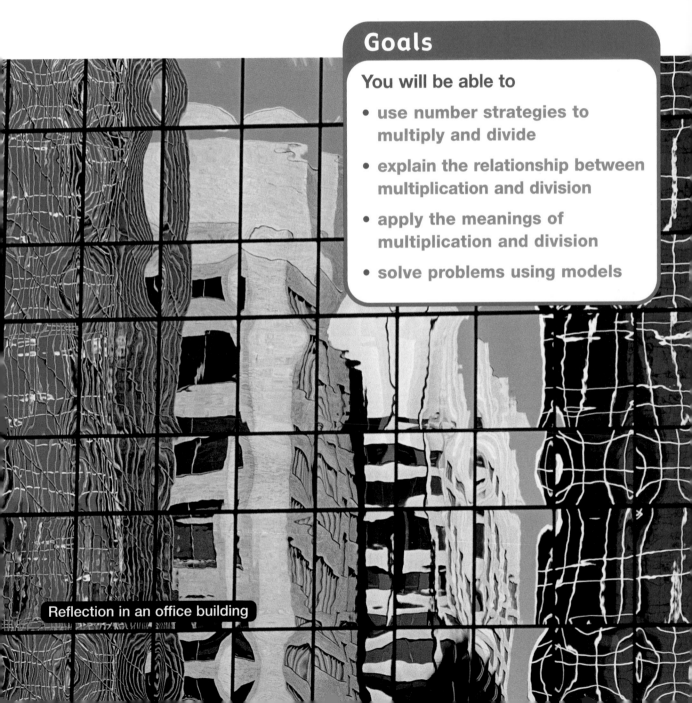

Reflection in an office building

Goals

You will be able to

- **use number strategies to multiply and divide**

- **explain the relationship between multiplication and division**

- **apply the meanings of multiplication and division**

- **solve problems using models**

You will need

• a multiplication table

×	1	2	3
1	1	2	3
2	2	4	6
3	3	6	9

Getting Started

Patterns in a Multiplication Table

? **What patterns can you find in a multiplication table?**

diagonal

column

row →

×	1	2	3	4	5	6	7
1	1	2	3	4	5	6	7
2	2	4		8		12	14
3	3	6	9		15	18	
4	4	8	12	16		24	28
5	5	10		20	25		35
6		12	18	24		36	42
7	7	14			35		49

A multiplication table includes many different kinds of patterns. Some of these are

• adding patterns
• subtracting patterns
• digit patterns

146

Miki's Pattern

I found an adding pattern.

Each number in row 3 is the sum of the 2 numbers above it.

A. Look for patterns and use them to complete the multiplication table.

B. What kinds of patterns did you use?
Make a list with examples.

C. Compare your patterns with someone else's.
What patterns can you add to your list?

D. Write 5 multiplication facts from the multiplication table.

Do You Remember?

1. Count on.
   a) 2, 4, 6, 8, ■, ■, ■
   b) 10, 20, 30, 40, ■, ■, ■
   c) 5, 10, 15, 20, ■, ■, ■
   d) 20, 18, 16, 14, ■, ■, ■

2. Multiply or divide.
   a) 5×2
   b) $10 \div 5$
   c) 5×4
   d) $20 \div 5$
   e) 6×5
   f) $30 \div 5$
   g) 5×5
   h) $25 \div 5$

3. Explain how factors and products are related.

$$4 \times 6 = 24$$
factor   factor   product

1 Using Doubling to Multiply

Goal Use repeated addition and doubling to multiply.

Carmen is using green and yellow triangles to make 9 squares for a quilt for her baby sister.

 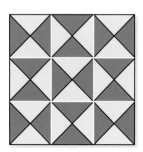

Carmen's Quilt Squares

I want to calculate the number of green triangles I need.

There are 9 squares in my quilt.

There are 2 green triangles in each square.

I need 9 × 2 green triangles to make my quilt.

I add or skip count to find the number of triangles.

$$9 \times 2 = 2 + 2 + 2 + 2 + 2 + 2 + 2 + 2 + 2$$
$$2, \quad 4, \quad 6, \quad 8, \quad 10, 12, 14, 16, 18$$

? **How many green and yellow triangles does Carmen use for her quilt?**

A. Write a multiplication equation for the number of green and yellow triangles.

B. What is the product of the equation in part A?

Reflecting

1. How does knowing 9 × 2 help you find 9 × 4?

2. Why do you think the strategy Carmen used is called the doubling strategy?

Checking

3. Carmen's new design is a square made of rectangles.
   a) How many yellow rectangles will Carmen use for 4 squares?
   b) Use doubling to find 8 × 3.

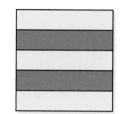

Practising

4. a) Count by 4s.
      4, 8, 12, ■, ■, ■, ■
   b) How many 4s did you count?
   c) How much is 7 × 4?
   d) How much is 7 × 8?

5. a) Count by 3s.
      3, 6, 9, ■, ■, ■, ■
   b) How much is 7 × 3?
   c) How much is 7 × 6?

6. Multiply.
   a) 2 × 7   b) 4 × 7   c) 8 × 7

7. Find each product. Explain your strategy.
   a) 8 × 4   b) 8 × 6   c) 5 × 8

8. a) Design your own quilt square by combining 2 or more shapes.
   b) Decide how many times your design will repeat in your quilt.
      Write multiplication equations that describe the number of shapes in your quilt.

2 Sharing and Grouping

You will need
- counters

Goal Use 2 meanings for division to solve problems.

Here are 2 meanings of division.

Sharing

You know the number **of groups**.
You are making 6 tarts. How many raisins should be in each tart?

30 ÷ 6 = 5 raisins

number of groups

Grouping

You know the number **in each group**.
You put 5 raisins in each tart.
How many tarts can you make?

30 ÷ 5 = 6 tarts

number in each group

Rami is making 6 butter tarts with 30 raisins.
He wants to put the same number of raisins in each tart.

? **How many raisins should be in each tart?**

Rami's Tarts

I'll put 1 raisin in each tart until there are no raisins left.

There are 6 groups of 5.

I can put 5 raisins in each tart.

Reflecting

1. Which meaning of division did Rami use? Explain your thinking.

2. a) When you divide by the number of groups, what does the **quotient** tell you?

   b) When you divide by the number in each group, what does the quotient tell you?

quotient
The result when you divide

$30 \div 6 = 5$

↑

quotient

Checking

3. a) Write a division equation for making 8 tarts with 32 raisins. How many raisins should be in each tart?

   b) Write a division equation for putting 4 raisins in each tart.

Practising

4. Draw pictures or use counters to show each problem. Write a division equation for each situation.

   a) There are 28 raisins. You put 4 raisins in each tart. How many tarts can you make?

   b) There are 42 raisins. You want to make 6 tarts. How many raisins should be in each tart?

5. Complete each division equation.

   a) $12 \div 6 = \blacksquare$ c) $18 \div 2 = \blacksquare$

   b) $24 \div 3 = \blacksquare$ d) $18 \div 3 = \blacksquare$

6. Rami has 24 raisins.
   He wants every tart to have more than 1 raisin.
   What is the greatest number of tarts he can make?
   Show your work.

7. Use the equation $42 \div 7 = \blacksquare$ to write 2 problems.
   Make one problem about grouping.
   Make the other problem about sharing.
   Solve the problems.

3 Division and Multiplication

Goal Relate multiplication to division.

Sarah and her friends were paid $20 to clean up a neighbour's yard. They each got $5.

? How many friends helped Sarah?

Rey's Solution

I need to divide $20 by $5.

I subtract 5s from 20 until I am out of money.

This is like working backward on a number line.

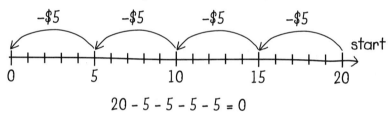

$$20 - 5 - 5 - 5 - 5 = 0$$

I take 4 groups of 5 from 20.

$$20 \div 5 = 4$$

This means 4 people got $5 each.

Since Sarah got $5, she must have had 3 helpers.

I can check by multiplying.

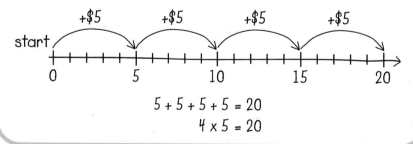

$$5 + 5 + 5 + 5 = 20$$
$$4 \times 5 = 20$$

Reflecting

1. How can you use multiplication to check the answer to a division problem?
   Use an example to help you explain.

Checking

2. A clean-up team was paid $16. Each person got $4. How many people are on the team?

3. a) Write a division equation for the number line.

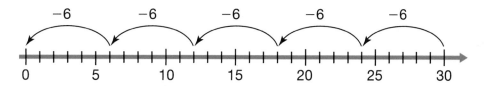

   b) Write a related multiplication equation.

4. Divide. Check by multiplying.
   a) 18 ÷ 3   b) 18 ÷ 6   c) 28 ÷ 7

Practising

5. Sarah and her 3 friends shared $20 equally.
   Rey and his 2 friends shared $18 equally.
   Which group would you choose to be in?
   Explain your answer.

6. a) Write a division equation for the number line.

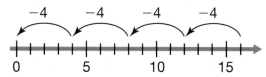

   b) Write a related multiplication equation.

7. a) Write a division equation for this equation.
   $$24 - 6 - 6 - 6 - 6 = 0$$

   b) Write a related multiplication equation.

4 Arrays for Fact Families

Goal Describe arrays using fact families.

In the game Concentration, cards are used to make an **array**.

A. How many rows does this card array have?

B. How many cards are in each row?

C. How many cards are in the whole array?

? **How can you use multiplication and division to describe this array?**

array
Objects arranged in the shape of a rectangle

Columns **go up and down.**

Rows **go across.**

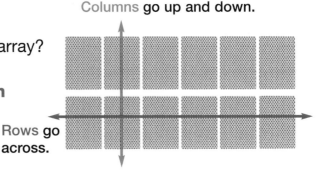

D. Complete the multiplication equations for the card array. Replace each symbol with the correct number.

  a) Read: ■ rows with ● cards in each row = ◆ cards in all
    Write: ■ × ● = ◆

  b) Read:
    ● columns with ■ cards in each column = ◆ cards in all
    Write: ● × ■ = ◆

E. Complete the division equations for the card array.

  a) Read: ◆ cards in ■ rows = ● cards in each row
    Write: ◆ ÷ ■ = ●

  b) Read:
    ◆ cards with ● columns = ■ cards in each column
    Write: ◆ ÷ ● = ■

F. Use cards to make your own array.
Write all the equations that describe the array.
These equations form the **fact family** for the array.

fact family
Equations that describe an array. Each equation is a member of the fact family.

3 rows and 4 columns:
$3 \times 4 = 12$ $12 \div 3 = 4$
$4 \times 3 = 12$ $12 \div 4 = 3$

Reflecting

1. How does knowing 6 × 2 = 12 help you to calculate 2 × 6 = ■?

2. How does knowing 6 × 2 = 12 help you to calculate 12 ÷ 6 = ■?

3. Can a fact family have only 2 equations? Explain your answer.

Checking

4. Complete the fact family.

$3 \times \bullet = \blacklozenge$ $2 \times \blacksquare = \blacklozenge$

$6 \div \blacksquare = \bullet$ $6 \div \bullet = \blacksquare$

Practising

5. Use the numbers 6, 7, and 42 to create a fact family.

6. Write the fact family that goes with the array on the right. Explain how each fact describes the array.

7. a) Draw a different card array.
   b) Write the fact family for your cards.

8. Use the given fact to write the whole fact family.

   a) 8 ÷ 2 = 4
   b) 3 × 8 = 24
   c) 45 ÷ 9 = 5

5 Using Facts to Multiply Larger Numbers

Goal Use basic facts, patterns, and mental math to multiply.

Vinh sleeps about 8 hours every day.

? **About how much time will Vinh spend sleeping in the month of April?**

APRIL 2004

S	M	T	W	T	F	S
				1	2	3
4	5	6	7	8	9	10
11	12	13	14	15	16	17
18	19	20	21	22	23	24
25	26	27	28	29	30	

Vinh's Solution

Understand
There are 30 days in April.
I sleep about 8 hours each day.
This is a multiplication problem because there are 30 groups of 8.

Make a Plan
30 groups of 8 is 30×8.
I know that $30 \times 8 = 8 \times 30$ because they are in the same fact family.
I will multiply 8×30 because it is easier.

Carry Out the Plan
I know that 30 = 3 tens.
I imagine 8 groups of 3 tens.
There are 24 tens.
I know that 24 tens = 240.
So $8 \times 30 = 240$.

8×3 tens = 24 tens

I will sleep about 240 hours in the month of April.

Reflecting

1. Explain how knowing $8 \times 3 = 24$ helps Vinh calculate 8×30.

2. Explain how Vinh could use his answer to find the number of hours he will sleep in May.

3. Explain how Vinh could calculate 8×300.

Checking

4. Show how each fact can help you multiply the others.

   a) 3×5
      3×50
      3×500

   b) 7×7
      7×70
      7×700

   c) 5×4
      5×40
      5×400

Practising

5. Find the products.

   a) 6×40
   b) 6×400
   c) 6×4000
   d) 2×60
   e) 2×600
   f) 2×6000
   g) 6×50
   h) 6×500
   i) 6×5000

6. Show why these products are equal.

   a) $4 \times 50 = 5 \times 40$
   b) $3 \times 500 = 5 \times 300$

7. a) How many tissues are in 7 boxes? Show your work.

   b) How many tablets are in 5 bottles? Show your work.

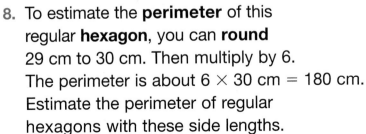

60 tissues

Vitamins

200 tablets

8. To estimate the **perimeter** of this regular **hexagon**, you can **round** 29 cm to 30 cm. Then multiply by 6. The perimeter is about 6×30 cm $= 180$ cm. Estimate the perimeter of regular hexagons with these side lengths.

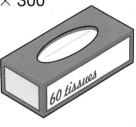

29 cm

hexagon

   a) 68 cm
   b) 42 m
   c) 196 cm

6 Solve Problems by Making Models

Goal Make models to solve problems.

Terry and his mother made 8 jars of jam.
Terry will put the jars on a shelf.

? How can Terry arrange the jam jars in arrays?

Terry's Arrays

Understand
I have to make different arrays of 8 jars.

Make a Plan
I can use linking cubes to make models.

Carry Out the Plan

1 by 8
$1 \times 8 = 8$

2 by 4
$2 \times 4 = 8$

I can arrange the jars in 1 row of 8 jars, or 2 rows of 4 jars.

Reflecting

1. How did making a model help Terry solve the problem?

2. Has Terry found all the ways to arrange the jars in an array? Explain how you know.

Checking

3. Show as many ways as you can to arrange 18 jars of jam in arrays.

Practising

4. Katie has 15 apples. How many more apples does she need to make 5 rows of 4 apples?
   Show your work.

5. Justin packs apples. After he packs every 5 apples, he stamps a  on the box.
   Show the number of stamps for 35 apples.

6. 12 fruit trees are planted in equal rows.
   Show all possible arrangements.

7. A 2-by-2 array of blocks has a square top. It uses 4 blocks.
   If you have 30 blocks, what is the biggest square you can make?
   Show your work.

8. A number of jars of jam can be shared equally by 4 people. The same number can also be shared equally by 3 people.
   How many jars might there be?
   Show your work.

9. 2 out of every 3 apples grown in Canada are sold fresh.
   1 out of every 3 apples is processed to make a product like juice or sauce.
   Out of 15 apples, how many will be sold fresh? Show your work.

10. Write and solve a problem about arranging fruit.
    Ask someone else to solve your problem.
    Check the answer.

Mid-Chapter Review

1. a) Count by 6s.

 6, 12, 18, ■, ■, ■, ■
 b) How many 6s did you count?
 c) How much is 6×4?
 d) How much is 6×8?

2. There are 42 apples in groups of 6.
 How many groups are there altogether?
 Show your work.

3. Give an example for each idea.
 a) You can use division to find out how many groups
 there are.
 b) You can use division to find out how many things
 are in each group.
 c) Multiplication and division are related.

4. Explain with words, pictures, or numbers.
 a) How is multiplication related to addition?
 b) How is division related to subtraction?

5. Use an array to show that $3 \times 4 = 4 \times 3$.

6. Complete each fact family.
 a) $3 \times 8 = 24$ b) $28 \div 7 = 4$

7. Complete each equation.
 a) $7 \times 2 = ■$ c) $7 \times 40 = ■$ e) $7 \times 800 = ■$
 b) $7 \times 20 = ■$ d) $7 \times 400 = ■$ f) $7 \times 8000 = ■$

8. Vikram is arranging 6 rows of 3 chairs for a
 puppet show.
 a) How many chairs are there?
 b) How many chairs will there be if he adds
 another row? Show your work.

Multiplying and Dividing with 0

You will need
- pennies
- a calculator

1
a) If you give 0 groups of pennies to your friend, how many pennies will your friend get?
b) Explain what happens when you multiply a number by 0.

2
a) If you share 0 pennies with some friends, how many pennies will each person get?
b) Explain what happens when you divide 0 by another number.

 4 Complete each equation. Which ones can't be completed?
a) $5 \times 0 = \blacksquare$ e) $0 \times 1 = \blacksquare$
b) $0 \div 5 = \blacksquare$ f) $1 \div 0 = \blacksquare$
c) $0 \times 5 = \blacksquare$ g) $0 \times 0 = \blacksquare$
d) $5 \div 0 = \blacksquare$ h) $2 \div 0 = \blacksquare$

3
a) If you have some pennies and you start to make groups of 0 pennies, when will you run out of pennies?
b) Explain why you can't divide by 0.

 5 Enter any number in your calculator. Divide by 0. What does your calculator show?

 6 Use an example to show how many facts can be in a fact family with 0.

7 Halving Strategies: Facts with 5 and 10

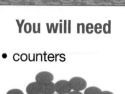

Goal Find patterns in multiplication and division facts with 5 and 10.

Natalie has 8 nickels. She wants to know how much money she has, but she can *never* remember 8×5.

? **What strategy could Natalie use to figure out how much money she has?**

Natalie's Strategy

I used 5 counters to represent each nickel.
8 groups of 5 is the same as 4 groups of 10.

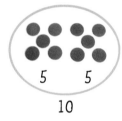 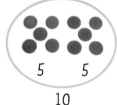 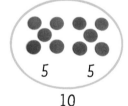 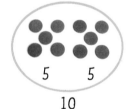

$$8 \times 5 = 4 \times 10$$

So now I know that $8 \times 5 = 40$.

Since 4 is half of 8 and 10 is double 5, Natalie's strategy is called **halve and double**.

halve
To divide a number by 2

Halve and Double Table

Multiply an even number by 5	Halve the even number and multiply by 10
2×5	1×10
4×5	2×10
6×5	3×10
8×5	4×10

Reflecting

1. What do you notice about the products in each row of the Halve and Double table?

2. What is the next row in the Halve and Double table? Explain your answer.

3. How could you use the table to find 7×5?

Checking

4. Show how to extend the Halve and Double table to find the value of 12 nickels.

5. Use the halve and double strategy to multiply.

   a) $8 \times 5 = \blacksquare \times 10$

   $8 \times 5 = \blacklozenge$

   b) $16 \times 5 = \blacksquare \times 10$

   $16 \times 5 = \blacklozenge$

Practising

6. Show how 4 groups of 5 is the same as 2 groups of 10.

7. a) What do you notice about the quotients in each row of this table?

   b) Explain how to use $40 \div 10$ to find $40 \div 5$.

Divide by 10	Divide by 5
$10 \div 10 = 1$	$10 \div 5 = 2$
$20 \div 10 = 2$	$20 \div 5 = 4$
$30 \div 10 = 3$	$30 \div 5 = 6$

8. Complete.

   a) $6 \times 5 = \blacksquare$

   b) $8 \times 5 = \blacksquare$

   c) $2 \times 5 = \blacksquare$

   d) $5 \times 4 = \blacksquare$

   e) $4 \times 5 = \blacksquare$

   f) $5 \times 8 = \blacksquare$

   g) $7 \times 5 = \blacksquare$

   h) $9 \times 5 = \blacksquare$

   i) $5 \times 3 = \blacksquare$

9. Complete.

   a) $5 \times 4 = \blacksquare$

   b) $5 \times 40 = \blacksquare$

   c) $5 \times 400 = \blacksquare$

   d) $6 \times 5 = \blacksquare$

   e) $6 \times 50 = \blacksquare$

   f) $6 \times 500 = \blacksquare$

   g) $7 \times 50 = \blacksquare$

   h) $7 \times 500 = \blacksquare$

   i) $7 \times 5000 = \blacksquare$

8 Adding On: Facts with 3 and 6

You will need

• counters

Goal Use addition strategies to multiply and divide with 3 and 6.

Paulette uses addition to find new facts from facts she already knows.

Paulette's Adding-On Strategy

I know that five 3s make 15.

 $5 \times 3 = 15$

If I want to know 6×3, I can add 1 group of 3.

 $6 \times 3 = 18$

So six 3s make 18.

? **How can you use the adding-on strategy to complete this multiplication table?**

×	3	4	5	6	7	8	9	10
5	15							
6	18							

A. Use counters to make 5 groups of 4. Write $5 \times 4 = \blacksquare$.

B. Add 4 counters to make 6 groups of 4.
Write $6 \times 4 = \blacksquare$.

C. Complete the 4 column in the multiplication table.

D. Repeat parts A, B, and C to complete the remaining columns.

Reflecting

1. How are the rows for 5× and 6× related?

Checking

2. a) Complete a multiplication table for 2 and 3.
   b) How are the rows for 2× and 3× related?

×	3	4	5	10
2	6			
3	9			

Practising

3. Show how knowing 6 × 3 = 18 can help you find 7 × 3.

4. a) Complete a multiplication table for 3 and 4.
   b) How are the rows for 3× and 4× related?

×	1	2	3	10
3				
4				

5. Explain how one fact can help you find the other.
   a) 3 × 3 = 9, so 4 × 3 = ■.
   b) 6 × 7 = 42, so 7 × 7 = ■.
   c) 6 × 5 = 30, so 7 × 5 = ■.

6. a) Describe a pattern in this table.
   b) Explain how to use 30 ÷ 3 to find 30 ÷ 6.

Divide by 3	Divide by 6
6 ÷ 3 = 2	6 ÷ 6 = 1
12 ÷ 3 = 4	12 ÷ 6 = 2
18 ÷ 3 = 6	18 ÷ 6 = 3
24 ÷ 3 = 8	24 ÷ 6 = 4

7. Complete the equations.
   a) 3 × 4 = ■
   b) 3 × 40 = ■
   c) 3 × 400 = ■
   d) 6 × 7 = ■
   e) 6 × 70 = ■
   f) 6 × 700 = ■
   g) 6 × 5 = ■
   h) 6 × 50 = ■
   i) 6 × 500 = ■

9 Subtracting Strategy: Facts with 9

You will need
• a 100 chart

1	2	3	4
11	12	13	14
21	22	23	24
31	32	33	34

Goal Use counting patterns to multiply and divide with 9.

9 is a special number for baseball players.
There are
• 9 positions on the field
• 9 innings in a game

? **Rey played 9 games in a tournament.
How many innings did he play?**

You can answer this question if you know the 9× facts.

Patterns can help you find the 9× facts.

A. Use a 100 chart.

B. Colour every 9th number green and every
10th number blue.

row 1	1	2	3	4	5	6	7	8	9	10
row 2	11	12	13	14	15	16	17	18	19	20
row 3	21	22	23	24	25	26	27	28	29	30

C. Describe the green pattern in the chart.

D. Explain how the numbers in the green and blue
squares in each row are related.

E. Describe how to use the relationship to find the
number of innings Rey played.

Reflecting

1. Describe how to use a 10× fact to find a 9× fact.

Multiplying with 9

Products Table

9×	Tens	Ones
1	0	9
2	1	8
3		
4		
5		
6		
7		
8		
9		

1

a) Complete the table.

b) Describe the patterns in the Tens and Ones columns.

c) Add the tens and ones digits in each product. What do you notice?

d) Describe how the numbers in the 9× column are related to the numbers in the Tens column.

e) Explain how to use patterns to find any 9× fact.

Adding the Middle

Sometimes 2 numbers can be added by adding the middle number to itself. To add 47 + 53:

50 is the middle number.
50 + 50 = 100
So 47 + 53 = 100.

A. How do you know that 50 is the middle number?

B. Would you use this method to add 37 and 38? Explain.

Try These

1. Use this method to add.

a) 39 + 41 c) 66 + 74 e) 153 + 147

b) 28 + 32 d) 297 + 303 f) 496 + 504

10 Number Neighbours: Facts with 7 and 8

Goal Use facts you know to multiply and divide with 7 and 8.

Shani's class is making bugs to decorate the set for a play. Shani is making 7 ladybugs. Each ladybug has 6 legs.

Shani's Ladybugs

I need 7×6 legs. I can't remember 7×6, but I know its neighbour, $6 \times 6 = 36$.

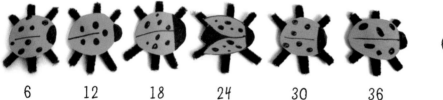

6   12   18   24   30   36

$6 \times 6 = 36$

I need another group of 6.

$7 \times 6 = ?$

$36 + 6 = 42$

So $7 \times 6 = 42$.

? **How can you use other facts to show that $7 \times 6 = 42$?**

A. Use $8 \times 6 = 48$.

B. Use $5 \times 7 = 35$.

C. Use $7 \times 7 = 49$.

Reflecting

1. List the neighbouring facts you could use to find 7 × 8. Explain your answers.

Checking

2. a) Complete the multiplication table.

×	5	6	7	8	9	10
6	30		42		54	
7		42		56		70
8	40		56		72	
9		54		72		90

   b) Explain how the rows for 6× and 7× are related.
   c) Explain how the rows for 8× and 9× are related.

Practising

3. Show how to use each fact to find 8 × 8.
   a) 9 × 8 = 72   b) 8 × 7 = 56   c) 4 × 8 = 32

4. Matt has enough pipe cleaners for 60 legs. Can he make 8 spiders? Explain your answer.

5. The Science Fair is in exactly 6 weeks. How many days is that? Show your work.

6. a) Write the numbers you say when counting by 8s to 64.
   b) Add the digits in each number until you get a 1-digit number.
   c) What is the pattern?

7. Multiply.
   a) 9 × 80   b) 800 × 7   c) 8 × 500

8. Write the fact family for each fact.
   a) 7 × 8 = ■   b) 7 × 9 = ■   c) 8 × 9 = ■

Circles and Digits

1

If you count by 2s from 0 to 20 and join the ones digits on a circle, the result looks like "Counting by 2s."

If you count by 8s from 0 to 80, the result looks like "Counting by 8s."

a) Make circles like these for all the other facts from $1\times$ to $9\times$.

b) Which pairs of circles look alike?

c) What happened with $5\times$?

Counting by 2s ($2\times$)

Counting by 8s ($8\times$)

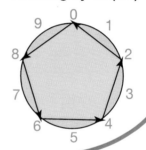

2

Look at fingers touching and not touching. How does it work? Try it with other facts.

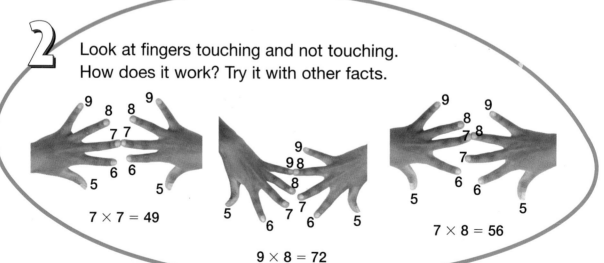

$7 \times 7 = 49$

$9 \times 8 = 72$

$7 \times 8 = 56$

Math Cat

Number of players: 2

How to play: Add the **quotients** on your cards.

You will need

- division fact cards

- counters

- Math Cat (optional)

Step 1 Deal 6 cards to each player.

Step 2 Each player keeps 4 cards and chooses 2 cards to give (face down) to Math Cat.

Step 3 Add the quotients for your cards to get your score. If you aren't sure of the quotients, think of patterns and fact families.

Step 4 Record the score for each player, including Math Cat. The player with the highest score gets 1 counter.

Allison	Vinh	Math Cat
28	30	29

Play until a player has 5 counters.

Allison's Turn

My quotients are 7, 8, 5, and 8.

My cards are worth 7 + 8 + 5 + 8, or 28 points.

42 ÷ 6	72 ÷ 9
25 ÷ 5	56 ÷ 7

Skills Bank

LESSON

1

1. Count on. Then multiply.

 a) 5, 10, 15, ■, ■, ■, ■, ■   8 × 5 = ■

 b) 7, 14, 21, ■, ■, ■   6 × 7 = ■

2. Multiply.

 a) 5 × 2 = ■   b) 2 × 8 = ■   c) 6 × 2 = ■

 5 × 4 = ■   4 × 8 = ■   6 × 4 = ■

2

3. Write a division equation for each situation.

 a) There are 21 cookies.

 There are 3 cookies in each package.

 How many packages are there altogether?

 b) There are 15 cookies.

 There are 5 packages altogether.

 How many cookies are in each package?

 c) There are 42 students.

 There are 6 groups altogether.

 How many students are in each group?

 d) There are 27 students.

 There are 3 students in each group.

 How many groups are there altogether?

3

4. Write a division and a multiplication equation for each.

 a)

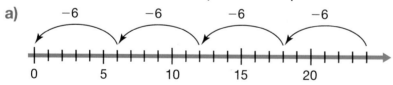

 b)

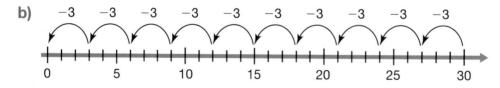

 c) $40 - 5 - 5 - 5 - 5 - 5 - 5 - 5 - 5 = 0$

5. Divide. Check by multiplying.

    a) 18 ÷ 2   **c)** 20 ÷ 4   **e)** 24 ÷ 4

    b) 18 ÷ 3   **d)** 20 ÷ 5   **f)** 24 ÷ 6

6. Write the fact family for each.

    a) 7, 3, 21   **d)** 8 ÷ 4 = ■   **g)** 40 ÷ 5 = ■

    b) 5 × 6 = ■   **e)** 4, 6, 24   **h)** 2 × 4 = 8

    c) 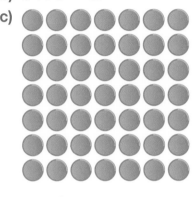   **f)**    **i)**

7. Draw the array to show the fact family for 7, 3, 21.

8. Find the product.

    a) 2 × 70   **d)** 5 × 700   **g)** 7 × 7000

    b) 2 × 700   **e)** 6 × 50   **h)** 4 × 60

    c) 5 × 70   **f)** 7 × 70   **i)** 4 × 6000

9. A box holds 200 straws.
How many straws are in 4 boxes?

10. Estimate the perimeter of a square if each side
length is 52 cm. Show your work.

11. Solve each problem. Show your work.

    a) 20 tulips are planted in equal rows.
        Show all possible arrangements.

    b) Kyle has 23 stamps. How many more stamps
        does he need to make 8 rows of 6 stamps?

    c) A number of marbles can be shared equally
        by 3 people. The same number of marbles
        can also be shared equally by 5 people.
        How many marbles might there be?

7 **12.** Complete.

    a) $4 \times 5 = \blacksquare \times 10$ **b)** $\blacksquare \times 5 = 3 \times 10$ **c)** $8 \times \blacksquare = 4 \times 10$

13. Complete.

    a) $4 \times 5 = \blacksquare$ **d)** $5 \times 5 = \blacksquare$ **g)** $8 \times 50 = \blacksquare$

    b) $6 \times 5 = \blacksquare$ **e)** $7 \times 5 = \blacksquare$ **h)** $20 \div 5 = \blacksquare$

    c) $8 \times 5 = \blacksquare$ **f)** $6 \times 50 = \blacksquare$ **i)** $40 \div 5 = \blacksquare$

8 **14.** Use the first fact to find the second fact.

    a) $4 \times 3 = \blacksquare$, so $5 \times 3 = \blacksquare$.

    b) $7 \times 3 = \blacksquare$, so $8 \times 3 = \blacksquare$.

    c) $3 \times 6 = \blacksquare$, so $4 \times 6 = \blacksquare$.

    d) $8 \times 6 = \blacksquare$, so $9 \times 6 = \blacksquare$.

15. Complete.

    a) $9 \times 60 = \blacksquare$ **b)** $36 \div 6 = \blacksquare$ **c)** $21 \div 3 = \blacksquare$

9 **16.** Complete.

    a) $8 \times 9 = \blacksquare$ **c)** $3 \times 9 = \blacksquare$ **e)** $63 \div 9 = \blacksquare$

    b) $9 \times 9 = \blacksquare$ **d)** $9 \times 20 = \blacksquare$ **f)** $9 \times 300 = \blacksquare$

17. Diana earns \$9 an hour working at a store.
How much does she earn in 40 hours?

10 **18.** Show how to use each fact to find 7×8.

    a) $7 \times 7 = 49$ **b)** $8 \times 8 = 64$ **c)** $7 \times 4 = 28$

19. Complete.

    a) $56 \div 7 = \blacksquare$ **c)** $7 \times 80 = \blacksquare$ **e)** $800 \times 9 = \blacksquare$

    b) $7 \times 9 = \blacksquare$ **d)** $8 \times 9 = \blacksquare$ **f)** $64 \div 8 = \blacksquare$

20. The perimeter of this octagon is 50 cm.
Is each side greater than or less than 7 cm?
Show your work.

octagon

174

Problem Bank

LESSON

2 1. Every 4th year is a leap year.
In leap years, there is an extra day on February 29.
Omar was born on February 29.
How many actual birthdays will Omar have had
when he is 28 years old?

3 2. Use these numbers to make 4 division equations.
Use each number only once.

9, 6, 28, 3, 7, 30, 24, 4, 2, 5, 8, 18

6 3. Some friends shared $35 evenly.
They received more than $5 each.
How many friends shared the money?
Show your work.

4. There are 50 boxes with
6 cans in each box.
How many cans are there in total?
Explain your answer.

5. 2 steps turn each of Jack's numbers
into one of Jill's numbers.
What are the 2 steps?
Explain using more examples.

Jack	Jill
3 ⟶	11
4 ⟶	15
5 ⟶	19
7 ⟶	27
10 ⟶	39

6. Write an equation for each statement.
   a) There are ■ sides in 8 hexagons.
   b) There are 24 sides in ■ hexagons.

7 7. Norah has 3 dimes and 9 nickels.
How much money does she have altogether?
Show your work.

8. a) Which number doesn't belong in this group?
      12, 16, 24, 30, 42
   b) Explain why you think so.
   c) Write another number that belongs.

9. A whole number multiplied by itself makes a
   square number.

1 × 1 **2 × 2** **3 × 3** **4 × 4**

Whole numbers	Green circles	Square numbers
1	1	1
2	3	4
3	5	9
4	7	16
5	9	
6	11	
7	13	
8	15	
9	17	
10	19	

   a) Describe the number pattern the green circles make.
   b) What do you add to a square number to get
      the next square number?
   c) Continue the pattern to complete the
      Square numbers column.
   d) What is the relationship between the numbers in
      the Whole numbers column and the numbers in
      the Green circles column?
   e) If you know 11 × 11 = 121, explain how you can
      find 12 × 12.

10. Estimate the number of times you can multiply
    2 by itself before you pass 1000.
    Check with a calculator.
    2 × 2 × 2 × 2 ...

Chapter Review

LESSON

2

1. 5 friends are sharing 20 jellybeans.
   How many jellybeans will each person get?

2. There are 6 eggs in 1 carton.
   How many eggs are in 3 cartons?

3

3. Which quotient is greater, $32 \div 4$ or $32 \div 8$?
   Explain how you can tell without dividing.

4

4. Tara made an array with 36 tiles.
   a) Show as many different ways to make
      the array as you can.
   b) Write the fact family for each array.

8

5. Find each result. Explain what you did.
   a) Use $4 \times 6 = 24$ to find $24 \div 6$.
   b) Use $6 \times 5 = 30$ to find 3×5.
   c) Use $2 \times 5 = 10$ to find 4×5.
   d) Use $10 \times 3 = 30$ to find 5×6.
   e) Use $5 \times 3 = 15$ to find 10×3.
   f) Use $7 \times 8 = 56$ to find 8×8.

6. Maggie says "5×8 is 40, so 6×8 must be
   $40 + 6$, or 46."
   Write a note to explain why her reasoning is wrong.

10

7. Are all these answers correct?
   Check by multiplying. Correct any errors.
   a) $12 \div 2 = 8$
   d) $24 \div 4 = 4$
   b) $63 \div 7 = 8$
   e) $81 \div 9 = 8$
   c) $25 \div 5 = 5$
   f) $60 \div 10 = 6$

$\times$	6	7	8	9	10
6					
7					
8					
9					
10					

8. a) Complete the multiplication table.
   b) Colour any square that contains a
      product that is an odd number.
   c) How are odd and even products related
      to their factors?

Chapter Task

Arrays on Parade

You will organize the school band so it can march in this year's community parade.

- The band will have between 60 and 85 people.
- The band will march in rows and columns.
- Each row has the same number of people in it.
- You cannot have rows or columns with more than 9 people.

? **How can you arrange the people in the band?**

A. Create all the arrays you can to fit between 60 and 85 people in the band.

B. Write the fact family for each of your arrays.

C. Explain how you know you found all the possible arrays in part A.

D. Choose 1 array. Explain how the fact family describes it.

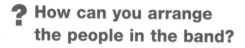

Task Checklist

☑ Did you find all the arrangements where rows and columns are not greater than 9?

☑ Did you organize your work so it is easy to follow?

☑ Did you explain your thinking?

☑ Did you use math language?

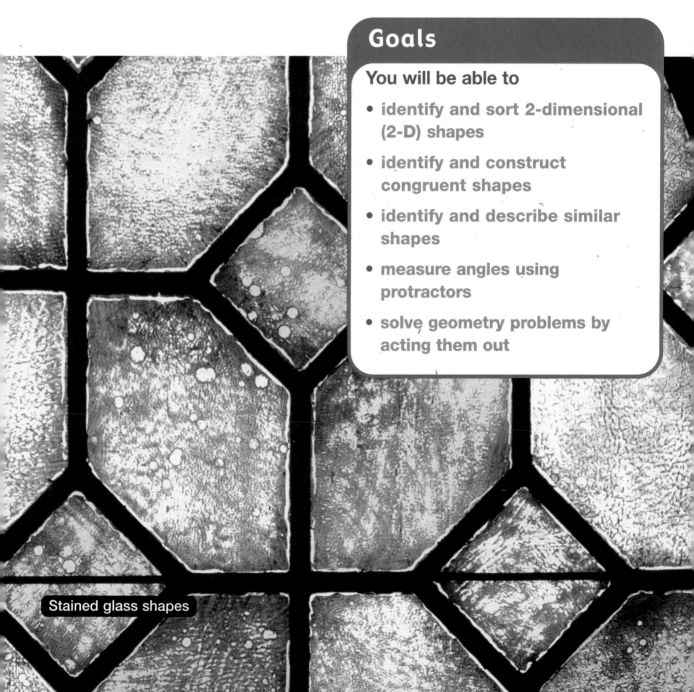

CHAPTER
2-D Geometry

7

Goals

You will be able to

- **identify and sort 2-dimensional (2-D) shapes**
- **identify and construct congruent shapes**
- **identify and describe similar shapes**
- **measure angles using protractors**
- **solve geometry problems by acting them out**

Stained glass shapes

Getting Started

Exploring Geometry with Puzzles

The butterfly puzzle is made of eight 2-D pieces.

? **How can you create a puzzle that follows these rules?**

• The whole puzzle must be a rectangle.
• There are 8 or more pieces.
• At least 2 pieces are **congruent**.
• At least 1 piece is a **parallelogram**.
• At least 1 piece is a **rectangle**.
• At least 1 piece is a **rhombus**.

A. Does the butterfly puzzle follow the rules?
   Explain your answer.

B. Sketch a plan for a puzzle that follows the rules.

C. Use a ruler to draw your puzzle pieces or trace
   around pattern blocks.

D. Create your puzzle.

E. Some of your pieces have **square corners**.
   What is the smallest number of these pieces
   that could be in your puzzle?
   Explain your answer.

F. Show how you could cut pieces in your puzzle in
   ways that would create more parallelograms.

Do You Remember?

1. Which shapes match each name?
   a) rectangle   b) hexagon   c) parallelogram   d) rhombus

   A   B   C   D   E

2. Which shapes have square corners?

3. Sort the 5 shapes using 2 **attributes**.
   Record and label your sorting.

4. Which 2 shapes are congruent?
   Explain your answer.

Classifying Quadrilaterals

Goal Identify and sort quadrilaterals.

A furniture store is creating a catalogue of its tables. Tables with these **quadrilateral** tops will be in the catalogue.

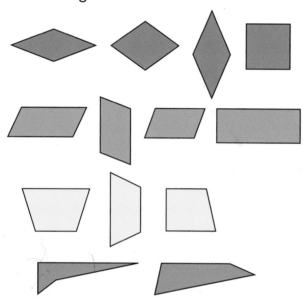

? **How are the tables organized?**

All the tables share the **attribute** of having 4 straight sides.

A. What other attributes do the purple tables share?

B. A square table is included with the purple tables. Is that a mistake? Explain your answer.

C. What other attributes do the blue tables share?

D. What other attributes do the yellow tables share?

E. Do the red tables share any attributes? Explain your answer.

quadrilateral
A closed shape with 4 straight sides

parallelogram
A quadrilateral with opposite sides that are **equal** and **parallel**

equal
The same length

Equal lines are marked with the same number of ticks.

parallel
Always the same distance apart

Parallel lines are drawn in the same colour.

F. Where does each shape belong in the Venn diagram?

a) a **rectangle**

b) a **rhombus**

c) a **square**

Sorting Quadrilaterals

parallelograms   all sides equal

G. What shape name would you give to each group of table tops?

a) purple   b) blue   c) yellow

Reflecting

1. In the word *quadrilateral*, what does *quad* mean?

2. Use examples to explain why a quadrilateral can have more than 1 shape name.

Checking

3. List all the possible shape names for each table top.

a) 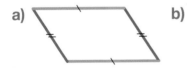   b)    c)

Practising

4. Draw your own table tops to show each shape.

a) a **trapezoid**

b) a quadrilateral that is not a **parallelogram** *or* a trapezoid

5. A table top has 4 sides, but only 2 square corners. What shape name can you use to describe it?

6. A table top has 2 pairs of **parallel** sides. What shape is it?

rectangle
A parallelogram with 4 square corners

square corner

rhombus
A parallelogram with 4 equal sides

square
A parallelogram with 4 equal sides and 4 square corners

trapezoid
A quadrilateral with only 1 pair of parallel sides

2 Building Quadrilaterals

Goal Relate properties of quadrilaterals to their side lengths.

You will need
- straws cut to 10 cm, 15 cm, and 20 cm lengths

? **What quadrilaterals can you model with different sets of straws?**

A. What quadrilaterals can you model with each set of straws?
   a) 4 short straws
   b) 2 short straws and 2 medium straws
   c) 2 short straws, 1 medium straw, and 1 long straw

B. Draw a picture of each model.

C. Label each picture with as many quadrilateral names as you can.

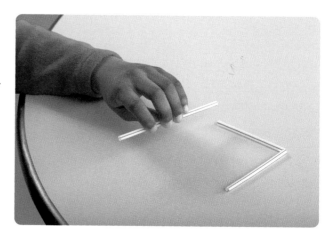

D. Use any of the straws to build a quadrilateral that is not a parallelogram or a trapezoid.

E. Draw the quadrilateral from part D, and list the straws you used to make it.

Reflecting

1. Name 2 different shapes that can be made with the same straws you used in part D.

2. Can you form a parallelogram and then a trapezoid with the same set of straws? Explain why or why not.

Tangram Quadrilaterals

This tangram puzzle is made up of 7 pieces, called tans.

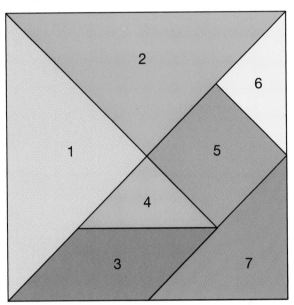

You will need

- a transparent mirror

- a tangram

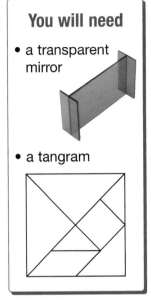

1
a) Identify which tans are quadrilaterals.
b) Name each quadrilateral.

2 You can join tans to make more quadrilaterals.
a) Draw quadrilaterals by tracing and combining tans.
b) Name each type of quadrilateral you make.

3 Use a transparent mirror to decide which quadrilaterals are symmetrical.
a) Name the quadrilaterals that are not symmetrical.
b) Name the quadrilaterals that have 1 line of symmetry.
c) Name the quadrilaterals that have more than 1 line of symmetry.

3 Congruent Shapes

Goal Identify and construct congruent shapes.

You will need
- a ruler
- geoboards
- dot paper

? Can you play the congruent shapes game?

A. Hide your geoboard from your partner.
Make a quadrilateral with no sides the same length.
Describe to your partner how to make a quadrilateral
that is **congruent** to yours.

B. Compare the shape your partner made to your shape.
Are the shapes congruent?

C. Explain how you can check whether the shapes
are congruent.

congruent
Identical in size
and shape

These quadrilaterals
are congruent to
each other.

Reflecting

1. These 2 shapes have equal side lengths.
Are they congruent? Explain your answer.

2. If 2 shapes are congruent, what attributes
must match?

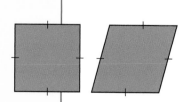

Checking

3. Which of these shapes are congruent?
   How do you know?

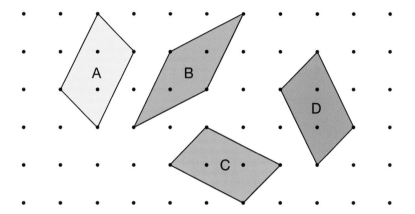

Practising

4. This geoboard shows a quadrilateral.
   a) Make a quadrilateral like this one on a geoboard.
      Copy the shape onto dot paper.
   b) Turn the geoboard upside down.
      Copy the new shape onto dot paper.
   c) Measure all the side lengths in both of your
      quadrilateral shapes. What do you notice?

5. These 2 quadrilaterals are congruent.
   a) Make 1 of the quadrilaterals on your geoboard.
      Copy the shape onto dot paper.
   b) Draw 5 other quadrilaterals that are congruent
      to the 1st quadrilateral.

6. Evan says that 2 rectangles with the same
   side lengths must be congruent.
   Do you agree? Explain why or why not.

4 Similar Shapes

Goal Identify and describe similar shapes.

You can use graphics software to enlarge or shrink a shape.
Sometimes the new shape is **similar** to the 1st shape.
Sometimes it is not similar.

similar
Identical in shape, but not necessarily the same size

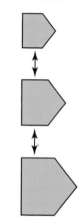

Natalie's Computer Triangles

I started with a small triangle.
I stretched the small triangle evenly.
The larger triangle has the same shape as the small triangle.
These triangles are similar.

Then I stretched only the bottom of the small triangle.
The larger triangle is too wide compared to the small triangle.
These triangles are *not* similar.

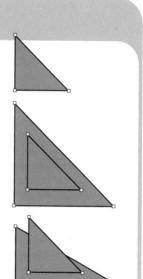

These shapes are similar to each other.

? **How would you describe a shape that is similar to each of these shapes?**

A. Compare these triangles.
   How do you know they are not similar?

B. Compare these rectangles.
   How do you know they are not similar?

C. Draw a shape that is similar to the blue triangle.
   Explain why the shape is similar.

D. Draw a shape that is similar to the yellow rectangle.
   Explain why the shape is similar.

Reflecting

1. Can a triangle and a square be similar?
   Explain your answer.

2. Are all squares similar?
   Explain your answer using pictures and words.

Checking

3. a) Which pairs of shapes look similar?
      Explain your answer.
   b) Explain why shapes D and J are not similar.

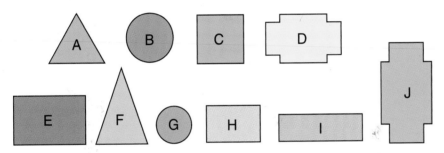

Practising

4. Which rectangle looks similar to the red rectangle?
   Explain your answer.

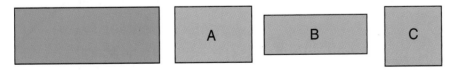

5. Which blue hexagon looks similar to the red hexagon?
   Explain your answer.

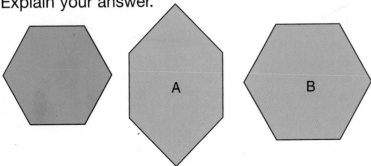

A Similarity Test

Use this test to decide if 2 rectangles are similar.

Step 1 Place 1 corner of the smaller rectangle on top of the matching corner of the larger rectangle.

Step 2 Draw a diagonal from that corner to the opposite corner of the larger rectangle.

If the diagonal passes through the opposite corner of the smaller rectangle, then the rectangles are similar. If it doesn't, the rectangles are not similar.

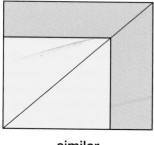

similar

not similar

1 Use the similarity test to find out if all squares are similar. What did you discover?

2 Isosceles triangles have 2 sides of equal length. Design a test that will help you decide if 2 isosceles triangles are similar.

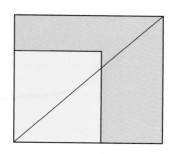

Mid-Chapter Review

1 1. Use each shape name once to make these
sentences true.

- parallelogram
- trapezoid
- rhombus

- square
- rectangle

a) A ■ is a special ■.

b) A ■ is never a ■.

c) A ■ always has 4 square corners.

3 2. Use dot paper to show that 2 congruent
quadrilaterals are still congruent even if they are
turned or flipped over. Draw pictures and explain
how you know your shapes are congruent.

4 3. Which of the shapes in this
figure fit each of the clues below?

a) The shapes are similar.

b) The shapes are congruent.

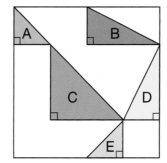

4. Use dot paper to draw 2 pictures of each shape.
The shapes should not be congruent or similar.

a) trapezoids   b) parallelograms

5. Brad said that these 2 frogs are similar.
Do you agree? Explain how you could check.

5 Measuring Angles

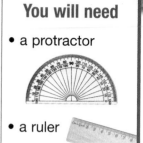
Goal Measure angles using a protractor.

When you spread 2 fingers, you make an **angle**.

? **What is the greatest angle you can make with your ring and middle fingers?**

angle

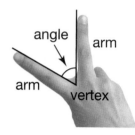

angle
arm
arm
vertex

 Vinh's Angle

I made an angle by tracing my ring and middle fingers.

I used a ruler to straighten out the arms of the angle.

I estimated the size of my angle by comparing it to 45°.

It looks like my angle is less than 45°.

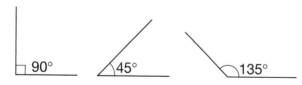

90°   45°   135°

I measured the angle with my **protractor**.

I put the line of my protractor with the 0° mark over 1 arm of the angle.

I read the **degree** measure where the other arm of the angle meets the protractor.

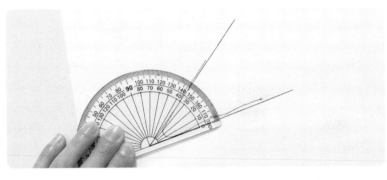

I can make a 35° angle with my ring and middle fingers.

protractor
A tool used to measure angles

degree
A unit for measuring angles

45°

45° is read as 45 degrees.

Reflecting

1. About how great an angle can you make between your thumb and your index finger?

2. Form a triangle with your fingers. How many angles in that triangle can be measured?

3. Do the arm lengths of an angle affect the angle measure? Measure these angles. Explain what you find.

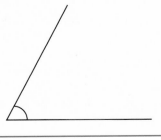

Checking

4. Measure each angle.

a)

b)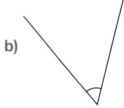

c)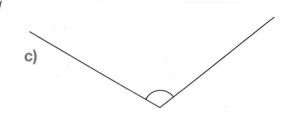

5. Measure the 3 angles inside the triangle.

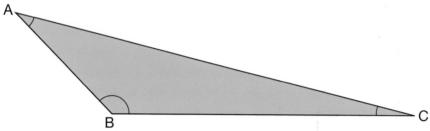

Practising

6. The yellow shapes are congruent. Measure the angles inside each shape. What do you notice about the angles inside congruent shapes?

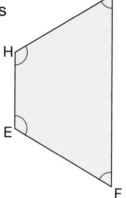

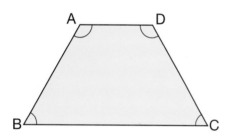

7. The blue shapes are similar. Measure the angles inside each shape. What do you notice about the angles inside similar shapes?

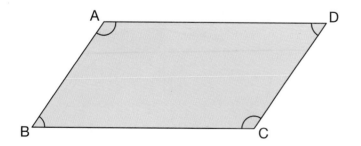

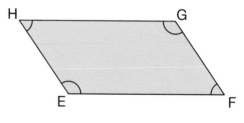

Building Shapes from Triangles

You will need
- pattern block triangles

 Shani's Hexagon

I created a hexagon with 6 triangles.

A. Use 6 pattern block triangles to make a hexagon like Shani's.

Try These

1. How many different hexagons can you make with 6 pattern block triangles?
Show your work.

2. Make each of these shapes with 6 triangle pattern block triangles.
   a) an octagon (8-sided)
   b) a parallelogram

6 Solve Problems by Acting Them Out

You will need
- pattern blocks

Goal Act out a problem to solve it.

Sarah is pushing together 20 tables shaped like trapezoids to make a single row.

? **How many people can sit at the tables if 1 person sits at each side?**

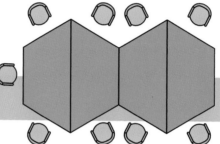

Sarah's Solution

Understand

It isn't possible to sit where 2 tables come together. That means I have to count only the open sides.

Make a Plan

I will act out the problem using trapezoid blocks for the tables.

Carry Out the Plan

First I count the number of open sides on top.

There are 20 open sides on top.

1 2 3 4 5 6 7 8 9 10 11 12 13 14 15 16 17 18 19 20

There are 20 more open sides on the bottom and 1 open side at each end.

20 + 20 + 1 + 1 = 42 open sides

42 people can sit at the tables.

Reflecting

1. Why didn't Sarah need to count the sides on the bottom?

2. If Sarah had arranged the tables in 2 rows of hexagons, would there have been more or fewer places to sit? Explain your answer.

3. How did acting out the problem help Sarah find a solution?

Checking

4. Rami is pushing together 7 tables shaped like hexagons to make 1 row. How many people can sit at the tables if 1 person sits on each open side? Show your work.

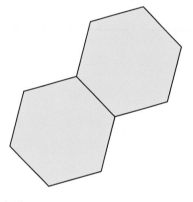

Practising

5. Terry is pushing together 9 tables shaped like rhombuses to make 1 row. How many people can sit at the tables if 1 person sits on each open side?

6. Tamara is making 1 big table by pushing together 6 small tables shaped like equilateral triangles. 1 person sits at each open side.
   a) How many people can sit at the larger table?
   b) Explain why there is more than 1 answer to this problem.

7 Lines of Symmetry

Goal Draw lines of symmetry.

Symmetry can be used to see patterns and solve puzzles.
These 2 names are half covered.
Which name is easier to figure out?

The name on the left is probably easier to figure out because each letter in TOM is symmetrical across the vertical line. The letters in JEN are not.

? **If you fold a shape on its line of symmetry, is it easy to visualize the whole shape?**

A. Trace a square pattern block or make a square on dot paper.

B. Draw all the **lines of symmetry** of the square.
Try each of these methods.

Use a transparent mirror.

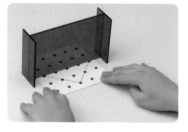

Measure with a ruler.

Cut it out and fold.

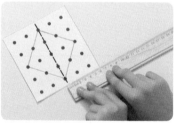

Use the dots on the grid.

line of symmetry
A line that divides a shape in half so that if you fold the shape on the line, the halves match

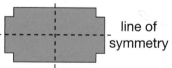

line of symmetry

line of symmetry

This shape has 2 lines of symmetry.

C. Repeat parts A and B with a triangle, a hexagon, and a rhombus.

D. Trace a trapezoid pattern block. Draw any lines of symmetry. Which method did you use? Why?

E. Fold each of the shapes in parts C and D on 1 of its lines of symmetry. Hide half of the shape. Is it easy to visualize the whole shape from the half? Why or why not?

F. Draw these 3 quadrilaterals on dot paper. For each quadrilateral, find all the lines of symmetry, if there are any.

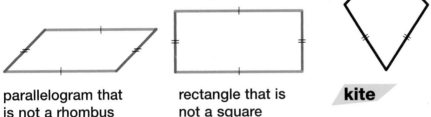

parallelogram that is not a rhombus

rectangle that is not a square

kite

kite
A quadrilateral with 2 pairs of equal sides and no sides parallel

Reflecting

1. What do you notice about the shapes that have more than 1 line of symmetry?

2. How does dot paper help you to find lines of symmetry?

3. What is an easier tool for drawing lines of symmetry, a transparent mirror or a ruler? Explain your thinking.

8 Classifying 2-D Shapes

Goal Identify and sort 2-D shapes.

You will need
- sheet of shapes

- a ruler
- a protractor

Think about attributes of some 2-D shapes.
- parallel sides
- number of sides
- equal sides
- symmetry
- similarity
- congruence
- angle size

? **How many different ways can you sort these shapes?**

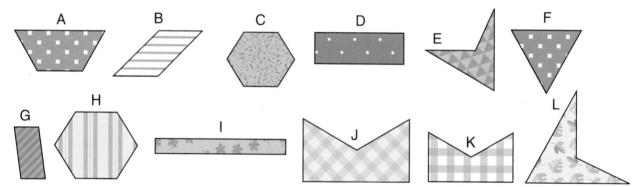

A. Sort the shapes using 2 or more attributes.

B. Show how you sorted the shapes.
You could make a chart or a list, or draw a Venn diagram.

C. Find at least 4 other ways to sort the shapes.
Show how you sorted the shapes each time.

Reflecting

1. Which attributes do most of the shapes have?

2. Which attributes do only a few of the shapes have?

Playing the Angles

You will need

- dice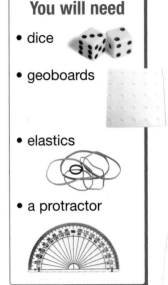
- geoboards
- elastics
- a protractor

Number of players: 2
How to play: Make a **polygon** with the greatest angle.

Step 1 Each player rolls 1 die. Add the numbers on the dice. If the sum is 2, roll again.

Step 2 Each player uses elastics to make a polygon with the number of sides equal to the sum of the dice.

Step 3 Each player chooses the greatest angle in his or her polygon and measures it.

Step 4 Compare the 2 angles. Subtract to find the difference between the greater and lesser angles.

Step 5 The player with the greater angle gets points equal to the difference between the 2 angles.

Play 5 rounds. The player with the higher score wins.

Terry's and Chantal's Polygons

Chantal and I rolled a 3 and a 4.
We made **heptagons**.
My greatest angle was 157°.
Chantal's greatest angle was 153°.
The difference is 4°.
My score is 4.

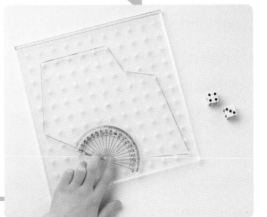

Skills Bank

LESSON

1

1. Complete the table. Find as many shapes as possible for each shape name.

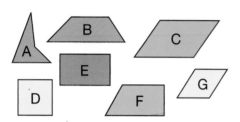

Shape name	Shape letter
parallelogram	
quadrilateral	
rectangle	
rhombus	
square	
trapezoid	

3

2. Which of these shapes are congruent?

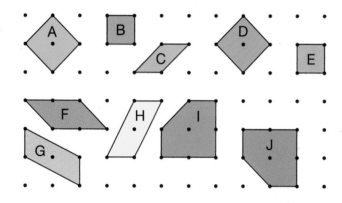

3. Draw 2 shapes that are congruent to this shape. Use dot paper.

4

4. Which green shape looks similar to the red shape?

a)

c)

b)

d)

5. Measure all the angles inside each shape.

a)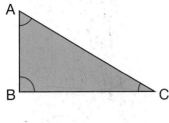

b)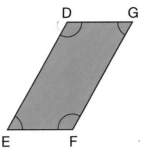

c)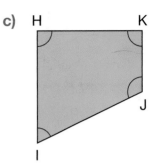

6. Draw each shape on dot paper.
Draw all the lines of symmetry.

a)

b)

c)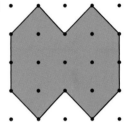

7. a) Complete the Venn diagram to sort the shapes.

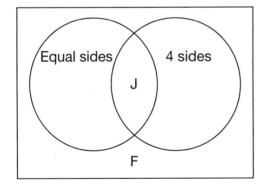

b) Sort the shapes another way.
Use a Venn diagram, a chart, or lists.
You can use 2 or more attributes such as
- number of sides
- equal sides
- parallel sides
- similarity
- congruence
- symmetry
- angle size

Problem Bank

1

1. Shani found a board shaped like a rhombus. Show how she can cut the board and rearrange the pieces to make a rectangle.

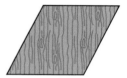

2. How many different sizes of parallelograms can you see in this figure?
Draw pictures with labels to record your answer.

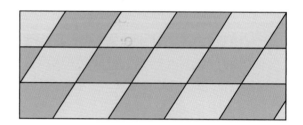

3. Imagine that you cut a quadrilateral into 2 pieces with a straight cut. How many sides can your resulting shapes have? Show all the possibilities you can think of.

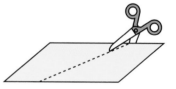

3

4. How many shapes can you draw on the grid that are congruent to this shape? The shapes can overlap. Draw pictures to show your answer.

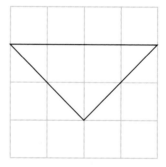

4

5. Trace these 2 similar triangles. Explain how to place the triangles on top of one another for each result.
   a) Only 1 triangle and 1 trapezoid can be seen.
   b) 4 congruent triangles can be seen.

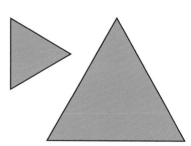

Chapter Review

1 1. Which of these shapes are parallelograms? Explain your thinking.

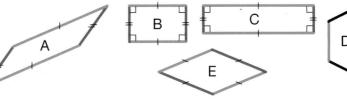

3 2. Use a geoboard or dot paper.
   a) Copy the quadrilateral.
   b) Create 2 other shapes that are congruent to this shape.
   c) Does this shape have a line of symmetry? Explain your answer.

4 3. Identify the shapes that look similar. Explain your thinking.

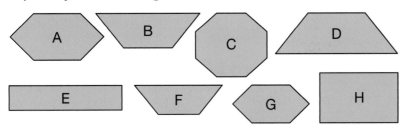

5 4. Draw a trapezoid that you think has 2 equal angles. Then draw a trapezoid that you think has no equal angles.
   Measure all the angles and record your measurements. Check your predictions.

6 5. Draw a cake like this one on dot paper. Show how to cut the cake in 2 pieces with a straight cut to get each result.
   a) Each piece is a parallelogram.
   b) Each piece is a trapezoid.

8 6. Describe 2 ways to sort the shapes from Question 3 using 2 attributes each time. Use a Venn diagram, a chart, or a list.

Chapter Task

Shape Names

Poly Gon is having a math party.
She wants a name tag for each of her guests,
but she has rules for the tags.

- More than half, but not all, of the name tags are quadrilaterals.
- 4 of the name tags have an angle greater than 90°.
- Only 3 of the name tags are congruent.
- 2 of the name tags are similar.
- 1 name tag has 2 angles where 1 angle is at least 50° greater than the other.

? **How can you make and describe 10 different name tags for Poly's party?**

A. Create 10 name tags to fit Poly's rules.

B. Completely describe each of the name tags you made.

Task Checklist

- ☑ Did you include diagrams?
- ☑ Did you use math language?
- ☑ Did you verify that your name tags agree with Poly's rules?
- ☑ Did you organize your work so it is easy to follow?

Cumulative Review

Cross-Strand Multiple Choice

1. Which calculations would help you find the missing digits?

   $$\begin{array}{r} 8\ 7 \\ +\ 9\ \blacksquare \\ \hline 1\ \blacksquare\ 8 \end{array}$$

   A. 8 + 9 and 7 + 8   C. 80 + 90 and 70 + 80
   B. 87 + 9 and 18 − 7   D. 8 − 7 and 80 + 90

2. Josh paid for all of these items using two $20 bills and one $10 bill. How much change should he get?

blank CDs	$30.00
magazine	$6.95
CD labels	$8.25

   E. $4.80   F. $4.90   G. $5.80   H. $5.87

3. Which measurements could describe the perimeter of a beach towel?

   A. 40 mm   B. 400 cm   C. 4 m   D. 4 km

4. Which statement does not describe this array?

   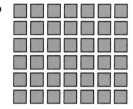

   E. 42 − 7 − 7 − 7 − 7 − 7 − 7
   F. 6 + 6 + 6 + 6 + 6 + 6
   G. 6 × 7
   H. 42 ÷ 6

5. How could you name the 2 groups on this sorting mat?

   A. quadrilaterals/not quadrilaterals
   B. polygons/quadrilaterals
   C. rectangles/not rectangles
   D. parallel sides/no parallel sides

   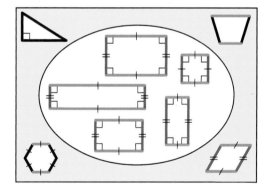

6. Which angle has the greatest measure?

   E.    F.   G.    H.

Cross-Strand Investigation

Canada's Supreme Court

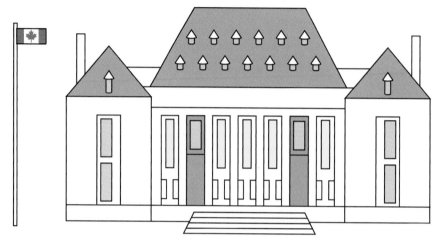

The Supreme Court of Canada in Ottawa

7. a) Identify 2 pairs of congruent shapes in the picture.
   Explain how you know the shapes are congruent.
   b) Could the yellow lit windows be similar to the
   blue unlit windows above the doors?
   Explain using a drawing and math words.
   c) Why are parts of buildings often congruent?
   Explain using math words.

8. Each lit window contains 6 rows of glass panes.
   There are 3 panes in each row. How many panes
   were needed to make all of the lit windows?
   Solve this problem using 2 different strategies.
   Explain your solution.

9. a) The Main Courtroom is a rectangle that is 16 m
   long and 12 m wide. How can the length and
   width help you find the perimeter?
   Explain using a labelled drawing.
   b) Draw a rectangle to fit exactly around the
   outside of the building on this page. Then draw
   a different rectangle with the same perimeter.
   Show how you know the perimeter is the same.

Area and Grids

Goals

You will be able to

- use 2 standard area units
- measure area with the appropriate unit
- investigate how changes in shape affect perimeter and area
- solve area problems using organized lists

Ploughed rectangular fields

Getting Started

Comparing Area

Your eyes can trick you into thinking something is a different size than it really is.

? **How can you compare the areas of the red and blue shapes?**

NEL

A. What do you think you will find when you compare the areas of the red and blue shapes? Give a reason for your answer.

B. Measure the areas of both shapes. What did you find?

C. The blue shape is inside a square.
   a) Estimate how much greater the area of the square is compared to the area of the blue shape. Measure to check.
   b) Estimate how much longer the perimeter of the square is compared to the perimeter of the blue shape. Measure to check.

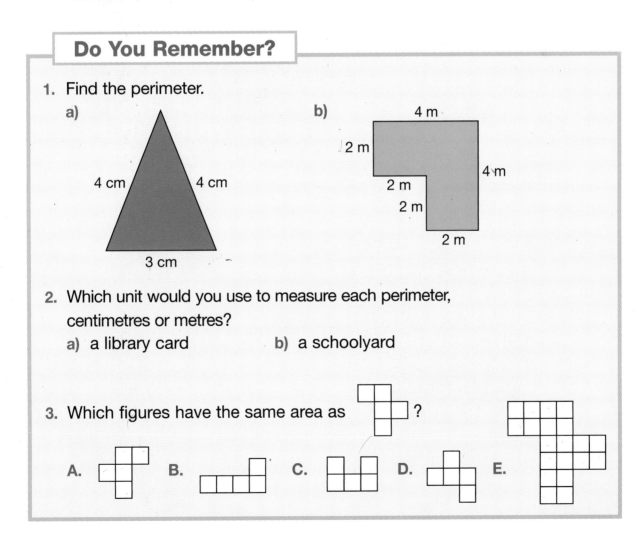

Do You Remember?

1. Find the perimeter.
   a) 4 cm   4 cm   3 cm
   b) 4 m   2 m   2 m   2 m   4 m   2 m

2. Which unit would you use to measure each perimeter, centimetres or metres?
   a) a library card
   b) a schoolyard

3. Which figures have the same area as ⌐ ?
   A.   **B.**   **C.**   **D.**   **E.**

1 Standard Area Units

You will need
- paper
- scissors

Goal Explain why we use standard units to measure area.

Shani and Josef are working together to make a card and an envelope for the card.

Shani's Instructions

I sent Josef an e-mail with instructions for making the card.

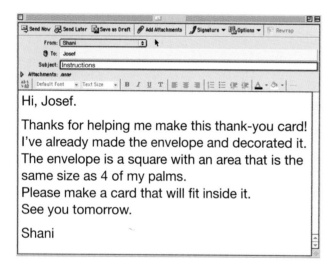

Send Now   Send Later   Save as Draft   Add Attachments   Signature ▾   Options ▾   Rewrap

From: Shani
To: Josef
Subject: Instructions
Attachments: none

Default Font ▾ Text Size ▾ **B** *I* U T

Hi, Josef.

Thanks for helping me make this thank-you card!
I've already made the envelope and decorated it.
The envelope is a square with an area that is the
same size as 4 of my palms.
Please make a card that will fit inside it.
See you tomorrow.

Shani

? **What size should Josef make the card?**

A. Measure a paper square that has an area of 4 palms. Cut out the square.

B. Compare your square with the squares of others in your class. What do you notice?

C. Write a note to Shani. Suggest a better way to describe the area of the envelope.

Reflecting

1. Why did your square have a different area than the squares made by others in your class?

2. Why is it important to measure area with units that are the same for everyone?

3. How could Shani use centimetres or millimetres to describe the size of the envelope?

Cutting and Moving

Zola's Movable Square

I cut this square into 4 triangles.

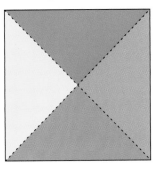

You will need

- grid paper

- scissors

I put the triangles together to make this shape.

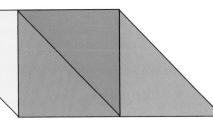

A. What is the name of Zola's second shape?

Try This

1. Make your own square and cut it into triangles.
   a) Make shapes with the triangles.
   b) Describe each shape.

2 Square Centimetres

Goal Estimate, measure, and compare area using square centimetres.

You will need

• a centimetre grid transparency

Mandy and Calvin are making stars for art class.
They are using shiny gold paper.
The paper comes in 2 shapes, square and rectangular.

Mandy's Square

I think the square paper has a greater area.

Calvin's Rectangle

I think the rectangular paper has a greater area.

? **How can Mandy and Calvin compare the areas of the 2 shapes of paper?**

A. Who do you think is right?
Explain your reasoning.

B. Place a centimetre grid transparency over each shape.
Measure the area by counting the number of **square centimetres** it takes to cover each shape.

C. How do the areas compare?

square centimetre
A **standard unit**
for measuring area

1 cm
1 cm

A square with sides of
1 cm has an area of
1 square centimetre.

Reflecting

1. Why was it difficult to compare the areas of Mandy's square and Calvin's rectangle without measuring?

2. Sometimes area is measured to the nearest whole square centimetre. The area of this triangle is about 7 whole square centimetres. Why does that make sense?

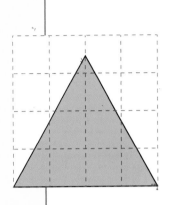

Checking

3. a) Which shape do you think has the greater area?

   b) Estimate the area of each shape.

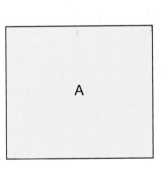

A

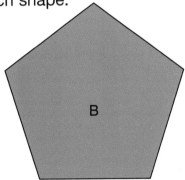

B

   c) Measure the area of each shape to the nearest whole square centimetre. Use a centimetre grid transparency.

Practising

4. Estimate the area of each shape. Measure the area of each shape to the nearest whole square centimetre.

   a)

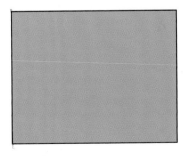

   b)

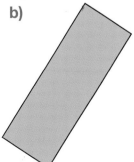

5. Estimate the area of each shape.
   Measure the area of each shape to the nearest whole
   square centimetre.

   a)

   c)

   b)

   d)

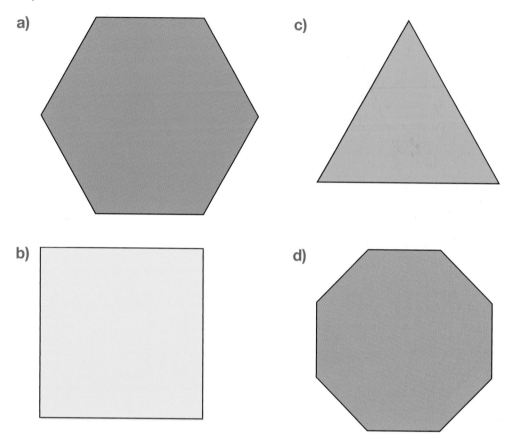

6. Choose 3 flat surfaces in your classroom that you
   can measure with a square centimetre grid.
   a) Estimate each area in square centimetres.
   b) Measure each area to the nearest whole
      square centimetre.

7. Does a shape with an area of 1 square centimetre
   have to be a square?
   Use an example to help you explain.

Area Logic

Number of players: 2 or 3
How to play: Colour areas on a grid.
Each player uses a different coloured pencil crayon.

Step 1 Roll 2 dice. Use the product of the 2 numbers as the area of a rectangle.

Step 2 Players try to colour their rectangles on the centimetre grid paper.
If there is no space left to colour a rectangle with this area, lose your turn.

Step 3 Continue taking turns until no player can go.

Count the coloured squares to see which player has coloured the greatest area.

You will need

- 2 dice
- grid paper
- pencil crayons or crayons

Paulette's Turn

I rolled 2 and 4.

I will need to colour a rectangle with an area of 8 square centimetres.

The rectangle could be 2 cm by 4 cm or 1 cm by 8 cm.

I will colour a 2 cm by 4 cm rectangle.

3 Square Metres

Goal Estimate area using an appropriate area unit.

When you buy wallpaper, you need to estimate how many square metres of paper it will take to cover the walls.

? **About how many square metres of wallpaper would you need to cover 1 wall in your classroom?**

A. Use chart paper to make a model of a **square metre**. Each side of the square should be 1 m long.

B. Use your model to estimate the area of 1 wall in your classroom.

C. About how many square metres of wallpaper would you need to cover the wall?

square metre
A standard unit for measuring area

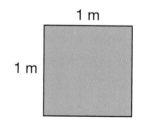

A square with sides of 1 m has an area of 1 square metre.

Reflecting

1. Explain how you estimated the area of the wall.

2. Suppose you estimated the area of the wall using square centimetres. Would your estimate be a greater or a smaller number of units? Explain your thinking.

Checking

3. Carpet is also measured in square metres. Use your model of a square metre to estimate the area of your classroom floor. About how many square metres of carpet would you need?

Practising

4. Find an object in your classroom that you estimate has an area between 6 square metres and 12 square metres. Estimate and record its area.

5. Which unit would you use to measure each area, square metres or square centimetres? Explain your answer.
   a) a baseball field
   b) a book cover
   c) a backyard
   d) an envelope

6. Name something that can be made from each material.
   a) about 1 square metre of cloth
   b) about 1 square centimetre of metal
   c) about 1 square metre of plastic

7. Josh cut his model of a square metre. He used the pieces to make a new shape.

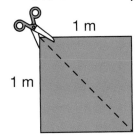 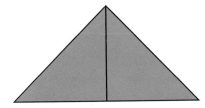

1 m

1 m

   a) What is the area of Josh's new shape? Explain how you know.
   b) What other shapes can you make with your model of a square metre? What do you know about the area of the shapes?

LESSON

Mid-Chapter Review

1

1. Would coins be useful units for measuring area? Explain your thinking.

3 cm

3 cm

2

2. Which shape has the same area as the red square? How do you know?

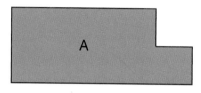

A

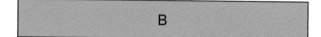

B

3. Measure each area to the nearest whole square centimetre. Use a centimetre grid transparency.

a)

b)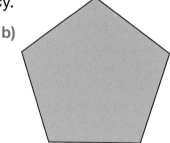

3

4. Identify 3 surfaces in your classroom each with an area between 10 square centimetres and 1 square metre. Estimate the area of each surface.

5. Which unit would you use to measure each area, square centimetres or square metres? Explain each answer.

   a) a photograph
   b) the library ceiling
   c) the surface of an ice rink

   d) the palm of your hand
   e) the school parking lot
   f) the chalkboard

Area on Board

1

This geoboard is divided in half.

a) Find 5 more ways to divide a 5 by 5 geoboard in half.

b) How do you know the halves have the same area?

c) Are the halves always congruent?

2

Do the parallelogram and the rectangle have the same area? Explain how you know.

3

Make as many squares as you can on a 5 by 5 geoboard. How many squares with a different area can you make?

4 Relating Linear Dimensions and Area

Goal Relate the area of a rectangle to its length and width.

Rami is making display bases for his model cars. He wants to use a special gold paint, but he isn't sure if he'll have enough.

? **Will Rami have enough paint to cover all 3 bases?**

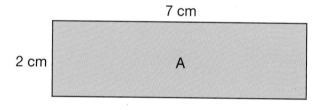

7 cm

2 cm

A

display base

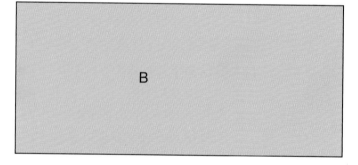

B

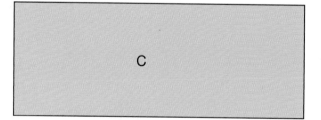

C

Rami's Paint

I have a small bottle of paint that will cover an area of 75 square centimetres.

I used a centimetre grid transparency to measure the area of rectangle A.
The area is 14 square centimetres.

Rectangle	Width	Length	Area
A	2 cm	7 cm	14 square centimetres
B			
C			

A. Measure the areas of rectangles B and C.

B. Complete Rami's table.

C. Will Rami have enough paint?
Explain your answer.

D. What relationships do you notice in the table?

E. If there is leftover paint, will there be enough to cover another rectangle that is 3 cm by 4 cm?
Explain how you know.

Reflecting

1. a) Explain how you can find the area of a rectangle using the length and width.
   b) How would finding the area of a square be the same as finding the area of a rectangle? How would it be different?

Checking

2. Carmen is also making display bases.
   She has paint that will cover 50 square centimetres.
   Does she have enough paint to cover these
   2 rectangles? Calculate the area of each rectangle.
   Use the relationship among length, width, and area
   of a rectangle. Show your work.

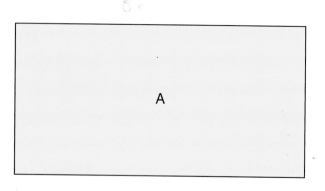

A

B

Practising

3. Calculate the area of each rectangle.
   Use the relationship among the length, width,
   and area of a rectangle. Show your work.

   a)

   6 cm

   3 cm

   b)

   7 m

   4 m

4. Complete the table. Show your work.

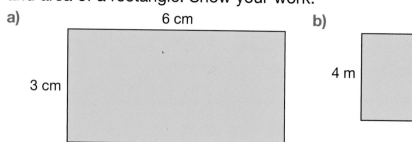

Rectangle	Width	Length	Area
A	4 cm	5 cm	
B	5 m	6 m	
C	5 cm		25 square centimetres
D	2 m		20 square metres

5 Relating Shape, Area, and Perimeter

Goal Investigate how changes in shape affect area and perimeter.

A pentomino is made up of 5 square tiles.
Each tile shares a side with at least 1 other tile.

These 4 pentominoes are congruent.
Each of these pentominoes has an area of
5 square units and a perimeter of 12 units.

pentominoes

? **Do all pentominoes have the same area and the same perimeter?**

A. Make as many different pentominoes as you can.

B. Draw your pentominoes on grid paper.

C. Record the area and perimeter of each pentomino.

D. Compare your results with other groups.
How many different pentominoes did you find?

E. Do all pentominoes have the same area and perimeter?

Reflecting

1. Is it possible for 2 different shapes to have the same perimeter? How do you know?

2. Is it possible for 2 different shapes to have the same area? How do you know?

3. a) What is the difference between perimeter and area?
   b) Give an example of when you might use each.

6 Solve Problems Using Organized Lists

Goal Use an organized list to solve area problems.

? How many different rectangles with an area of 12 square tiles can you make?

Rey's Solution

Understand

I know I can make a rectangle that is 1 row of 12 tiles.

I can also make a rectangle that is 2 rows of 6 tiles.

Make a Plan

If I keep trying different numbers of rows in order, I should be able to find all the rectangles that are possible.

I can keep track of what I do in an **organized list**.

Carry Out the Plan

I started with 1 row and then tried all the numbers of rows to 12.

I crossed out the rectangles that were the same as another rectangle.

I can make 3 different rectangles with 12 square tiles.

Organized List of Rectangles

1 row of 12 ✓

2 rows of 6 ✓

3 rows of 4 ✓

~~4 rows of 3~~ (same as 3 rows of 4)

5 rows (rectangle impossible)

~~6 rows of 2~~ (same as 2 rows of 6)

7, 8, 9, 10, 11 rows (rectangle impossible)

~~12 rows of 1~~ (same as 1 row of 12)

organized list
The strategy of following a certain order to find all possibilities

Reflecting

1. How did Rey's organized list help him find all the different rectangles?

2. Suppose each tile has a design on it. Would there still be only 3 different rectangles? Explain your thinking.

Checking

3. How many different rectangles with an area of 36 square tiles can you make? Show your work.

Practising

4. How many different rectangles can you draw with an area of 40 square centimetres? Show your work.

5. This square has an area of 16 square centimetres. Hidden in the square are other squares with different areas. Complete the organized list to find the total number of squares.

Size of square	Area of square	Number of squares
4 by 4	16 square centimetres	1 square
3 by 3	▪ square centimetres	4 squares
2 by 2	▪ square centimetres	▪ squares
1 by 1	▪ square centimetres	▪ squares

6. Charlotte has 55¢ in quarters, dimes, and nickels. She has at least one of each type of coin. How many coins could she have? Show your work.

7. Write a problem that can be solved with an organized list. Give your problem to a partner to solve.

LESSON

Skills Bank

2   1. Estimate the area of each shape. Then measure
    the area to the nearest whole centimetre.
    Use a centimetre grid transparency.

a)

e)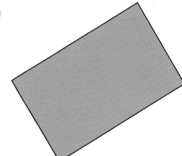

b)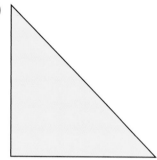

f)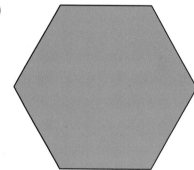

c)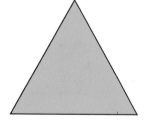

g)

d)

h)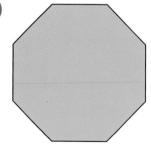

2. Find an object that you estimate has each area.
Estimate and record the area of your object.
a) between 1 square metre and 4 square metres
b) between 4 square metres and 9 square metres
c) between 9 square metres and 16 square metres
d) greater than 16 square metres

3. Name at least 5 things that you would measure using each area unit.
a) square metres
b) square centimetres

4. Measure the length and width of each rectangle.
Calculate the area of each rectangle.
Show your work.

a)

b)

5. Calculate the area of each rectangle.
Show your work.

a)

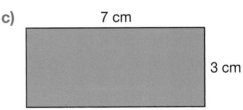

5 cm
3 cm

c)

7 cm
3 cm

b)

6 m
3 m

d)

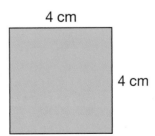

4 cm
4 cm

Problem Bank

1   **1.** Justin designed this tile on grid paper.
His tile is 4 units by 4 units.
He laid 3 tiles side by side.

a) What is the perimeter of the 3 tiles?

b) How much area is green in the 3 tiles?

c) How much area is orange in the 3 tiles?

1 tile

5   **2.** A rectangular centimetre grid is 6 cm long by 5 cm wide.
It is cut along a grid line to create 2 smaller rectangles.
What could the areas of the smaller rectangles be?
Give as many different answers as you can.
Show your work.

3. The floor of a room is a rectangle.
It has a perimeter of 22 metres and an area of
24 square metres.

a) What are the length and width of the room?
Show your work.

b) Is it possible for a floor to have the same
perimeter but a larger area?
Give an example to explain your answer.

6   **4.** There are 5 possible tetrominoes. Here are 2 of them.

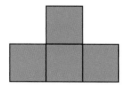 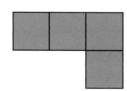

tetrominoes (4 squares)

a) Draw the other 3 tetrominoes.

b) What is the total area of all 5 tetrominoes?

c) Can the 5 tetrominoes fit together to make a
rectangle? Show your work.

Chapter Review

LESSON

2

1. Measure the area of each shape to the nearest whole square centimetre.

   a)

   b)

3

2. What unit of measurement would you use for each? Explain your answer.
   a) the amount of paint needed to paint a model car
   b) the amount of carpet needed to cover a floor

4

3. Draw a rectangle on centimetre grid paper that is 3 cm wide and has an area of 12 square centimetres.

4. a) How many different rectangles with an area of 32 square tiles can you make? Show your work.
   b) Did you find all the rectangles? Explain how you know.

5

5. Indicate whether each statement is true or false. Explain your answer.
   a) Rectangles that are not congruent can have the same area.
   b) If you know the perimeter of a square, you can find its area.

6

6. 32 square patio tiles are used to make a walkway around a rectangular garden.
   Each tile is 1 square metre.
   a) What are the area and perimeter of the garden? Show your work.
   b) Find at least one more answer.

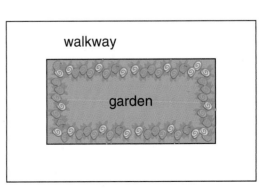

Chapter Task

Design a Petting Zoo

You are designing a petting zoo for the Spring Fair.
Each type of animal should be in its own pen.
You have only 80 m of fencing.

- The pony and calf each need a large pen.
- The chickens and rabbits need small pens.
- The lambs and piglets need medium pens.
- The pens must have some space between them.

? **How can you design the petting zoo so that it is well planned, and doesn't take up too much space?**

Understand

A. How many pens are needed?

B. What do you know about the areas and the perimeters of the pens?

Make a Plan

C. Use square tiles to model the pens.
Each square represents 1 square metre.

Carry Out the Plan

D. Draw your model on grid paper.

Look Back

E. Does your design meet the requirements?

Communicate

F. Explain why you think your design is a good one.

Task Checklist

- ☑ Did you use a model?
- ☑ Did you include diagrams?
- ☑ Did you show the right amount of detail?
- ☑ Did you explain your thinking?
- ☑ Did you use math language?

Multiplying Greater Numbers

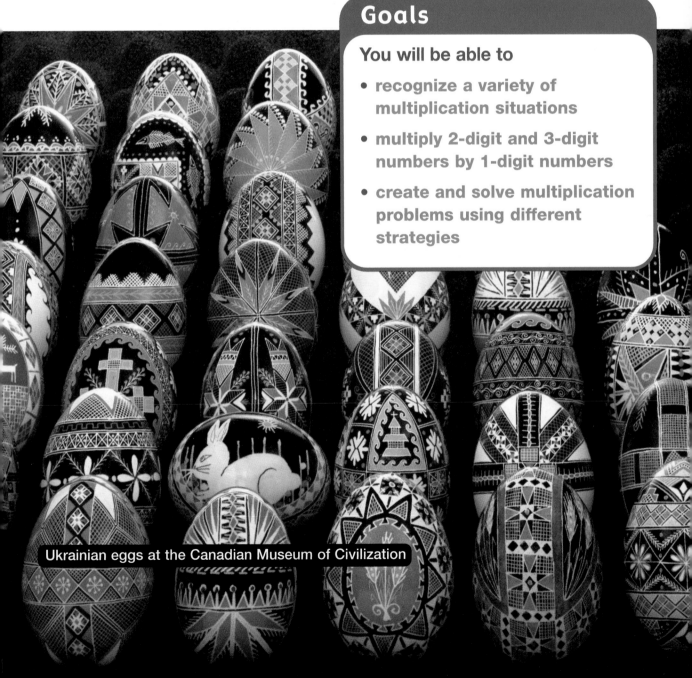

Goals

You will be able to

- recognize a variety of multiplication situations

- multiply 2-digit and 3-digit numbers by 1-digit numbers

- create and solve multiplication problems using different strategies

Ukrainian eggs at the Canadian Museum of Civilization

Getting Started

You will need

• dice

• tiles

• a multiplication table

×	1	2	3
1	1	2	3
2	2	4	6
3	3	6	9

Making Multiplication Facts

A single array represents 2 multiplication facts. Some arrays can be rearranged to show other multiplication facts.

? **How many multiplication facts can you find by making and rearranging arrays?**

A. Roll 2 dice. Record the results.

B. Use tiles to make an array. Use the numbers you rolled as the numbers of rows and columns.

C. Write 2 multiplication sentences for the array. Circle the products on a multiplication table.

Josef and Pedro's Array

Pedro and I rolled a 2 and a 6. We made this array.

We wrote our multiplication sentences.

$2 \times 6 = 12$ $6 \times 2 = 12$

Then we circled 12 for 2×6 and 12 for 6×2 on a multiplication table.

We think we can make a different array with the 12 tiles.

D. If possible, rearrange the array to make other arrays.

E. Write 2 multiplication sentences for each new array. Circle the products on a multiplication table.

F. Repeat parts A to E six times to see how many different facts you can make.

Do You Remember?

1. Multiply. Explain the strategy that you used.
   a) Use 3 × 4 = 12 to find 3 × 8.
   b) Use 2 × 10 = 20 to find 4 × 5.
   c) Use 5 × 3 = 15 to find 6 × 3.
   d) Use 3 × 5 = 15 to find 6 × 5.
   e) Use 8 × 9 = 72 to find 9 × 8.

2. Multiply.

   a) 7 × 8   d) 2 × 8   g) 0 × 0
   b) 9 × 3   e) 9 × 7   h) 8 × 8
   c) 6 × 0   f) 6 × 5   i) 1 × 9

3. Multiply.

   a) 7 × 10   c) 9 × 100   e) 2 × 1000
   b) 3 × 50   d) 7 × 20   f) 5 × 200

4. Write the fact family that goes with this array.

1 Exploring Multiplication

Goal Solve multiplication problems using models.

A grade 4 class is planning a pizza party.
There are 28 students in the class.
They want 3 slices of pizza each.

ZIPPY PIZZA
8-Slice Pizza
$9.00 Every Day!

? **How many pizzas should the class order, and how much will the pizzas cost?**

Use base ten blocks to model the problem.

A. How many slices of pizza will the class need?

B. How many slices will they have when the pizzas arrive?

C. How much will the pizzas cost?

Reflecting

1. How do you know parts A, B, and C are multiplication questions?

2. How does changing 28 groups of 3 to 3 groups of 28 help you to model the solution?

Persistent Numbers

To find the persistence of a number, you multiply the
digits of the number until you get a 1-digit number.

Step 1	Step 2

723 $\longrightarrow$ $7 \times 2 \times 3 = 42$ $\longrightarrow$ $4 \times 2 = 8$

The persistence of 723 is 2 because it
takes 2 steps to get a 1-digit number.

1 Use a calculator to find the
persistence of each number.
a) 54 c) 328 e) 5063
b) 12 d) 4528

2 What is the least number
with a persistence of 2?

Sum and Product

1 What 3 numbers have a
sum equal to their product?

■ + ▲ + ● = ■ × ▲ × ●

2 5 different numbers
have a sum of 15.
Those same 5 numbers
have a product of 120.
What are the 5 numbers?

2 Multiplying with Arrays

Goal Use easier numbers to simplify multiplication.

You will need
- grid paper

- pencil crayons

? How many squares are on Natalie's game?

Natalie's Solution

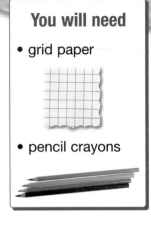

There are 8 rows of squares in my game. There are 12 columns of squares. I can multiply 8 × 12 to find how many squares there are altogether.

First, I estimate that 12 is about 10.

8 × 10 = 80. There are more than 80 squares.

I can model the game on grid paper.

I noticed there are 2 arrays *inside* the 8 × 12 array. I colour the 8 × 10 array red. I colour the 8 × 2 array blue. I find the products for the 2 smaller arrays and add them together.

8 x 12 = ■

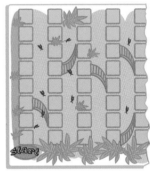

8 x 12 = 8 x 10 + 8 x 2

A. Use 8 × 10 + 8 × 2 to find 8 × 12.

The array can also be broken into other smaller arrays.

B. Draw an 8 × 12 array on grid paper.
Starting in the 1st column, colour in an 8 × 8 array.
Then colour in an 8 × 4 array.

C. Write 8 × 12 as the sum of 2 products to represent what you coloured.

8 × 12 = 8 × ■ + 8 × ■

8 × 12 = ■ + ■

8 × 12 = ■

D. Draw another 8×12 array on grid paper. Find and colour 2 arrays inside it. Use different arrays than in parts A and B. Write 8×12 as the sum of 2 products to represent what you coloured.

Reflecting

1. **a)** How does using smaller arrays help you to multiply?

   b) Which arrays were easier to multiply? Why?

2. Describe the pattern in the multiplication sentences from parts A, C, and D.

Checking

3. A game has 7 rows and 14 columns.

   a) Estimate the number of squares on the game.

   b) Draw the array on grid paper. Find and colour smaller arrays that have easier numbers to multiply.

   c) Write 7×14 as the sum of 2 products to represent what you coloured.

Practising

4. A tree planter has planted 7 rows of 18 trees. How many trees did he plant? Solve using arrays.

5. Complete.

   a) $6 \times 21 = 6 \times 20 + 6 \times 1$
   $6 \times 21 = \blacksquare$

   b) $4 \times 16 = 4 \times 8 + 4 \times \blacksquare$
   $4 \times 16 = \blacksquare$

   c) $5 \times 32 = 5 \times \blacksquare + 5 \times \blacksquare$
   $5 \times 32 = \blacksquare$

   d) $5 \times 28 = \blacksquare \times \blacksquare + \blacksquare \times \blacksquare$
   $5 \times 28 = \blacksquare$

6. Multiply.

   a) 9×17 **b)** 2×15 **c)** 8×11

3 Multiplying in Expanded Form

Goal Multiply 1-digit numbers by 2-digit numbers using expanded form.

Thousands	Hundreds	Tens	Ones

Paulette is making 54 leather bags for gifts at a celebration.
She sews 3 medallions on each bag.

? **How many medallions will Paulette need?**

Paulette's Solution

54 bags with 3 medallions on each bag is 54 groups of 3.

When I have equal groups, I can multiply.

54 × 3 and 3 × 54 have the same product, so I'll multiply 3 × 54 instead.

I'll multiply using expanded form and check my work using blocks.

Step 1 I write 54 in expanded form. I make 3 groups of 54.

$$
\begin{array}{r} 54 \\ \times\, 3 \end{array}
\qquad
\begin{array}{r} 50 + 4 \\ \times\, 3 \end{array}
\qquad
\begin{array}{r} 5 \text{ tens} + 4 \text{ ones} \\ \times\, 3 \end{array}
$$

Tens	Ones
‖‖‖‖‖	▫ ▫
‖‖‖‖‖	▫ ▫
‖‖‖‖‖	▫ ▫

Step 2 I multiply 5 tens by 3. I see 3 groups of 5 tens, or 15 tens.

$$
\begin{array}{r} 54 \\ \times\, 3 \end{array}
\qquad
\begin{array}{r} 50 + 4 \\ \times\, 3 \\ \hline 150 \end{array}
\qquad
\begin{array}{r} 5 \text{ tens} + 4 \text{ ones} \\ \times\, 3 \\ \hline 15 \text{ tens} \end{array}
$$

Tens	Ones
‖‖‖‖‖	▫ ▫
‖‖‖‖‖	▫ ▫
‖‖‖‖	▫ ▫

Step 3 I multiply 4 ones by 3. I see 3 groups of 4 ones, or 12 ones.

```
 54      50 + 4        5 tens + 4 ones
x 3       x 3                    x 3
         150          15 tens + 12 ones
        + 12
```

Tens	Ones
▌▌▌▌	▪ ▪
▌▌▌▌	▪ ▪
▌▌▌▌	▪ ▪

Step 4 I add the 2 products. I regroup the blocks.

1 hundred + 5 tens + 1 ten + 2 ones

```
 54      50 + 4        5 tens + 4 ones
x 3       x 3                    x 3
         150          15 tens + 12 ones
        + 12
         162               162
```

Hundreds	Tens	Ones
▨	▌▌▌▌▌	▪ ▪

1 hundred + 6 tens + 2 ones

Reflecting

1. How did writing 54 in expanded form help
   Paulette to multiply?

Checking

2. Stanley serves 4 trays of salmon at a feast.
   Each tray holds 32 pieces of salmon.
   How many pieces of salmon does Stanley serve?
   Use expanded form to multiply. Use blocks to check.

Practising

3. Alasie made a necklace with 6 rows of 64 beads.
   How many beads did she use altogether?

4. Estimate. Then calculate each product.
   a) 17 × 5   b) 14 × 7   c) 56 × 6

Mid-Chapter Review

LESSON

1 1. Which problem can be solved using multiplication?
Explain how you know.
   a) A basketball player played in 3 games.
      In each game, he scored 22 points.
      How many points did he score altogether?
   b) A basketball player scored 27 points.
      Each basket was worth 3 points.
      How many baskets did she make?
   c) A basketball player scored 26 points.
      Another player scored 32 points.
      How many points did they score together?

2 2. Calculate each product. Show your work.
   a) 3×18 b) 6×11 c) 7×14

3. Olivia made a 6×16 tray of Nanaimo bars.
Write a set of smaller arrays to find the number
of bars she made.

$6 \times 16 = \blacksquare \times \blacksquare + \blacksquare \times \blacksquare$

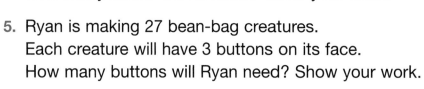

3 4. Kaytan is helping to make a brick pathway.
It is going to have 19 rows with 7 bricks in each row.
How many bricks will he need? Show your work.

5. Ryan is making 27 bean-bag creatures.
Each creature will have 3 buttons on its face.
How many buttons will Ryan need? Show your work.

6. Complete.
   a)   7 tens + 9 ones
          $\times$ 6 ones
      —————————————
      42 tens + ▬▬▬

   b)   60 + 7
          $\times$ 8
      ——————————
      480 + ▪

   c)   3 tens + 2 ones
              $\times$ 3
      —————————————
      ▬▬▬ + 6 ones

7. Justine estimates that 8×72 is more than 560.
Explain her thinking.

Adding Numbers Near 100

What is the total?

Rey's Calculation

I calculated the total using mental math.

I added this way:

$2.99 + $4.98 + $3.99 = ■

$2.99 is $3.00 – 1¢ ⎫
$4.98 is $5.00 – 2¢ ⎬ → $3.00 + $5.00 + $4.00 = $12.00
$3.99 is $4.00 – 1¢ ⎭   1¢ + 2¢ + 1¢ = 4¢
                                  $12.00 – 4¢ = $11.96

$2.99 + $4.98 + $3.99 = $11.96

A. Describe Rey's method using a different example.

B. Why is Rey's mental math method useful for adding money?

C. How could you use Rey's method to add whole numbers such as 198 + 699?

Try These

1. Calculate each total.
   a) $1.98 + $6.99
   b) $8.98 + $7.99 + $3.98
   c) $4.97 + $6.99
   d) $10.97 + $3.99 + $9.96

2. Add.
   a) 499 + 398
   b) 399 + 497 + 296
   c) 598 + 497
   d) 199 + 598 + 497

4 Communicate About Solving Problems

Goal Explain your thinking when solving a problem.

? How can Chantal explain how she solved a problem?

Chantal's Problem

I heard that horses age differently.
A 1-year-old horse is like a 3-year-old human.

I wondered how old our 16-year-old horse would be in human years, so I figured it out.

Chantal's Explanation

I asked Vinh to help me improve my explanation.

I made sure I understood the problem.

A horse this old ...	... is like a human this old
1	3
2	6
3	9

I made a plan. I will multiply.

I carried out the plan. The answer was 48,

so I knew my horse would be like a 48-year-old human.

Then I looked back to check.

I think 48 years old is a reasonable answer.

> You showed the problem-solving steps.

> How did you know you could multiply?

> What numbers did you multiply?

> You looked back to check your answer.

> How do you know 48 is reasonable?

A. What strengths did Vinh see in Chantal's explanation?

B. What did Vinh think was missing from Chantal's explanation?

C. How would you answer Vinh's purple questions?

Reflecting

1. How did Chantal's table help to show what she was thinking?

2. Which question in the Communication Checklist was each of Vinh's purple questions about?

Checking

3. A 1-year-old bear is like a 4-year-old human. Vinh calculated the age of a 19-year-old bear in human years.

   a) Identify at least 1 strength in Vinh's explanation.

   b) What questions would you ask Vinh to help him improve his explanation?

Vinh's Explanation

I made sure I understood the problem.

A bear this old ...	... is like a human this old
1	4
2	8
3	12

I made a plan. I multiplied 19 × 4.

I carried out the plan. 19 × 4 = 76

I looked back to check. 76 is right because

20 × 4 = 80, so 19 × 4 must be a bit less.

Practising

4. A 1-year-old deer is like an 8-year-old human.

   a) Calculate the age of a 13-year-old deer in human years.

   b) Explain how you solved the problem. Use the Communication Checklist.

5 Multiplying 3 Digits by 1 Digit

Goal Multiply 3-digit numbers by 1-digit numbers using expanded form.

Miki lives near a beach.
She collects 114 shells in 1 week.

? **How many shells will Miki have in 4 weeks?**

Miki's Solution

Collecting 114 shells each week
for 4 weeks is like 4 groups of 114.

When I have equal groups, I can multiply.

Step 1 First, I estimate.
4×114 is about $4 \times 100 = 400$.
I will have more than 400 shells.

Step 2 I write 114 in expanded form.

$$114 \qquad\qquad 100 + 10 + 4$$
$$\underline{\times\ 4} \qquad\qquad\quad \underline{\times\ 4}$$

Step 3 I multiply 4 by the hundreds digit.

$$114 \qquad\qquad 100 + 10 + 4$$
$$\underline{\times\ 4} \qquad\qquad\quad \underline{\times\ 4}$$
$$\qquad\qquad\qquad\qquad\quad 400$$

Hundreds	Tens	Ones
▨	▮	▫▫
▨	▮	▫▫
▨	▮	▫▫
▨	▮	▫▫

A. Complete Miki's multiplication.

B. Check your answer with base ten blocks on a place value chart.

Reflecting

1. Suppose you solved Miki's problem by multiplying this way. Would the product be the same? Explain.

$$
\begin{array}{r}
114 \\
\times\ 4 \\
\hline
\end{array}
\qquad
\begin{array}{r}
100 + 10 + 4 \\
\times\ 4 \\
\hline
16
\end{array}
$$

2. Was your final product in Question 1 greater or less than Miki's estimate? Explain why.

Checking

3. Craig polishes small rocks in a rock tumbler.
   He polishes 115 rocks each month.
   How many rocks will Craig polish in 6 months?
   a) Estimate how many rocks Craig will polish in 6 months.
   b) Calculate how many rocks Craig will polish in 6 months. Multiply using expanded form.
   c) Check your answer using base ten blocks.

Practising

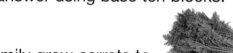

4. Kristi and her family grow carrots to sell at the farmer's market.
   They plant 350 carrots each month from May to July.
   How many carrots do they plant altogether?

5. In a school parade, 485 students will each carry 3 balloons. 125 students will each carry 2 flags.
   How many balloons and flags should the students buy?

6. Create a 3-digit by 1-digit multiplication problem about collecting cards. Estimate the answer.
   Then calculate the product.

7. Estimate. Then calculate each product.

   a) $\begin{array}{r} 986 \\ \times\ 3 \\ \hline \end{array}$
   b) $\begin{array}{r} 181 \\ \times\ 5 \\ \hline \end{array}$
   c) $\begin{array}{r} 332 \\ \times\ 7 \\ \hline \end{array}$

6 Multiplying with an Algorithm

Goal Multiply using a procedure.

Terry has 256 hockey cards. Pedro has twice as many.

? **How many hockey cards does Pedro have?**

Terry's Calculations

Twice as many means 2 times as many.

I'll multiply to find how many cards Pedro has.

Step 1 First, I estimate.

256 is about halfway between 200 and 300.

$2 \times 200 = 400$ $2 \times 300 = 600$

500 is halfway between 400 and 600.

Pedro has about 500 cards.

Step 2 I calculate by making 2 groups of 256.

I see 2×6 ones blocks.

Hundreds	Tens	Ones

← 12 ones

$$\begin{array}{r} 256 \\ \times\ 2 \\ \hline \end{array}$$

Step 3 I regroup 10 ones as 1 tens block.

Hundreds	Tens	Ones

1 ten

2 ones

$$\begin{array}{r} 1 \\ 256 \\ \times\ 2 \\ \hline 2 \end{array}$$

Step 4 I see 2 × 5 tens blocks + 1 tens block.

10 tens + 1 ten = 11 tens

Hundreds	Tens	Ones
▫ ▫ ▫ ▫	▐▐▐▐▐ ▐▐▐▐	▪ ▪

11 tens

$$\begin{array}{r} 1 \\ 256 \\ \times\ 2 \\ \hline 2 \end{array}$$

Step 5 I regroup 10 tens as 1 hundreds block.

Hundreds	Tens	Ones
▫ ▫ ▫ ▫	▫ ▐	▪ ▪

1 hundred

1 ten

$$\begin{array}{r} 11 \\ 256 \\ \times\ 2 \\ \hline 12 \end{array}$$

Step 6 I see 2 × 2 hundreds blocks + 1 hundreds block.

4 hundreds + 1 hundred = 5 hundreds

Hundreds	Tens	Ones
▫ ▫ ▫ ▫ ▫	▐	▪ ▪

5 hundreds

$$\begin{array}{r} 11 \\ 256 \\ \times\ 2 \\ \hline 512 \end{array}$$

512 is just a bit more than my estimate of 500, so my answer is reasonable. Pedro has 512 hockey cards.

Reflecting

1. In Step 3, why did Terry record a 1 above the 5?

2. Terry calculates that Shani has 2 × 756 cards.
   a) What is the next step of his new multiplication?
   b) How is this next step different from when he multiplied 2 × 256?

$$\begin{array}{r} 11 \\ 756 \\ \times\ 2 \\ \hline 12 \end{array}$$

Checking

3. Chantal likes horses. She has 145 plastic horses.
   She says she has 3 times as many other animals
   as she has horses.
   How many other animals does she have?
   Give an estimate. Then calculate the answer.

Practising

4. 2 art classes are making mugs.
   The 1st class made 154 mugs.
   The 2nd class made 4 times as many mugs.
   How many mugs did the 2nd class make?

5. Jamal multipied 384 × 4.
   He used 4 × 400 for his estimate.
   a) Was his estimate high or low?
      Explain your answer.
   b) Write 3 other 3-digit by 1-digit multiplications that
      would have the same 4 × 400 estimate.

6. Write the multiplication sentence for this model.

Hundreds	Tens	Ones

7. Estimate. Then calculate each product.

   a) 225   b) 863   c) 594   d) 943
      × 9   × 3   × 7   × 8

8. Make up a 3-digit by 1-digit multiplication problem
   about a hobby or game that interests you.
   Solve your problem.

Greatest Product

Number of players: 2 to 4
How to play: Create the greatest product.

Step 1 Each player rolls 1 die and records the digit in 1 of the boxes of their own game card.

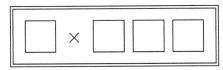

Step 2 Players keep rolling and recording until all 4 boxes of the game card are filled. Once a digit is recorded in a box, it cannot be changed.

Step 3 Calculate the product. The player with the greatest product wins.

Mandy's Turn

I rolled 2, 5, 1, 4.
My product is
5 × 412, or 2060.

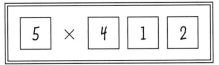

Other ways to play:
- Find the least product.
- Use a 1-digit by 2-digit game card.
- Use a spinner or digit cards instead of dice.

7 Choosing a Method to Multiply

You will need
• a calculator

Goal Choose and justify a multiplication method.

Did you know that in 1 minute …
• 250 babies are born in the world
• a cartoon uses 1430 animated pictures
• Mary can walk 67 m

? **How can you choose the best multiplication method for calculating each event?**

For each situation, would you
• estimate or calculate?
• use mental math, pencil and paper, or a calculator?
Explain your choices.

A. You want to find out how many babies will be born in the next 4 minutes.

B. You want to find out how many babies will be born in the next 15 minutes.

C. You want to find out how many pictures are needed to show a cartoon that is 15 minutes long.

D. You want to find out how many pictures are needed to show a cartoon that is 2 minutes long.

E. You want to find out how far Mary walks in each of the times below.
   a) 2 minutes
   b) 10 minutes
   c) 17 minutes
   d) 20 minutes

Reflecting

1. Suppose the number of babies born had been 247 in 1 minute instead of 250. Would you have answered parts A and B the same way? Explain.

2. a) Why might the number of minutes change the calculation method you choose?
   b) Why might the number of times in 1 minute change the calculation method you choose?

Egyptian Multiplication

Here is a curious way to multiply.
It is called Egyptian multiplication.

Suppose you want to multiply 314 by many different numbers.
Begin by making a list starting with $314 \times 1 = 314$.
Double the red number and the product to make each new line in the list.
Decide what number you want to multiply 314 by.
Find red numbers that add up to your value.
Add the numbers to the right of the equals sign from those rows.

$$314 \times 1 = 314$$
$$314 \times 2 = 628$$
$$314 \times 4 = 1256$$
$$314 \times 8 = 2512$$

For example, $9 = 8 + 1$, so
$$9 \times 314 = 8 \times 314 + 1 \times 314$$
$$9 \times 314 = 2512 + 314$$
$$9 \times 314 = 2826$$

1 Calculate. Show your work.
   a) 7×314 b) 6×314

Skills Bank

2 **1.** Complete.

a)

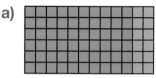

$6 \times 12 = 6 \times 10 + 6 \times \blacksquare$

$6 \times 12 = \blacksquare$

c)

$3 \times 18 = 3 \times \blacksquare + 3 \times \blacksquare$

$3 \times 18 = \blacksquare$

b)

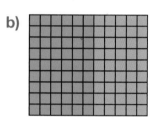

$9 \times 11 = \blacksquare \times 6 + \blacksquare \times \blacksquare$

$9 \times 11 = \blacksquare$

d)

$5 \times 27 = \blacksquare \times \blacksquare + \blacksquare \times \blacksquare$

$5 \times 27 = \blacksquare$

2. Multiply to find how many in each array.
a) 3 rows of 19 stamps
b) 5 rows of 21 carrots
c) 6 rows of 18 trading cards
d) 4 rows of 12 books
e) 9 rows of 17 new cars
f) 8 rows of 16 bottles

3. Multiply.
a) $3 \times 17 = \blacksquare$
b) $2 \times 16 = \blacksquare$
c) $4 \times 15 = \blacksquare$
d) $7 \times 11 = \blacksquare$
e) $7 \times 29 = \blacksquare$
f) $8 \times 14 = \blacksquare$
g) $9 \times 14 = \blacksquare$
h) $9 \times 23 = \blacksquare$
i) $9 \times 19 = \blacksquare$

3 **4.** Complete using expanded form.

a)

$$\begin{array}{r} 6 \text{ tens} + 2 \text{ ones} \\ \times\ 8 \\ \hline 48 \text{ tens} + \blacksquare \text{ ones} \end{array}$$

$\blacksquare$ hundreds + $\blacksquare$ tens + $\blacksquare$ ones

b)

$$\begin{array}{r} 70 + 4 \\ \times\ 6 \\ \hline 420 + \blacksquare \end{array}$$

c)

$$\begin{array}{r} 30 + 8 \\ \times\ 4 \\ \hline \end{array}$$

5. Estimate. Then multiply using expanded form.

a) 73
    × 4

c) 72
    × 2

e) 61
    × 3

g) 92
    × 2

b) 29
    × 5

d) 16
    × 3

f) 14
    × 7

h) 87
    × 3

6. Solve each problem. Show your work.
   a) There are 5 pencils in each box.
      How many pencils are in 85 boxes?
   b) There are 4 bookshelves and 21 books
      on each shelf.
      How many books are there altogether?

7. Complete each multiplication.

a) 300 + 20 + 7
    _____ × 5
         1500
          100
    +   ■
    ▬▬▬

b) 200 + 80 + 3
    _____ × 7
         1400
         ▬
    +   ■
    ▬▬▬

c) 400 + 60 + 9
    _____ × 9
         ▬
         ▬
    +   ■
    ▬▬▬

8. Estimate. Then multiply using expanded form.

a) 361
    × 7

c) 421
    × 4

e) 618
    × 3

g) 333
    × 6

b) 125
    × 8

d) 753
    × 5

f) 618
    × 7

h) 275
    × 3

9. Solve each problem. Show your work.
   a) A jumbo jet travels 885 km in 1 hour.
      How many kilometres does the jet travel in 5 hours?
   b) Kia earns $678 a week working at a greenhouse.
      How much will she earn in 5 weeks?
   c) There are 341 mL of orange juice in each litre
      of punch. How many millilitres of orange juice will
      be needed for 7 L of punch?

6 **10.** Estimate. Then calculate each product.

a) 762
× 7

c) 491
× 3

e) 611
× 9

g) 383
× 5

b) 145
× 7

d) 952
× 6

f) 937
× 9

h) 268
× 7

11. Solve each problem. Show your work.

a) An art class made 267 plates.
Another art class made 4 times as many plates.
How many plates did the 2nd class make?

b) Some jets can carry 131 passengers.
A jumbo jet can carry about 4 times as
many passengers.
How many passengers can a jumbo jet carry?

7 **12.** Estimate or calculate. Show your work.
Explain why you chose your multiplication method.

a) 1 bucket contains 5000 nails.
How many nails are in 3 buckets?

b) 1 houseboat costs $18 325.
How much do 6 houseboats cost?

c) 72 minutes of music can be burned on 1 CD.
How many minutes of music can be burned
on 7 CDs?

d) The drugstore ordered 76 cases of shampoo.
Each case has 36 bottles of shampoo.
How many bottles did they order altogether?

e) Jonah has $387 in his bank account.
His brother saved about 5 times as much money.
About how much money has Jonah's brother saved?

f) Ms. Stein drives the school bus about 217 km
each day. How many kilometres does she drive
in 5 days?

256

Problem Bank

2

1. A greenhouse has
3 rows of 11 vegetables,
3 rows of 13 vegetables,
3 rows of 18 flowers, and
3 rows of 16 flowers.
Are there more vegetables
or flowers? Show your work.

3

2. Ava is playing Scrabble.
She can get a triple word score with F I X
or a double word score with F R I E N D
Which word would score more points?

6

3. Talima and Mark are making dreamcatchers.
Mark uses 880 cm of thread.
Talima uses 3 times as much thread.
How much thread does Talima use?

4. Create the greatest product you can by putting the
digits 2, 4, 6, and 8 once into this multiplication.
Show your work.

■■■
× ■

5. The digits 3, 4, 5, and 8 are missing from these
problems. Enter digits to make the products correct.

a) ■■■
  × 5
 4 2 1 5

b) ■■■
  × 3
 1 6 4 4

c) ■■■
  × 4
 1 5 4 0

6. What is the greatest possible product that can be
made by putting the digits 6, 7, 8, and 9 once into
this multiplication? Use a calculator. Show your work.

■ × ■■■

Chapter Review

LESSON

2

1. Matthew multiplied using this array.
   a) What multiplication does
      the array model?
   b) Show the array as 2 smaller arrays.
   c) Write the arrays as the sum of
      2 products.

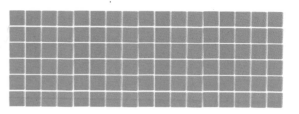

2. Laura has 12 books on each of her 7 shelves.
   How many books does Laura have?
   Show your answer as arrays.
   Write the arrays as the sum of 2 products.

3

3. Which estimate is closer to the actual product?
   Explain your choice.
   a) 79×9
      A. 80×10 B. 80×9
   b) 47×7
      A. 50×7 B. 47×10
   c) 18×4
      A. 20×4 B. 18×5

4. There are 28 students in a class.
   Each student brought in 5 items for a food drive.
   a) Estimate the number of items the class collected.
   b) Solve the problem. Show your work.
   c) Is your answer reasonable?
      Check your answer using your estimate.

5

5. An illustrator of science books is drawing
   7 centipedes with 354 legs each.
   How many legs will she need to draw altogether?
   Multiply using the expanded form of 354.

6. Pierre is fencing off a square field for his horse.
Each side of the field is 152 m long.
What is the length of the fence?

7. Sound travels 344 m in 1 second.
How far does sound travel in 7 seconds?

8. In the 1st month of business, a movie
rental store rented out 985 movies.
In the next month, it rented out 3 times
as many movies.
How many movies did it rent out in
the 2nd month?

9. Estimate. Then calculate each product.

a) 35
×9

b) 654
×3

c) 29
×2

d) 185
×4

10. Determine the missing digits in each multiplication.
Show your calculations.

a) ■8
×8
30■

b) ■24
×5
26■■

c) ■8■
×4
1128

11. Chris is multiplying 348 × 7.
He estimates that the product
is more than 2100 because
7 × 300 is 2100.

a) Is Chris's answer reasonable?
Why or why not?

b) Do the exact multiplication.

c) Explain how you did the calculation.

Chris's Multiplication

348
x 7

300 + 40 + 8
x 7
56
280
+ 210
546

12. Multiply. Explain your calculation method.

a) 50
×4

b) 312
×6

c) 479
×8

d) 2896
×3

Chapter Task

Describing a School Year

There are 3 recesses each day, including lunch.
There are about 190 days in 1 school year.
So, there are about 3 × 190 = 570 recesses in 1 year.

? **How can multiplication be used to describe other things that happen in a school year?**

A. List 4 other things about school that can be described using multiplication.

B. How many times does each thing happen in a day, a week, or a month?

C. What 2 pieces of information do you need to determine how often each thing happens in a year?

D. Describe each thing using multiplication.

E. Explain why you chose your multiplication methods.

Task Checklist

☑ Did you explain how you estimated and calculated?

☑ Did you use math language?

☑ Did you organize your work so it is easy to follow?

CHAPTER 10

Dividing Greater Numbers

Goals

You will be able to

- use the relationship between multiplication and division to solve problems
- use different methods to divide 2-digit and 3-digit numbers by 1-digit numbers
- explain the strategies you use to solve division problems

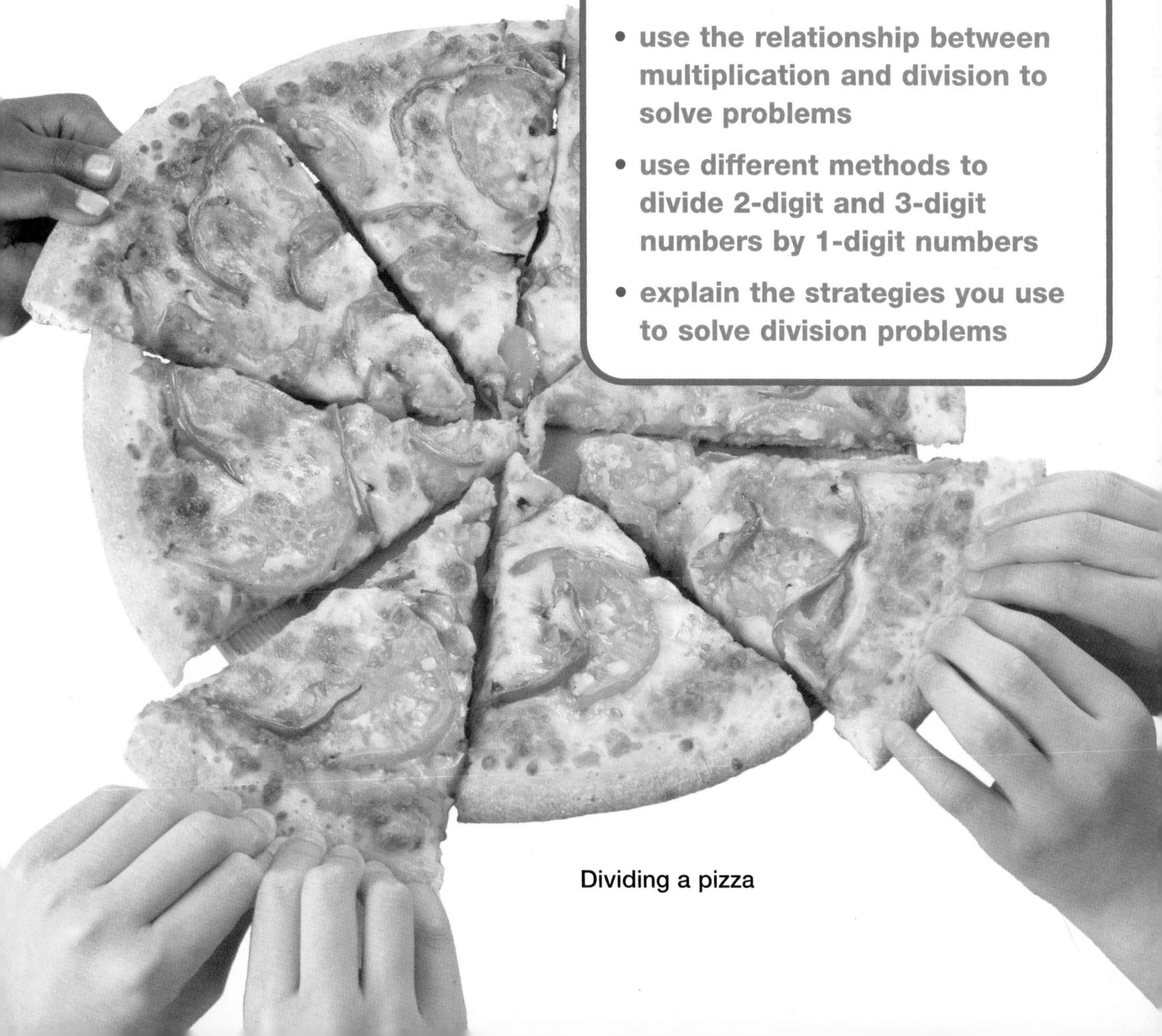

Dividing a pizza

Getting Started

Planning a Play Day

The students are planning a Play Day.
There will be 54 students participating.

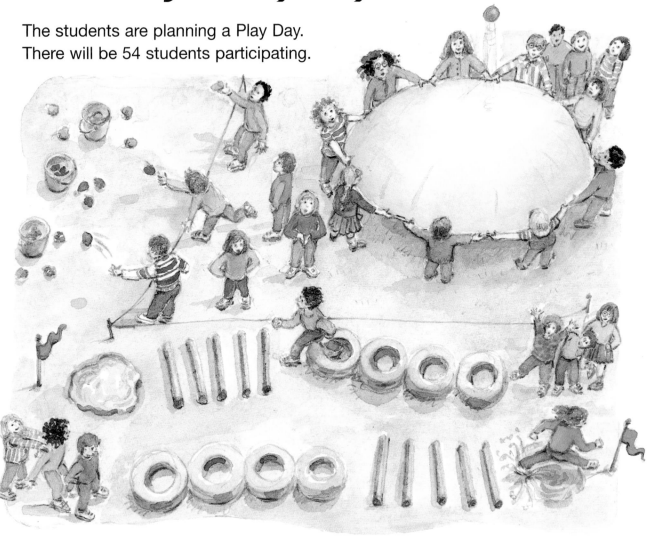

Think of an event that would be fun for 54 students
to do at the Play Day.

? **How many groups would there be in your event?
How many people would be in each group for
your event? How many items need to be shared?**

A. Miki is planning a relay race for the 54 students.
She wants 2 equal teams.
How many students should she put on each team?
Explain your thinking.

B. Rey is planning a beanbag toss.
If he puts the 54 students in teams of 6, how many
teams can he make? Explain your thinking.

C. Sometimes you divide to find the number of
groups. Sometimes you divide to find the
number in each group.
Which type of division did you use in part A?
Which type of division did you use in part B?

D. Write a division sentence to represent what you did
in part A. Write another division sentence for part B.

E. Make up a Play Day event for 54 students. Describe
your event and tell how it will involve equal groups.
Explain how you used division or multiplication.

Do You Remember?

1. Complete.
   a) $9 \times 6 = \blacksquare$ d) $35 \div 5 = \blacksquare$ g) $54 \div 6 = \blacksquare$
   b) $18 \div 2 = \blacksquare$ e) $8 \times 8 = \blacksquare$ h) $12 \div 4 = \blacksquare$
   c) $64 \div 8 = \blacksquare$ f) $18 \div 3 = \blacksquare$ i) $3 \times 7 = \blacksquare$

2. Write the multiplication and division **fact family**
   to describe this **array**.
   Remember to include 2 multiplication equations
   and 2 division equations.

3. Use the multiplication equation to divide.
   a) $8 \times 7 = 56$, so $56 \div 7 = \blacksquare$.
   b) $6 \times 8 = 48$, so $48 \div 8 = \blacksquare$.

1 Exploring Division

You will need
- How to Make a Kaleidoscope
- counters

- base ten blocks

- grid paper

- a 100 chart

1	2	3	4
11	12	13	14
21	22	23	24
31	32	33	34

Goal Solve division problems using models.

The students in the Science Club made kaleidoscopes. Each kaleidoscope had a reflector shaped like a triangle-based prism.
Each reflector is made of 3 plastic rectangles.
The students used between 70 and 90 plastic rectangles. There were no plastic rectangles left over.

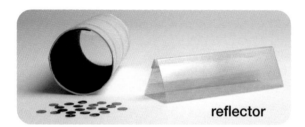

reflector

? **How many kaleidoscopes could the students have made?**

A. Why can you solve this problem using division?

B. What will the **divisor** be? Explain how you know.

C. Use any materials available to solve the problem. Find more than 1 answer. Show your work.

divisor
The number you divide by in a division equation
$$6 \div 2 = 3$$
↑
divisor

Reflecting

1. Why is there more than 1 answer to this problem?

2. Did you divide every number between 70 and 90? Why or why not?

3. Write a division equation and a multiplication equation to describe 1 of your answers.

Adding in Steps

When you want to add numbers in your head,
it sometimes helps to add the numbers in steps.

 Manitok's Mental Addition

I want to add 23 + 18.

First I'll add 10. That's easy.

$23 + 10 = 33$

Then I'll add 7 to get to 40.

$33 + 7 = 40$

I have 1 left because 18 = 10 + 7 + 1.

So 23 + 18 = 41.

A. Why do you think Manitok added 10 first?

B. How else can you add 23 + 18 in steps?
Explain how your way makes the addition easier.

C. How can you add 23 + 18 + 12 in your head?

Try These

1. Use mental math to add. Describe your steps.

a) 38 + 11   c) 42 + 21   e) 45 + 25   g) 12 + 18 + 11
b) 25 + 15   d) 16 + 18   f) 51 + 19   h) 26 + 12 + 18

2. Show the steps you could use to subtract
63 − 15 using mental math.

2

Using Repeated Subtraction to Divide

Goal Use repeated subtraction to divide.

Zola is making decorations for a banquet.
She is tying balloons together in bunches of 4.

? **How many bunches of 4 balloons can Zola make with 77 balloons?**

Zola's Division

I can model the balloons with 77 counters.

Then I can use repeated subtraction to subtract bunches of 4 until there aren't enough balloons to make any more bunches.

$$4\overline{)77}$$ ← I start with 77 balloons.
$$-40$$ 10 ← I can make at least 10 bunches because 10 x 4 = 40.
$$37$$ ← Now I have 37 balloons left.
$$-\blacksquare\blacksquare$$ 5 ← I can make 5 more bunches because ...

remainder
The number left over after an amount is divided into equal parts

When you divide 7 into 3 groups, you get 2 in each group and a remainder of 1.

Write $7 \div 3 = 2$ **R1**

↑
remainder

A. Why does Zola think she can make 5 bunches next? Show how you would continue Zola's recording to complete the division.

B. How many bunches of 4 balloons can Zola make in all? Explain how you know.

C. What will the **remainder** be? Explain how you know.

Reflecting

1. Why did Zola start by subtracting 10 groups of 4?

2. When Zola had 37 balloons left, she decided to subtract 5 bunches. Was this the quickest way to finish the division? Explain your answer.

3. Why does it make sense to subtract **multiples** of 4 to find out how many 4s there are in 77?

multiples
The products when a number is multiplied by other numbers

The multiples of 4 are 4, 8, 12, 16, 20, 24, ...

Checking

4. Zola has 99 balloons to put in bunches of 6.
   a) How many bunches could she subtract first? Why? How many balloons would that be?
   b) How many bunches can she make in all? Show all your steps.
   c) What will the remainder be? Explain how you know.

Practising

5. Zola has 62 balloons to put in bunches of 5. How many bunches can she make? What will the remainder be? Show your steps.

6. Use repeated subtraction to divide. Show your steps.
   a) 3)64   b) 4)50   c) 6)62   d) 2)95   e) 4)87

7. Zola used a calculator to solve 441 ÷ 21. She used pencil and paper to solve 96 ÷ 8. Do you agree with Zola's choice of methods? Explain your answer.

8. Zola had about 70 balloons. When she made groups of 4 balloons, she had no balloons left over. How many balloons could Zola have had? Explain how you know.

3 Interpreting Remainders

Goal Decide how to treat the remainder in a division problem.

Each student wrote a problem that can be solved by calculating $6\overline{)51}$.

? **How does the problem help you decide what to do with the remainder?**

$$
\begin{array}{r}
6\overline{)51} \\
-42 \\
\hline
9 \\
-6 \\
\hline
3
\end{array}
\quad
\left.
\begin{array}{l}
7 \\
\\
1
\end{array}
\right\}
\; 7 + 1 = 8
$$

$51 \div 6 = 8 \text{ R3}$

Chris's Problem
51 students went for a ride on the Super Coaster. Each car holds 6 people. How many cars did they need?
Solution: $51 \div 6 = 8 \text{ R3}$
Answer: 9 cars

Miki's Problem
A restaurant served 51 slices of pepperoni pizza. There are 6 slices in each pizza. How many pizzas did they serve?
Solution: $51 \div 6 = 8 \text{ R3}$
Answer: 8 and $\frac{1}{2}$ pizzas

Jon's Problem
Sarah had 51 stickers to give to 6 friends. She wanted to give the same number to each friend. How many stickers did each friend get?
Solution: $51 \div 6 = 8 \text{ R3}$
Answer: 8 stickers each

Reflecting

1. Describe what happened to the remainder in each problem. Explain why it happened.

Checking

2. **a)** Chantal has 58 photographs to
arrange in an album.
She wants to put 4 pictures
in each spread.
How many spreads will she need?
Show your work.

   b) Explain what you did with the
remainder and tell why.

3. Write a new problem about 58 ÷ 4 where you would
do something different with the remainder.
Explain what you would do differently.

Practising

4. **a)** 4 friends will share 25 licorice strings.
How many strings will each friend get if they
share equally and all the strings are eaten?

   b) Explain what you did with the remainder
and tell why.

5. **a)** Raffle tickets cost 5¢.
How many tickets can Michael buy with 72¢?

   b) Explain what you did with the remainder
and tell why.

6. **a)** The rafts for the Scary Tunnel ride hold 4 people.
If 62 children go on the ride at the same time,
how many children will be on the last raft?

   b) Explain what you did with the remainder
and tell why.

7. Use a calculator to divide. What do you notice about
the result when there is a remainder?
   a) 24 ÷ 2   **b)** 27 ÷ 2   **c)** 40 ÷ 4   **d)** 27 ÷ 8

8. Write a problem about 53 ÷ 3. Show how to solve it.
Explain what you did with the remainder and tell why.

4 Dividing 2 Digits by 1 Digit

Goal Use base ten blocks and pencil and paper to divide a 2-digit number by a 1-digit number.

There are 94 stickers for 4 people to share equally.

? **How many stickers will each person get?**

Rami's Division

I think each person will get about 25 stickers because $4 \times 25 = 100$.

To find out, I can model the **dividend** with base ten blocks and divide the blocks into 4 equal groups.

Step 1 I model 94 stickers.
I need to put them in 4 equal groups.

$4\overline{)94}$

dividend
The number you divide into equal parts

$6 \div 2 = 3$
↖ dividend

Step 2 First I share the tens in 4 groups.

I put 2 tens in each group so I write 20 in the quotient.

$$\begin{array}{r} 20 \\ 4\overline{)94} \\ -80 \\ \hline 14 \end{array}$$

I've shared 80 stickers.

I have 14 stickers left.

Step 3 Now I regroup the ten and share the 14 ones.
I can put 3 ones in each group.

Each person will get 23 stickers with 2 stickers left over.

This is reasonable because 23 is close to my estimate of 25.

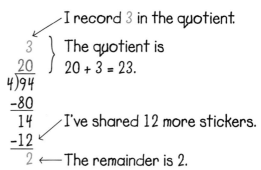

I record 3 in the quotient.

The quotient is 20 + 3 = 23.

$$\begin{array}{r} 3 \\ 20 \\ 4\overline{)94} \\ -80 \\ \hline 14 \\ -12 \\ \hline 2 \end{array}$$

I've shared 12 more stickers.

The remainder is 2.

Reflecting

1. Why did Rami regroup 1 ten as 10 ones in Step 3?

2. Why did Rami subtract 12 in Step 3?

Checking

3. 6 people will share a bowl of 75 grapes.
   a) Model the sharing of the grapes.
      Record the division on paper.
   b) How many grapes will each person get?
   c) Will there be any grapes left over? Explain.

Practising

4. There are 83 jellybeans in a jar.
   5 people will share the jellybeans equally.
   a) Will any jellybeans be left over? Explain.
   b) Estimate the number of jellybeans each person will get.
   c) Divide to find out how many jellybeans each person will get. Show all your steps.

5. Divide. Show your work.
   a) $6\overline{)78}$ b) $3\overline{)95}$ c) $7\overline{)93}$ d) $4\overline{)65}$

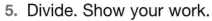

5 Solve Problems by Guessing and Testing

Goal Use a guess-and-test strategy to solve problems.

Terry put the candles on his mother's
birthday cake in an array.
He used 1 candle for each year of her age.
He made 5 equal rows of candles.
He put 6 candles around the edges because there
weren't enough candles to make another row.

? **How old could Terry's mother be if she is younger than 50?**

Mandy's Solution

Understand

Since there are the same number of candles in 5 rows,
I can think about multiplying or dividing.

The number of candles in each row must be more than 6 or
Terry could make another row with the 6 extra candles.
The least number of candles that could be in each row is 7.

Make a Plan

I'll try multiplying 5 rows by 7 candles. Then I'll add the 6 extra
candles to see if the total number is less than 50.

Carry Out the Plan

5 rows of 7 = 35
35 + 6 extra candles = 41
41 is less than 50, so Terry's mother could be 41.

Could there be another answer?

5 rows of 8 = 40
40 + 6 = 46
Terry's mother could be 46.

5 rows of 9 = 45
45 + 6 = 51
She is younger than 50, so this array isn't a solution.

There are 2 possible answers.
Terry's mother could be 41 years old or 46 years old.

Reflecting

1. How did Mandy know there were at least 7 candles in each row? How did she know there were fewer than 9 candles?

2. How did Mandy use information from the problem to make sure her guesses were reasonable?

Checking

3. Terry packed cookies in equal-sized bags.
   He packed more than 40 cookies but less than 50.
   He filled 4 bags and had 5 cookies left over.
   How many cookies could he have packed?

Practising

4. Terry had between 50 and 60 square tiles.
   He made a rectangle that was 6 units long.
   He had 4 tiles left over.
   Draw Terry's rectangle. Label the side lengths.

5. Create your own guess-and-test problem.
   Give your problem to a partner to solve.

Mid-Chapter Review

1

1. Melissa has 40 counters.
   How many groups of 5 can she make?
   Show your work.

2

2. Tony has 43 jars of jam to pack in boxes of 6.
   How many boxes can he fill? Show your steps.

3

3. Write a problem about 92 ÷ 8.
   a) Show how to solve your problem.
   b) Explain what you did with the remainder
      and tell why.

4

4. Divide. Show all your steps.
   a) 52 ÷ 7   b) 74 ÷ 9   c) 8)‾75‾   d) 5)‾48‾

5. Replace the words with numbers to make a
   true equation:
   dividend ÷ divisor = quotient R2

6. Which quotient is closest to 10?
   Explain how you know.
   A. 92 ÷ 6   **B.** 71 ÷ 3   **C.** 64 ÷ 5   **D.** 83 ÷ 9

7. Would you use pencil and paper, mental math,
   or a calculator for each division?
   Explain your thinking.
   a) 72 ÷ 8   b) 84 ÷ 3   c) 546 ÷ 6

5

8. Students are put in equal groups for a field trip.
   There are 4 students in all the groups except
   for 1 group, which has only 3 students.
   The number of students on the trip is between
   30 and 40.
   a) How many students are on the trip?
   b) Explain how you know you've found all the
      possible answers.

Remainder Hunt

You will need
- number cards

Number of players: 2 to 5

How to play: Arrange 3 cards in a division frame to get the least possible remainder.

Step 1 Each player makes a division frame that looks like $\square\overline{)\square\square}$. The boxes should be large enough to fit the number cards.

Step 2 Deal 3 cards to each player.

Step 3 Arrange your cards on your division frame. Try to make the division calculation that will have the least possible remainder.

Step 4 Complete the division and find the remainder.

Step 5 Have the other players check your remainder.

The player with the least remainder wins 1 point. The game ends when a player has 5 points.

Pedro's Turn

I can't make a division equation with a remainder of 0.

I'm going to make $3\overline{)25}$ because the remainder is 1.

2 3 5

Another way to play: Try to make the greatest possible remainder.

6 Estimating with 3-Digit Dividends

Goal Use multiplication and division facts to estimate quotients.

Allison loves the Stevie Diamond books by Linda Bailey. She made a list of the books she would like to read.

 Allison's Reading Plan

I want to read *How Can a Brilliant Detective Shine in the Dark?* in 7 days.

I plan to read the same number of pages every night.

Stevie Diamond book	Pages
1. How Come the Best Clues Are Always in the Garbage?	176
2. How Can I Be a Detective if I Have To Babysit?	160
3. Who's Got Gertie? And How Can We Get Her Back!	176
4. How Can a Frozen Detective Stay Hot on the Trail?	168
5. What's a Daring Detective Like Me Doing in the Doghouse?	192
6. How Can a Brilliant Detective Shine in the Dark?	200
7. What's a Serious Detective Like Me Doing in Such a Silly Movie?	192

? **About how many pages does Allison need to read each night?**

A. How do you know that Allison has to read more than 10 pages each night?

B. How do you know that Allison has to read fewer than 50 pages each night?

C. How does knowing $21 \div 7 = 3$ help Allison estimate?

D. About how many pages should Allison read each night?

Reflecting

1. Why might it be useful for Allison to think of 200 as 20 tens?

2. Suppose Allison had only 6 nights to read the book.
   a) What division equation would Allison have to estimate?
   b) What multiplication or division fact would help Allison find the number of pages she would need to read each night?

Checking

3. Allison wants to read *What's a Daring Detective Like Me Doing in the Doghouse?* in 9 days. She plans to read the same number of pages each day.
   a) Why will she read more than 10 pages each day?
   b) What fact would help Allison estimate the number of pages she needs to read each day?
   c) About how many pages should she read each day?

Practising

4. Allison wants to read all of the first 3 books on her list in 8 days. She plans to read the same number of pages each day.
   a) What fact would help Allison estimate the number of pages she should read each day?
   b) About how many pages should she read each day?
   c) About how many pages would she have to read each day to finish in 7 days instead of 8?

5. Estimate each quotient. Explain your thinking.
   a) $6\overline{)574}$ b) $8\overline{)307}$ c) $7\overline{)511}$

6. Gerry can finish his book if he reads about 90 pages every day for 6 days. About how long is the book?

7 Dividing in Parts

Goal Divide in steps using simpler numbers.

Josef and Shani both collect postcards. Josef has 3 times as many postcards as Shani.

Greetings from Shediac, New Brunswick!

? **If Josef has 285 postcards, how many postcards does Shani have?**

Calvin's Solution

I can rename 285 as 270 + 15.

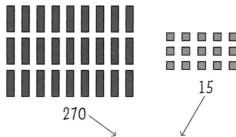

270

15

$3\overline{)285}$ is the same as $3\overline{)270}$ + $3\overline{)15}$.

Shani has 90 + ■ postcards.

A. Why did Calvin divide 285 by 3?

B. Why is dividing 285 into 3 parts the same as dividing 270 by 3 and then dividing 15 by 3?

C. Finish Calvin's division. Why did Calvin rename 285 as 270 + 15 and not as 200 + 85?

Reflecting

1. Would this be a good way to rename 285 to solve the problem? Explain your answer.

   $3\overline{)285} = 3\overline{)240} + 3\overline{)30} + 3\overline{)15}$

2. How else could you rename 285 to solve the problem?

3. How did knowing multiplication facts for 3 help Calvin divide?

Checking

4. Shani and Josef both collect hockey cards.
   Shani has 4 times as many cards as Josef.
   If Shani has 272 cards, how many does Josef have?
   a) How could you rename 272 to solve the problem?
   b) How many cards does Josef have? Show your work.

Practising

5. Shani has 368 stickers in her sticker book.
   How many stickers does Josef have if Shani
   has this many stickers? Show your work.
   a) 4 times as many   b) 8 times as many

6. Calvin used this method to share
   297 postcards equally in 3 albums.
   a) Is his method correct? Explain.
   b) Use his method to divide
      392 into 4 parts.

7. Would you divide in parts?
   Why or why not?
   a) $6\overline{)312}$ b) $7\overline{)511}$ c) $9\overline{)900}$

8. Show 2 ways to rename 376 to
   make it easier to divide by 8.

Calvin Divides Again

I can rename 297 as 300 − 3.
$3\overline{)297}$ is the same as $3\overline{)300} - 3\overline{)3}$.
I can put 100 − 1 = 99 postcards
in each album.

Dividing 3 Digits by 1 Digit

You will need

- base ten blocks

Goal Use base ten blocks and pencil and paper to divide a 3-digit number by a 1-digit number.

Grandma has 269 jingle cones to put on the jingle dresses of her 3 grandchildren.

? **If Grandma shares the jingle cones evenly, how many cones will be on each dress?**

A jingle dress

Rey's Division

I estimate that each dress will get about 100 cones because there are about 300 cones and $300 \div 3 = 100$.

I can model the division with base ten blocks and record each step.

Step 1 I modelled 269. I need to put the blocks in 3 equal groups.

$$3\overline{)269}$$

Step 2 I only have 2 hundreds, not 3. There aren't enough to give 100 cones to each dress. I'll regroup the 2 hundreds as 20 tens.

$$3\overline{)269}$$

Step 3 Now I can give each dress 8 tens.
There are 2 tens and 9 ones left.

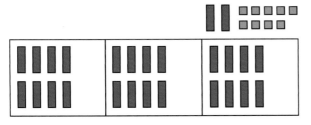

$$\begin{array}{r} 8 \\ 3\overline{)269} \\ -240 \\ \hline 29 \end{array}$$

Step 4 I can't share 2 tens in 3 groups, so I need to regroup the 2 tens as 20 ones.

Step 5 Now I can give each dress 9 ones.

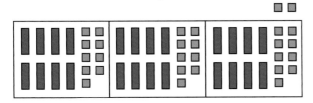

$$\begin{array}{r} 89 \\ 3\overline{)269} \\ -240 \\ \hline 29 \\ -27 \\ \hline 2 \end{array}$$

Each dress got 89 cones and there were 2 left over.

This is reasonable because I estimated that each dress would get about 100 cones.

Reflecting

1. In Step 3, why did Rey record the 8 tens he gave each dress above the 6 and not above the 2?

2. Why did Rey subtract 240 from 269?

3. Why didn't Rey record any numbers in Step 4?

4. When did Rey need to regroup to divide?

Checking

5. Suppose grandma has 282 jingle cones for 4 jingle dresses.
   a) Model the sharing of the cones with your base ten blocks and record the division on paper.
   b) How many cones would each dress get?
   c) Would there be any cones left over? Explain your answer.

Practising

6. Grandpa has made 218 cookies for 7 families to share.
   a) Estimate the number of cookies each family would get.
   b) Use base ten blocks or divide on paper to find the exact share for each family. Are there any cookies left over?
   c) How many more cookies would each family get if there were 288 cookies instead of 218? Explain your answer.

7. Divide. Record your work.
   a) $7\overline{)812}$
   b) $6\overline{)433}$
   c) $8\overline{)517}$
   d) $3\overline{)726}$

8. You want to calculate $4\overline{)736}$.
   Show 2 different ways to do the division.
   Tell which way you like better and why.

9. Grandpa baked 318 cookies for 8 families to share.
   Mom baked 152 cookies for 3 families to share.
   Who gave each family more cookies, grandpa or mom?
   Explain your answer.

10. Would you use pencil and paper, mental math, or a calculator for each division? Why?
    a) $56 \div 7$
    b) $180 \div 9$
    c) $86 \div 3$
    d) $2400 \div 4$
    e) $656 \div 6$
    f) $4842 \div 5$

Finding the Mean

The students are selling magazine subscriptions to raise money for a school trip. One class made this graph to keep track of the number of subscriptions they sold each day.

Subscriptions Sold Each Day

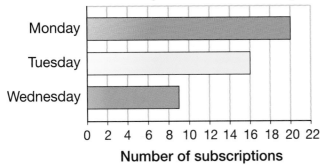

Monday
Tuesday
Wednesday

0 2 4 6 8 10 12 14 16 18 20 22

Number of subscriptions

The **mean** is 1 way to find the typical or average number in a set of data.

1 Use linking cubes to make bars that match the bars on the graph. Now rearrange the cubes until all the bars are the same length. How long is each bar? This number is the mean.

2 You can also find the mean for the bar lengths by adding the lengths and dividing by the number of bars.

a) Use this method to find the mean.

b) Why does this give the same result you got with the cubes?

3 The table shows the number of subscriptions sold in 1 week by all the students in the school.
What is the mean for this set of data?
Show your work.

Day	Subscriptions sold
Monday	143
Tuesday	87
Wednesday	116
Thursday	245
Friday	254

Skills Bank

2

1. Use repeated subtraction to divide.
   Show your steps.
   a) $2\overline{)80}$ c) $6\overline{)78}$ e) $3\overline{)46}$ g) $8\overline{)87}$
   b) $4\overline{)56}$ d) $5\overline{)58}$ f) $4\overline{)53}$ h) $7\overline{)89}$

2. Solve each problem.
   Show your work.
   a) Carlos has 65 balloons
      to put in bunches of 3.
      How many bunches
      can he make?
      What will the remainder be?
   b) Carlos had about 80 balloons.
      He put them in bunches of 6 and
      had none left over.
      How many balloons could he have had?

3

3. Divide to solve each problem. Show your work.
   For each problem, explain what you did
   with the remainder.
   a) Nadine uses 4 pieces of wood for
      each picture frame.
      How many frames can she make with
      58 pieces of wood?

   b) Cupcakes come in packages of 6.
      Jessie needs 57 cupcakes.
      How many packages should he buy?
   c) Lisa and 3 friends have earned $25.
      They have to share the money
      equally. How much money will
      each person get?

4. Divide. Show your work.
   a) $3\overline{)43}$ d) $5\overline{)91}$ g) $6\overline{)89}$
   b) $6\overline{)73}$ e) $7\overline{)96}$ h) $9\overline{)97}$
   c) $7\overline{)82}$ f) $4\overline{)73}$ i) $8\overline{)95}$

5. Solve each problem.
   Show your work.
   a) There are 95 collector cards to be shared
      among 6 people.
      How many cards will each person get?
   b) The music teacher is arranging the 87 children in
      the choir in 6 equal rows.
      Any children that are left over will help the teacher.
      How many helpers will the teacher have?

6. Estimate each quotient.
   Show your work.
   a) $416 \div 5$ d) $785 \div 8$ g) $232 \div 4$
   b) $7\overline{)500}$ e) $8\overline{)635}$ h) $9\overline{)715}$
   c) $307 \div 4$ f) $6\overline{)654}$ i) $617 \div 5$

7. Vilay has a book with 248 pages.
   He plans to read the same number of pages each day.
   Estimate how many pages he should read each day
   if he wants to finish the book in each number of days.
   a) 6 days   b) 4 days   c) 8 days

8. Estimate. Then divide in parts.
   Show your work.
   a) $5\overline{)475}$ d) $9\overline{)729}$ g) $7\overline{)364}$
   b) $6\overline{)384}$ e) $4\overline{)356}$ h) $8\overline{)464}$
   c) $7\overline{)588}$ f) $7\overline{)434}$ i) $9\overline{)882}$

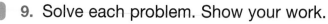

7 **9.** Solve each problem. Show your work.

a) Greg has 339 marbles.
He has 3 times as many marbles as Kelly.
How many marbles does Kelly have?

b) Oliver has read 829 pages for a
read-a-thon.
Oliver has read about 4 times as
many pages as Kyle.
About how many pages has Kyle read?

8 **10.** Estimate. Then divide.
Show your work.

a) 456 ÷ 4   **d)** 796 ÷ 8   **g)** 484 ÷ 6

b) 6)135   **e)** 3)183   **h)** 5)662

c) 239 ÷ 5   **f)** 5)916   **i)** 8)599

11. a) Explain how you know the quotient
in this division is incorrect.

b) Show how to find the correct
quotient.

c) Why do you think the mistake
happened?

```
    124
3)472
   -300
    72
   -60
    12
   -12
     0
```

12. Solve each problem. Show your work.

a) Terry baked 312 cookies for 6 families
to share. How many cookies will each family get?

b) Suppose there were 618 cookies instead of 312.
How many more cookies would each of the 6
families get?

13. Would you use pencil and paper, mental math,
or a calculator for each division? Why?
Use your chosen method to solve the question.
Show your work.

a) 150 ÷ 5   **c)** 539 ÷ 8   **e)** 484 ÷ 7

b) 6)48   **d)** 37)1813   **f)** 600 ÷ 3

Problem Bank

LESSON

1 1. When plush toy elephants are shipped to stores, the manufacturer can pack up to 6 elephants in 1 box. How many boxes will be needed to ship 95 elephants?

2. Choose any 4 numbers in this pattern on a 100 chart. Divide each number by 4. How many of the numbers have no remainder? Try some others. What pattern can you find? Can you explain it?

14	15	16	17	18	19
24	25	26	27	28	29
34	35	36	37	38	39

5 3. Find the missing values. Show how to test your values to make sure they fit.

a) Find a divisor for ■)81 that has no remainder.

b) Find a divisor for ■)81 that has a remainder of 3.

8 4. Find at least 1 way to complete this division equation so the digits are all different. Explain the strategy you used.

■■■ ÷ 7 = ■■ R5

5. Each box represents the same digit.
a) What is the digit?
b) Explain how you solved the problem.

$$\begin{array}{r} ■6■ \\ ■)\overline{5■4} \end{array}$$

6. The triangle and the square each have a perimeter of 312 cm.
a) How much longer is 1 side of the triangle than 1 side of the square?
b) Explain how you solved the problem.

Chapter Review

LESSON

1

1. How does knowing $7 \times 8 = 56$ help you to find $560 \div 8$?

5

2. There were more than 40 and less than 60 people at a team banquet. There were 4 people at the head table and 6 people at each other table.
   a) How many tables of 6 were there?
      Find more than 1 answer. Show your steps.
   b) Explain how you know you found all the possible answers.

6

3. Which of these divisions would you solve using mental math? Explain your answer.
   A. $420 \div 6$ B. $397 \div 3$ C. $537 \div 3$

7

4. How does knowing $525 = 500 + 25$ help you to find $525 \div 5$?

8

5. Estimate and then divide. Show your work.
   a) $96 \div 8$ c) $99 \div 7$ e) $368 \div 3$
   b) $6\overline{)96}$ d) $4\overline{)125}$ f) $5\overline{)576}$

6. Mary plans to pack 185 cookies in bags of 4.
   a) Mary says she will be able to make more than 40 bags. Is she correct? Explain your answer.
   b) Mary says there will be a remainder. Is she correct? Explain your answer.
   c) How many full bags can Mary pack? Show your work.

7. Devon prepared 458 cm of yarn for the Craft Club. He cut the yarn into pieces that are 5 cm long.
   a) How many 5 cm pieces did he cut if he used up all the yarn? Show your work.
   b) How much yarn was left over? Explain how you know.

8. Julia got a quotient of 206 when she divided.
   What numbers might she have been dividing?
   List 3 possibilities.

9. Solve. Explain what you did with the remainder
   and tell why.
   a) 63 students went on a trip to the Art Gallery.
      The students toured the gallery in groups of 5.
      How many groups went to the Art Gallery?
   b) Hong is mixing batter for a Pancake Lunch.
      He needs 5 scoops of flour to make the
      batter for 1 batch of pancakes.
      If he has enough flour for 182 scoops,
      how many batches of pancakes can he make?
   c) Alex has 182 quarters. She is putting the quarters
      in piles of 4 to count the dollars.
      How much money does she have?

10. Adrian has 4 times as many coins in his collection
    as Sunita. If Adrian has 204 coins, how many coins
    does Sunita have?

11. Which quotient is greatest?
    Explain how you know.
    A. 92 ÷ 4   B. 83 ÷ 9   C. 118 ÷ 2   D. 158 ÷ 4

12. Would you use pencil and paper, mental math,
    or a calculator for each division?
    Explain your thinking.
    a) 350 ÷ 7   c) 51 ÷ 3   e) 1400 ÷ 7
    b) 648 ÷ 8   d) 800 ÷ 5   f) 3669 ÷ 3

Chapter Task

Printing Pages

Book pages are printed on large sheets of paper called *forms*. Each form contains the same number of pages, so the number of pages in a book will always divide by that number with no remainder. After the forms are printed, they are cut apart so the pages can be bound.

? **How many pages can be on a form? Explain your answer.**

Book	Pages
1. How Come the Best Clues Are Always in the Garbage?	176
2. How Can I Be a Detective if I Have To Babysit?	160
3. Who's Got Gertie? And How Can We Get Her Back!	176
4. How Can a Frozen Detective Stay Hot on the Trail?	168
5. What's a Daring Detective Like Me Doing in the Doghouse?	192
6. How Can a Brilliant Detective Shine in the Dark?	200
7. What's a Serious Detective Like Me Doing in Such a Silly Movie?	192

Task Checklist

- ☑ Did you show all your steps?
- ☑ Did you use math language?
- ☑ Did you explain your thinking?

CHAPTER 11

3-D Geometry and 3-D Measurement

Goals

You will be able to

- draw, build, and describe 3-dimensional (3-D) shapes

- describe attributes of 3-D shapes

- estimate, measure, and compare the volume, capacity, and mass of 3-D shapes

- make connections between 2-D and 3-D geometry and between geometry and measurement

Cree Village at Moose Factory Island

Getting Started

Describing Packages

These students are describing and comparing packages of different sizes and shapes.

? **How can you describe the sizes and shapes of the packages?**

A. Examine 2 packages in the picture. Make a list of math words that describe each package.

B. Compare the 2 packages. Write at least 1 thing that is the same and 1 thing that is different about the packages.

C. List 2 things that might come in each package.

D. Circle the words in your list that have to do with shape. Underline the words that have to do with measuring.

Do You Remember?

1. Match each name with a shape.
   a) rectangle-based prism
   b) triangle-based prism
   c) triangle-based pyramid
   d) cone

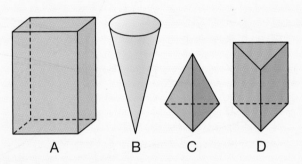

A   B   C   D

2. Which shapes in Question 1 have congruent bases?

3. Complete the chart for 1 pyramid and 1 prism.

3-D shape	Number of faces	Number of edges	Number of vertices
▬ prism			
▬ pyramid			

4. Would you use grams or kilograms to measure the mass of each object?
   a) a refrigerator   b) a can of soup

5. Would you use millilitres or litres to measure the capacity of each object?
   a) a refrigerator   b) a can of soup

1 Sketching Faces

You will need

• 3-D models

Goal Describe relationships between 3-D shapes and their 2-D faces.

? What can you learn about a 3-D shape from its 2-D faces?

A. Choose a prism. How many **edges** does it have?

B. Trace each **face** of the prism.
   Find the total number of **sides** of all of its faces.

C. Record the data in a chart like this one.

D. Repeat parts A, B, and C for a different prism.

E. Repeat parts A, B, and C for 2 different pyramids.

	3-D shape	2-D faces
Name of 3-D shape	Number of edges	Total number of sides of the faces
triangle-based prism	9	18

F. Compare the number of edges in each 3-D shape to the total number of sides in its 2-D faces. What do you notice?

Reflecting

1. When you join faces to create a 3-D shape, how many shapes are joined at 1 edge? How does your chart show this?

2. The total number of sides of a pyramid's faces is 20. How many edges does the pyramid have? How do you know?

Faces, Edges, and Vertices

1

a) If you know the shape of
the base of a pyramid,
how can you predict
the number of edges?

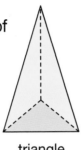  

triangle   quadrilateral   pentagon

b) If you know the shape of the
base of a prism, how can you
predict the number of edges?

2

A historical equation says the sum of the faces and vertices
of a prism or pyramid is 2 more than the number of edges.

number of faces + number of vertices − number of edges = 2

Check the equation for yourself by completing a chart for
2 prisms and 2 pyramids.

3-D shape	Number of faces	Number of vertices	Number of edges

2

Building 3-D Shapes with Congruent Faces

Goal Build 3-D shapes and describe relationships between faces and vertices.

Some geodesic domes are made of congruent triangles.

? **What 3-D shapes can you build using only congruent triangles with equal sides?**

A. Join different numbers of triangles to create **nets**. Try 2 faces, 3 faces, and so on up to 10 faces. Fold your nets to see if they make complete 3-D shapes.

B. For each successful 3-D shape, count and record these attributes:
  • the number of faces
  • the number of vertices
  • the number of faces that meet at each vertex

C. Repeat parts A and B using congruent squares.

You will need

• triangles and squares

• tape

Geodesic dome at Ontario Place

Reflecting

1. Did you build more 3-D shapes with the triangles or the squares? Why do you think that is?

2. Compare the number of faces to the number of vertices in each shape. What do you notice?

3. What did you notice about the number of faces that meet at the vertices of each shape?

Cross-Sections

You will need

- modelling clay

- dental floss

Rey's Cube

I tried to imagine what new faces I would get if I cut a cube diagonally. I also wondered what 3-D shapes I would get.

I guessed that I would get rectangle faces because the shape would still have square corners.

I checked my prediction by cutting a clay cube with dental floss.

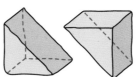

The new faces are rectangles and the cut made 2 triangle-based prisms.

Predict the shapes of the faces for each cut.
Check your predictions. Describe the 2 new 3-D shapes.

A. Cut a cube vertically.

B. Cut a cube horizontally.

C. Cut a corner off a cube.

Try These

1. What new faces will you get if you cut a triangle-based prism horizontally?

2. Describe the new face and the shapes you get when you slice the top off a pentagon-based pyramid.

3 Making Skeleton Models

Goal Build 3-D skeletons and describe relationships between edges and vertices.

Skeletons are used in building structures.
Teepees have skeleton frameworks.
A skeleton is a good model for exploring relationships between the edges and vertices of 3-D shapes.

Allison's Model

I made a skeleton model of a prism with 6 vertices.

Rami's Model

I made a skeleton model of a pyramid with 6 vertices.

? **Can you make different 3-D shapes with the same number of vertices?**

A. Make a shape with 6 vertices that is not a prism or a pyramid.

B. Complete the chart with what you know about Allison's and Rami's shapes. Then add what you know about your shape from part A.

	Number of vertices	Number of edges	Description of 3-D shape
Allison's shape	6		prism with triangle base
Rami's shape	6		pyramid with pentagon base
my shape	6		

C. Make 2 or more different 3-D shapes, each with the same number of vertices.
Add the new information to your chart from part B.

Reflecting

1. Compare the number of edges to the number of vertices for each shape. What do you notice?

2. Is it possible to build a 3-D shape with 4 vertices? Explain your answer.

3. Suppose you know the number of vertices of a shape. Can you predict what the shape will look like? Explain your thinking.

Curious Math

Making Shadows

A shadow is made when light shines through a skeleton. What shapes could the skeletons that made these shadows be? Explain your answers.

1. a) 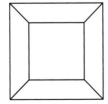   b) 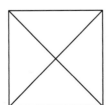   c)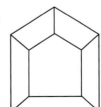

4 Drawing 3-D Shapes

Goal Draw prisms and pyramids.

Mandy is writing a story about her family's camping trip.
She wants to draw a realistic picture of the campsite.

Mandy's tent

? **How can Mandy draw a tent that looks 3-dimensional?**

Mandy's Drawings

My tent is a triangle-based prism.

Step 1 I trace a triangle block to draw the front face.

Step 2 I slide the block and trace it to draw the back face.

Step 3 I join the vertices to form the edges.

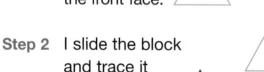

My brother's tent is a square-based pyramid.

Step 1 I trace a square block to draw the floor.

Step 2 I draw a dot where the top vertex should be.

Step 3 I join the vertices to form the edges.

NEL

Reflecting

1. What else can Mandy do to make her drawings more realistic?

2. How is drawing a prism different from drawing a pyramid?

Checking

3. Draw each shape. Try drawing the shapes several times until you have drawn one that you think is your best.
   a) a square-based prism
   b) a triangle-based pyramid

Practising

4. Draw 2 different views of Mandy's tent with the back face in different places.

5. Draw 2 different views of Mandy's brother's tent.

6. a) Draw a square-based prism with only the visible faces showing.
   b) Draw any pyramid with only the visible faces showing.

7. Roll 2 dice. Draw the dice.
   Make sure to include the dots on the visible faces.

8. Draw a house made of each pair of shapes.
   a) a rectangle-based prism and a triangle-based prism
   b) a cube and a square-based pyramid

9. a) Terry says that drawing a cylinder is just like drawing a prism. Why would he say that?
   b) Draw a cylinder.
   c) Draw a cone. How is drawing a cone like drawing a pyramid?

5

Communicate an Understanding of Geometric Concepts

Goal Use math language to show what you know about a 3-D shape.

The famous inventor Alexander Graham Bell had a cabin shaped like a triangle-based pyramid, or **tetrahedron**. Calvin wrote about what it would be like to live in a tetrahedron.

? **How can Calvin show what he knows about tetrahedrons in his writing?**

Calvin's Writing

First I made a skeleton model of a tetrahedron. Then I talked with a classmate about my ideas. After that, I wrote my rough copy. Then I looked for ways to improve it for my good copy.

> I like the way I explained about the pictures hanging.

> I should use math words to explain why there are only 2 walls.

> I should explain why I only need 6 pieces of wood using math words and a picture.

Living in a Tetrahedron (Rough Copy)

If I lived in a tetrahedron house, the pictures would hang down away from the walls because the walls are slanted. There are only 2 walls to hang things on. I would only be able to stand up in the middle because of the slanted walls.

To make my house, I would only need 6 pieces of wood. I wouldn't want to live in a tetrahedron house, but a tent would be fun.

A. Use the Communication Checklist to decide how to improve Calvin's rough copy.
How would you answer each question in the checklist? Explain your thinking.

B. What changes could Calvin make when he writes his good copy?

Reflecting

1. Why is it helpful to talk with someone about your ideas?

2. What do Calvin's rough copy and comments show you about his knowledge of tetrahedrons?

Checking

3. Write about what it would be like to live in one of these buildings. Make a model of the shape.
Talk with a classmate about your ideas before you write your rough copy.

Cree Eco-Lodge on Moose Factory Island

Cube house in Toronto

Practising

4. Look at the rough copy you wrote for Question 3.
   a) What do you like about your writing?
   b) What could you do to improve your writing?
   c) Write your good copy.

Mid-Chapter Review

1. Complete the chart.

3-D shape and name	Drawing of 2-D faces	Number of vertices	Number of edges
triangle-based prism			
	☐ ☐ ☐ ☐ ☐ ☐		
			12
		5	

2. Use your completed chart from Question 1.
   a) What do you notice about the number of edges and vertices in any shape?
   b) How are prisms and pyramids the same? How are they different?
   c) Which 3-D shapes have all congruent faces?

3. How many straws do you need to make the skeleton of each shape?
   a) a square-based pyramid
   b) a triangle-based prism
   c) a pentagon-based pyramid
   d) a hexagon-based prism

4. Show that there is more than 1 possible 3-D shape with 6 faces.

6 Measuring Mass

Goal Estimate, measure, and record the mass of objects.

 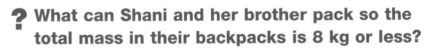
Shani's Backpack

My brother and I are going on a bicycle hike. We need food for 3 meals and extra clothing. I can't carry more than 2 kg in my backpack. My brother can't carry more than 6 kg.

? **What can Shani and her brother pack so the total mass in their backpacks is 8 kg or less?**

A. Find an object in your classroom with each **mass**. Measure using a balance scale.
   a) about 5 g   b) about 500 g   c) about 1 kg

B. Make a list of food and clothing items Shani and her brother might take on the hike.

C. Find the mass of each item on your list.

D. Choose what to pack in each backpack.

E. Find the total mass. Is the total mass 8 kg or less?

mass

A measure of the amount of matter in an object. Mass is measured in grams (g) or kilograms (kg).

1000 g = 1 kg

Reflecting

1. Why does it make sense that 1000 g is called one kilogram?

2. Name a familiar object with each mass.
   a) 5 g   b) 500 g   c) 1 kg   d) 2 kg

7 Measuring Capacity

You will need

- empty containers, including a 250 mL measuring cup and a 1 L bottle
- water
- a funnel

Goal Estimate, measure, and record the capacity of containers.

Pedro's Water Intake

I measured how much water I drank each day.
On Saturday, I drank 4 mugs of water.
On Sunday, I drank 4 large glasses of water.
On Monday, I drank a 1 L bottle of water.
On Tuesday, I drank a 1 L bottle, 1 mug, and 2 glasses of water.

? **How can Pedro measure and keep track of the amount of water he drinks each day?**

A. Find a container with each **capacity**.
- less than 250 mL
- about 250 mL
- about 500 mL
- about 1000 mL
- more than 1 L

Use a 250 mL container to measure the capacity.

B. Estimate the number of mugs of water that would fill a 1 L bottle.

capacity
The amount a container can hold. Capacity is measured in millilitres (mL) and litres (L).

1000 mL = 1 L

C. Estimate the number of glasses of water that would fill a 1 L bottle.

D. Measure the number of mugs of water it takes to fill a 1 L bottle. About how many millilitres does the mug hold?

E. Measure the number of glasses of water it takes to fill a 1 L bottle. About how many millilitres does the glass hold?

F. About how much water did Pedro drink each day? Complete a chart like this.

Day	Number and container	Capacity (mL or L)
Saturday	4 mugs	
Sunday	4 glasses	

Reflecting

1. On what day did Pedro drink the most water?

2. Each of these containers has a capacity of 2 L.

a)  b)  c)

Suppose 1 L of water was poured into each container. Where would the water line be for each container?
• halfway between the top and bottom
• closer to the top than the bottom
• closer to the bottom than the top
Explain your thinking.

3. a) What unit would you use to measure the capacity of a large container of milk or juice?
   b) What unit would you use to measure the capacity of a juice glass?

8 Using Mass and Capacity

Goal **Choose appropriate capacity and mass units.**

Sarah's Pancake Breakfast

Our class is having a pancake breakfast.

We will be using this recipe to make chocolate chip pancakes.

Pancakes	
Makes about 16 pancakes. Each pancake is 10 cm across.	
milk	175 mL
melted butter	30 mL
large egg	1
flour	250 mL
baking powder	10 mL
sugar	30 mL
salt	2 mL
chocolate chips	100 g (optional)

10 cm

? **How can Sarah use mass and capacity in recipes?**

A. The recipe uses these measurements.
Explain where and why each measurement is used.
a) mass   **b)** capacity   **c)** length

B. Why is the milk measured in millilitres rather than litres?

C. Why are the chocolate chips measured in grams rather than kilograms?

D. Suppose 2 L of salt and 1 kg of chocolate chips were used by accident to make the pancakes.
a) What would happen?
b) How do you know these are unreasonable amounts?

E. One of Sarah's classmates thinks 1 mL of maple syrup and 500 kg of butter should be served with the pancakes. Are these amounts reasonable? Explain your thinking.

Reflecting

1. Why is it important to know the width of 1 pancake?

2. What 2 things do you need to know when measuring an ingredient?

Checking

3. Which unit would you use for each, millilitres or litres?

a)   b)   c)

4. Which unit would you use for each, grams or kilograms?

a)    b)    c)

Practising

5. Which unit would you use for each, millilitres or litres?

a)    b)    c)

6. Which unit would you use for each, grams or kilograms?

a)    b)    c)

7. Which measurements seem unreasonable? Explain.

   A. a 500 g ostrich feather
   B. a 4 kg newborn baby
   C. a 2 L kitchen pot
   D. an 800 mL garbage can

9 Modelling Volume

Goal Model 3-D shapes to measure volume.

A box is a 3-D shape because it has 3 dimensions: length, width, and height.

? How do we measure the size of 3-D shapes?

height

width   length

Zola's Model

I will make a model of the box with cubes to measure its **volume**.

I can count the cubes.
The volume of the box is 16 cubes.

I can record my work by drawing a top view of my model.
The number in each square tells the number of cubes that are in that column.

2	2	2	2
2	2	2	2

volume
The measure of the amount of space taken up by a 3-D shape

This shape has a volume of 5 cubes.

A. Find a small rectangle-based prism to measure.

B. Make a model of the prism using cubes. Your model can be an estimate of the size of the prism. Record your work.

C. What is the volume of the prism in cubes?

D. Use the same number of cubes as in part C to model a new shape with the same volume. Your new shape cannot be a rectangle-based prism.

E. Compare the 2 models you made. How are they the same? How are they different?

Reflecting

1. If you turn a 3-D shape upside down or sideways, does its volume change? Give a reason for your answer.

2. Zola created these 2 prisms. Both prisms use the same number of cubes. Do they have the same volume? Explain.

3. If you know only the volume of a 3-D shape, can you describe its shape? Explain.

Checking

4. a) Find a square-based prism. Estimate its volume by making a model with cubes. Record your work.

   b) Use the same cubes to model 2 other shapes with the same volume. Make one a rectangle-based prism and the other a different shape. Record your work for both shapes.

Practising

5. Build each shape. What is the volume of each shape?

   a)    b)    c)

6. Make 2 different prisms with each volume. Record your work.

   a) 18 cubes   b) 30 cubes

7. Create a model of a 3-D shape using cubes. Record your work. Describe your model using measurement and geometry words.

LESSON

Skills Bank

1

1. Which shapes match each description?
   a) There are an even number of edges.
   b) The total number of sides of its faces is greater than 25.
   c) The total number of sides of its faces is twice the number of edges.

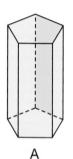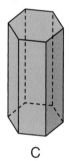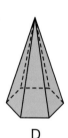

| A | B | C | D |

2

2. Which shapes in Question 1 match each description?
   a) The same number of faces meet at each vertex.
   b) The number of faces is the same as the number of vertices.

3

3. Which shapes in Question 1 match each description?
   a) There are an odd number of vertices.
   b) There are more edges than vertices.

4

4. Draw each shape.
   a) a prism with a trapezoid base
   b) a pyramid with a rhombus base

5. Name a familiar item with each mass.
a) about 10 g   c) about 100 g   e) about 10 kg
b) about 30 g   d) about 5 kg   f) about 75 kg

6. Name something with each capacity.
a) about 5 mL   c) about 50 L   e) about 100 mL
b) about 5 L   d) about 50 mL   f) about 750 mL

7. Which unit would you use to describe the capacity of each object, millilitres or litres?
a) a swimming pool   c) a bowl of soup   e) a sink
b) a tea pot   d) a bottle of glue   f) a bathtub

8. Which unit would you use to describe the mass of each object, grams or kilograms?
a) a hamster   c) a necklace   e) a personal CD player
b) a sack of potatoes   d) a car   f) a bag of dog food

9. Which measurements seem unreasonable? Explain your answer.
A. a 50 kg pencil sharpener   C. a 2 kg radio
B. a 100 g candy bar   D. a 50 mL juice box

10. Build each shape. What is the volume of each shape?

a)
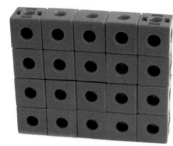

b)

c)

11. For each shape in Question 10, build another shape with the same volume. Record your work.

Problem Bank

1

1. Suppose all the vertices of a triangle-based prism were cut off.
   How many faces would the new shape have?
   How do you know?

2

2. I have 8 faces and 12 vertices.
   2 of my faces are different from the other 6 faces.
   What shape am I?

3

3. Paulette is using modelling clay and toothpicks to make skeletons. She wants to make a skeleton with 3 toothpicks in each piece of modelling clay.
   a) Name 1 shape she could make.
   b) How many toothpicks will she need for her shape?
   c) How many pieces of modelling clay will she need?

4. Vinh is stacking apples for a grocery display.
   The finished display looks like a square-based pyramid.
   a) How many apples will he need?
   b) Why is there more than 1 answer?

5. We both have 6 vertices.
   We have different numbers of edges.
   What shapes are we?

6

6. 1 medium egg has a mass of about 50 g.
   An empty egg carton weighs about 25 g.
   Denny is holding about 5 kg of eggs, including cartons.
   How many full cartons of eggs is he holding?

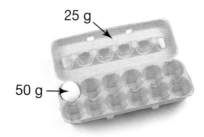

25 g

50 g →

314

7. Which foods might go in each bag?

8. 100 pennies have a mass of 250 g.
Is your own mass closer to the mass of $100 in
pennies or $1000 in pennies? How do you know?

9. Would the mass of a hot dog
and bun be greater than
or less than 50 g?
Show your work.

10. A can holds 350 mL of frozen orange juice
concentrate. To make juice, 3 cans of
water must be added to the concentrate.
Will a pitcher with a capacity of 1 L
be large enough to hold the juice?
Show your work.

11. The tap in the health room drips 1 mL of water
every 15 seconds.
   a) How many millilitres does the tap drip every minute?
   b) How many millilitres does the tap drip every hour?
   c) About how many litres of water are wasted
   each day?
   d) 1 L of water has a mass of 1 kg.
   What mass of water is wasted each day?

Chapter Review

1

1. A 3-D shape has 7 faces. It is either a prism or a pyramid.
   a) What 3-D shapes could it be?
   b) Sketch all the faces of each shape.
   c) How many edges does each shape have?
      How do you know?

2. a) Examine a triangle-based prism and a
      square-based pyramid.
      Look at each shape from different angles.
      Which shape has more faces that can be
      seen at one time? Why do you think this is?
   b) Compare other prisms and pyramids.
      What do you notice?

3

3. a) Complete a chart to organize data about these prisms.

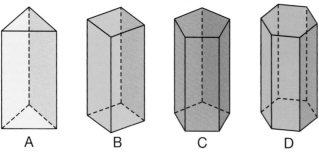

A   B   C   D

Name of prism	Number of sides of base	Number of faces	Number of edges	Number of vertices

   b) Describe any relationships you see.
   c) Are the relationships the same for a pyramid?

4

4. Make a skeleton of a prism.
   Draw your skeleton.

5. Write a description of this shape for someone who has never seen it. Do not include a drawing.

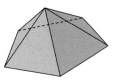

6. Angela was preparing an order of 500 g of meat. She estimated and then measured 3 times. She measured 462 g, then 521 g, and finally 498 g.
   a) Did her estimates get closer each time?
   b) Why did she stop measuring after 498 g?

7. Which mass is closest to 2 kg? How do you know?
   A. 1950 g   B. 2020 g   C. 1590 g

8. Estimate the amount of liquid in each container.

a)

b)

c)

d)

9. Which unit would you use to measure each object?
   a) a tree (grams or kilograms)
   b) a cat (grams or kilograms)
   c) an egg (grams or kilograms)
   d) a tube of toothpaste (millilitres or litres)
   e) a pitcher of juice (litres or grams)
   f) a spoonful of oil (millilitres or grams)

10. a) Make a rectangular prism that is 3 cubes long, 3 cubes wide, and 1 cube high.
    b) What is the volume of this prism?
    c) Make a new shape with the same cubes. What is the volume of the new shape?

Chapter Task

Cube Creature

Create a Cube Creature following these guidelines.
- Your creature must have at least 1 head, 2 or more arms, a body, and 2 or more legs.
- Each body part of your Cube Creature must be at least 2 cubes wide and 2 cubes long. For example, the smallest head would have a volume of 4 cubes.

? **How can you describe your Cube Creature so that someone can make a copy of it?**

Task Checklist
☑ Is your description clear and organized?
☑ Did you include diagrams?
☑ Did you use math language?
☑ Did you include the mass and volume of your Cube Creature?

Cumulative Review

Cross-Strand Multiple Choice

1. Which list shows areas that should *all* be measured in square metres?
   - A. field, parking lot, skating rink, basketball court
   - B. basketball court, field, playground, sandwich
   - C. napkin, field, playground, skating rink
   - D. field, sandbox, skateboard, parking lot

2. Choose another way to write 5×24.
   - E. 4×25
   - F. $5 \times 20 + 5 \times 4$
   - G. $5 \times 2 + 5 \times 4$
   - H. 5×2 ones $+ 5 \times 4$ tens

3. 352 slices of cake were sold at the school fun fair. Each cake was cut into 8 slices. How would you calculate the number of cakes that were used?
   - A. Multiply 352×8.
   - B. Divide 352 by 8.
   - C. Add $352 + 8$.
   - D. Subtract 8 from 352.

4. Describe the faces of a pentagon-based prism.
   - E. pentagons only
   - F. pentagons and triangles
   - G. pentagons and trapezoids
   - H. pentagons and rectangles

5. Which object is best measured in millilitres?
   - A. a juice box
   - B. a bag of milk
   - C. the water in a swimming pool
   - D. the water in an aquarium

6. Choose the measurement that doesn't make sense.
   - E. bag of potatoes: 5000 g
   - F. truck: 454 g
   - G. small paper salt package: 23 g
   - H. bag of uncooked spaghetti: 500 g

Cross-Strand Investigation

We Need a Playground

The children had nowhere to play. They wanted a playground that was big enough for all of them.

7. a) 456 children marched to City Hall in 2 arrays.
   The 1st array had 8 rows. The 2nd array had 5 rows.
   Draw a diagram to show the arrays.
   Write the multiplication equation for each array.
   b) The children walked home in groups of 6.
   How many groups were there? Show your calculations.

8. Carlitos designed a playground on a centimetre grid.
   a) Is there enough room for the children to walk and run?
   Compare the areas for walking, running, and playing on equipment.
   Show your work.
   b) Find 2 parts of the playground that have the same area.
   Explain how you know the areas are the same.

9. What 2-dimensional and 3-dimensional shapes can you see in this playground equipment? Use geometry words.

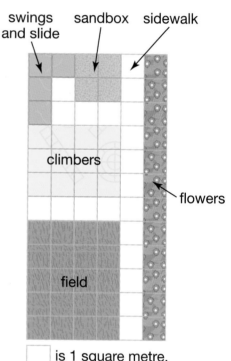

is 1 square metre.

Fractions and Decimals

Goals

You will be able to

- **describe fractions of an area and of a set**

- **use mixed numbers and fractions to describe wholes and parts**

- **describe and create areas and sets using decimal tenths and decimal hundredths**

- **compare and order fractions and decimals**

- **add and subtract decimals**

Sea sails

Getting Started

Fractions

? How many ways can you show $\frac{2}{3}$?

2 of 3 students are wearing green shirts.

$\frac{2}{3}$ of the students are wearing green shirts.

2 of 3 three students are boys.

$\frac{2}{3}$ of the students are boys.

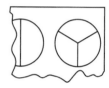

A. Look at the picture. Create more descriptions of the students that are examples of the **fraction** $\frac{2}{3}$.

B. Use materials to make as many models of $\frac{2}{3}$ as you can.

C. Work with a partner. Do your models show $\frac{2}{3}$ of a set, $\frac{2}{3}$ of an area, or $\frac{2}{3}$ of a length?

Sort your models of $\frac{2}{3}$ using a chart like this.

$\frac{2}{3}$ of a set	$\frac{2}{3}$ of an area	$\frac{2}{3}$ of a length
	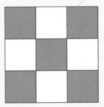	

D. Find examples in your classroom that you can describe with fractions.

Do You Remember?

1. Explain what each word means and give an example.
   a) numerator   b) denominator

2. Which picture cannot be described by the fraction $\frac{3}{4}$? Explain your thinking.

   A.   B.   C.

3. Use a fraction to estimate how full each glass is. Explain your answer.

   a)   b)   c)   d)

   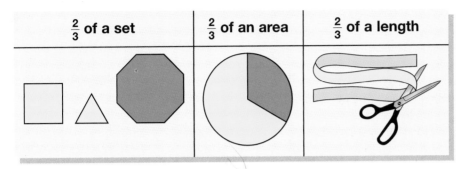

1 Fractions of an Area

Goal Describe and compare fractions as part of an area using words, objects, pictures, and symbols.

$\frac{1}{3}$ of the area of the flag of Belgium is red.
More than $\frac{1}{3}$ of the area of the flag of
Colombia is yellow.

Belgium

Colombia

? **Which flags show thirds?**

Flags of the World

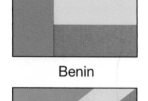

Benin

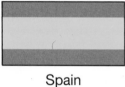

Spain

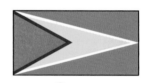

Guyana

Congo

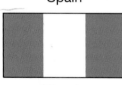

Nigeria

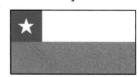

Chile

A. How many colours does each flag have?

B. Describe a colour in any flag that looks like $\frac{1}{3}$ of the flag's area.

C. Describe a colour in any flag that looks like more than $\frac{1}{3}$ of the flag's area. Explain your answer.

D. Use fractions and words to describe the flag of Spain so a friend could draw it without looking.

E. Use fractions and words to describe the flag of Colombia so a friend could draw it without looking.

Reflecting

1. Does each red part of this made-up flag show $\frac{1}{4}$? Explain why or why not.

2. How could you use the flag of Nigeria to show that $\frac{2}{3}$ is greater than $\frac{1}{3}$?

Checking

3. a) Draw a flag that is $\frac{3}{8}$ red and the rest yellow.
   b) What fraction is yellow?
   c) Is there more red or more yellow on your flag? Explain how you know.
   d) Which fraction is greater, $\frac{3}{8}$ or $\frac{5}{8}$? Explain your thinking.

Practising

4. Explain why each flag does or does not show fourths.

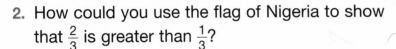

a)	b)	c)
Mauritius	Seychelles	Canada

5. Which fraction is greater? Show how you know.
   a) $\frac{3}{5}$ or $\frac{2}{5}$ b) $\frac{1}{4}$ or $\frac{3}{4}$ c) $\frac{3}{6}$ or $\frac{4}{6}$ d) $\frac{1}{8}$ or $\frac{7}{8}$

6. Arrange these fractions in order from least to greatest. $\frac{3}{10}, \frac{7}{10}, \frac{1}{10}, \frac{4}{10}, \frac{9}{10}, \frac{5}{10}$

7. Is $\frac{1}{3}$ of flag A the same area as $\frac{1}{3}$ of flag B? Why or why not?

Flag A   Flag B

2 Mixed Numbers and Improper Fractions

Goal Model, write, and compare improper fractions and mixed numbers.

Chris's Trapezoids

I have 5 trapezoids.

I cover hexagons with trapezoids to find out how many hexagons I have.

2 trapezoids cover a whole hexagon. A trapezoid is half a hexagon.

I can say 2 trapezoids, or $\frac{2}{2}$, makes 1 whole hexagon.

5 trapezoids cover $\frac{5}{2}$ hexagons. I have $\frac{5}{2}$ hexagons.

$\frac{5}{2}$ is an **improper fraction**.

I can also say 5 trapezoids cover 2 whole hexagons and another half hexagon. I have $2\frac{1}{2}$ hexagons.

$2\frac{1}{2}$ is a **mixed number**.

improper fraction
A fraction with a numerator that is greater than or equal to its denominator

$\dfrac{7}{4}$ ← numerator
← denominator

an improper fraction

mixed number
A whole number with a fraction. A mixed number describes an amount between 2 whole numbers.

$1\dfrac{3}{4}$ ← fraction

↑
whole number (not 0)

? **What mixed numbers can you create with hexagons and other pattern blocks?**

A. Cover hexagons with 8 **green** triangles.
   Write an improper fraction for the hexagons covered.
   Write a mixed number for the hexagons covered.

B. Repeat part A using 8 **blue** rhombuses to cover hexagons.

C. Repeat part A using 3 **red** trapezoids to cover hexagons.

D. Which is greater, $\frac{5}{2}$ or $\frac{3}{2}$?
Use pattern blocks to show how you know.

E. Which is greater, $1\frac{2}{6}$ or $2\frac{1}{6}$?
Use pattern blocks to show how you know.

Reflecting

1. a) What does the numerator in an improper fraction tell you?
   b) What does the denominator in an improper fraction tell you?
   c) If the denominators are equal, how do the numerators help you to compare improper fractions?

2. How can you tell that $\frac{13}{6}$ is between 2 and 3?

Checking

3. Instead of a hexagon, think of the blue rhombus as the whole.
   a) What fraction of the rhombus is 1 green triangle?
   b) How many rhombuses do 5 triangles cover? Write an improper fraction and a mixed number.

Practising

4. Think of the red trapezoid as the whole. What fraction of the trapezoid is 1 green triangle?

5. How many trapezoids are covered? Write an improper fraction and a mixed number for each.

   a) 4 triangles   c) 6 triangles   e) 8 triangles
   b) 5 triangles   d) 7 triangles   f) 9 triangles

6. Which is greater? Show how you know.
   a) $3\frac{2}{3}$ or $2\frac{1}{3}$ b) $\frac{8}{3}$ or $\frac{5}{3}$ c) $\frac{7}{3}$ or $2\frac{2}{3}$

3 Fractions of a Set

You will need

• counters

• paper squares

 Goal Describe parts of sets using proper and improper fractions and mixed numbers.

Rey is having a party.
He bought invitations that come in boxes of 6.
He sent 8 invitations.

? **How many boxes of invitations did Rey use?**

A. How many full boxes did he use?
What fraction of another box did he use?
Explain your answer.

B. Write an improper fraction for the number of boxes he used.

C. Write a mixed number for the number of boxes he used.

D. Show how to find the missing amounts in this table.

Number of invitations	17			24
Number of boxes of 6 (improper fraction)	$\frac{17}{6}$		$\frac{21}{6}$	
Number of boxes of 6 (mixed number)		$3\frac{1}{6}$		

Reflecting

1. a) What does the numerator in the improper fraction tell you about the invitations?
   b) What does the denominator tell you?

2. What does the whole number part of the mixed number tell you about the invitations?

3. How can you draw a picture to find the mixed number if you know the improper fraction?

Checking

4. Pop cans come in cartons of 12.
   Rey needs 15 cans of pop for his party.
   How many cartons will he use for his party?
   Use counters or draw a picture.
   Show your answer as an improper fraction and a
   mixed number.

Practising

5. Party favours come in packages of 4.
   Samantha gave 1 party favour to
   each of her guests.
   She handed out the favours from
   $3\frac{3}{4}$ packages.
   How many guests were at her party?
   Show your work.

6. Write a mixed number for each improper fraction.

   a) $\frac{5}{3}$ b) $\frac{9}{4}$ c) $\frac{13}{8}$ d) $\frac{29}{10}$

7. Cho has $3\frac{1}{5}$ packages of noisemakers.
   How many noisemakers could she have?
   Explain your answer.

8. Think about the mixed numbers $2\frac{1}{6}$ and $1\frac{5}{6}$.

   a) Write each mixed number as an improper fraction.

   b) Is it easier to compare the size of numbers when
      they are written as mixed numbers or as improper
      fractions? Explain your answer.

9. Arrange the numbers in order from least to greatest.

   a) $2\frac{1}{6}$, $1\frac{5}{6}$, $2\frac{3}{6}$, $3\frac{2}{6}$, $2\frac{4}{6}$

   b) $2\frac{2}{4}$, $\frac{9}{4}$, $\frac{3}{4}$, $1\frac{2}{4}$, $\frac{5}{4}$

10. The number $\frac{\blacksquare}{3}$ is between 3 and 4.
    What could the numerator of this number be?
    Draw a picture to explain your answer.

4 Decimal Tenths

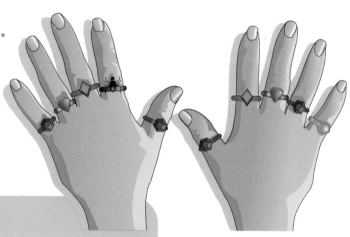

Goal Write tenths as decimals using words and symbols.

Miki has rings on all of her fingers.

? **How can Miki represent the number of blue rings on her fingers?**

Miki's Blue Rings

I have blue rings on 2 fingers.
That's two tenths of my fingers.
I can write two tenths as a fraction.

$$\frac{2}{10}$$

← 2 fingers have blue rings

← 10 fingers in all

I can also write two tenths as a **decimal**.

Zero means there is less than one whole set. → 0.2 ← number of tenths

decimal point

When I write tenths as **decimals**, the digit after the decimal point is the numerator of the fraction.

I can show two tenths on a fraction rectangle.

| 0.0 | 0.1 | 0.2 | 0.3 | 0.4 | 0.5 | 0.6 | 0.7 | 0.8 | 0.9 | 1.0 |

| $\frac{0}{10}$ | $\frac{1}{10}$ | $\frac{2}{10}$ | $\frac{3}{10}$ | $\frac{4}{10}$ | $\frac{5}{10}$ | $\frac{6}{10}$ | $\frac{7}{10}$ | $\frac{8}{10}$ | $\frac{9}{10}$ | $\frac{10}{10}$ |

Two tenths is closer to 0 than it is to 1.

decimal
A way to describe fractions and mixed numbers using place value. A decimal point separates the ones place from the tenths place.

Reflecting

1. Why are 2 hands a good model to show decimal tenths?

2. Why is 0.2 different from $\frac{0}{2}$?

3. What decimal is halfway along the fraction rectangle?

Checking

4. a) Describe Miki's other rings using words, fractions, and decimals.
   b) Tell which of your decimals is greatest and which is least.

Practising

5. Write a fraction and a decimal that tells that all of Miki's fingers have rings.

6. Write fractions, decimals, and words for the shaded parts of the fraction rectangles.

   a)

   b)

   c)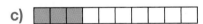

   d)

7. Write each as a fraction and a decimal.
   a) four tenths   b) eight tenths   c) zero tenths

8. Tell whether each decimal is closer to 0, $\frac{1}{2}$, or 1.
   a) 0.9   b) 0.4   c) 0.7   d) 0.1

9. a) Trace your hands and draw rings on your fingers.
      Leave some fingers without rings.
      Make less than half of your rings the same colour.
   b) Use words and decimals to describe your rings.

5 Decimal Tenths Greater Than 1

 Goal Model, write, and compare decimal tenths greater than 1.

Josef wants to enter his frog in a jumping contest.
Sarah's champion frog can jump 1.6 m.
Sarah says, "My frog jumped one-and-six-tenths metres."

? **Do you think Josef's frog can win?**

Josef's Frog Jump

I placed 2 metre sticks end-to-end to measure my frog's best jump.

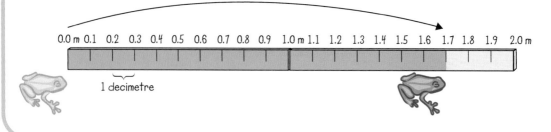

1 decimetre

A. What fraction of the metre stick is shaded between 1.0 m and 2.0 m?

B. Write the jump distance of Josef's frog as a mixed number.

C. Why would the decimal for this distance be 1.■ m?

D. Write the jump distance of Josef's frog as a decimal.

E. Whose frog can jump farther, Sarah's or Josef's? Show how you know.

F. Write each jump distance in **decimetres**.

Reflecting

1. **a)** Explain how you know 1.7 is greater than 1.2.
   b) Explain how you know 0.9 is less than 1.2.

Checking

2. A frog jumped 2.3 m.
   a) What does the 2 tell you?
   b) What does the 3 tell you?
   c) Write the jump distance in decimetres.
   d) Write the jump distance as an improper fraction.

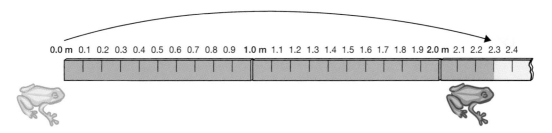

Practising

3. A frog jumped three-and-two-tenths metres.
   a) Use a tape measure or a draw a picture to show where the frog landed.
   b) Use decimals to write the jump distance.
   c) Write the decimal as a mixed number.

4. Write a decimal for each mixed number.
   Find the lengths in metres on a measuring tape.
   a) $2\frac{5}{10}$ **b)** $1\frac{1}{10}$ **c)** $2\frac{7}{10}$ **d)** $1\frac{14}{10}$

5. Write each measurement in metres.
   a) one metre three decimetres   **c)** three metres
   b) twenty three decimetres   **d)** two-and-four-tenths metres

6. Arrange these measurements from longest to shortest.
   2.1 m, 3.5 m, 0.9 m, 1.8 m, 2.6 m, 2.0 m

Mid-Chapter Review

1 1. 1 circle represents 1 whole.
Write a fraction or mixed number for each shaded area.

a)

$\frac{1}{3}$

b)

$1\frac{1}{2}$

c)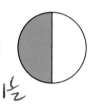

2. Use a 2 by 4 grid to make a flag.

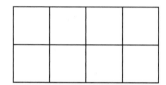

a) Colour one eighth of the flag **yellow**.
b) Colour half of the flag **red**.
c) Colour one quarter of the flag **green**.
d) What fraction of the flag is not coloured?

2 3. There are 35 buttons. 6 buttons make 1 set for a shirt.
a) How many sets can be made?
Write your answer as a mixed number.
b) How many buttons would be in $3\frac{5}{6}$ sets?

4 4. Tell whether each number is closest to 0, $\frac{1}{2}$, or 1.
Explain your answer.
a) $\frac{5}{6}$ b) 0.2   c) 0.4   d) $\frac{3}{10}$ e) $\frac{11}{10}$

5 5. Write each decimal as a fraction.
Write each fraction as a decimal.
a) 2.1   b) 0.2   c) $\frac{8}{10}$ d) $1\frac{2}{10}$ e) 2.5

6. Write the numbers in Question 5 from least to greatest.
Use pictures or a tape measure to help.

0.0 m 0.1 0.2 0.3 0.4 0.5 0.6 0.7 0.8 0.9 1.0 m 1.1 1.2 1.3 1.4 1.5 1.6 1.7 1.8 1.9 2.0 m 2.1 2.2 2.3 2.4 2.5 2.6 2.7 2.8 2.9 3.0 m

Find the Match

How to make the game:

A. Roll 2 dice. Then make a fraction or decimal with the numbers. For example, if you roll a 2 and a 5, you can make $\frac{2}{5}$, $\frac{5}{2}$, 5.2, or 2.5.

B. Write your fraction or decimal on a blank card.

C. On a 2nd card, draw a picture that matches your decimal or fraction.

D. Roll the dice again and make 2 new cards. Keep going until you have 5 pairs of cards.

Number of players: 2 or more
How to play: Match pairs of cards.

Step 1 Shuffle the cards and spread them out face down.

Step 2 Take turns turning over 2 cards at a time.
If the cards match, keep them.
If the cards don't match, turn them over again.

Keep playing until all the cards are matched.
The player with the most cards wins.

6 Adding Decimal Tenths

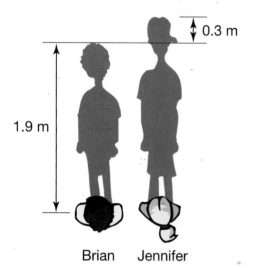

You will need

• a measuring tape

Goal Add decimals in tenths.

Brian's shadow is 1.9 m long.
Jennifer's shadow is 0.3 m longer than
Brian's shadow.

? **How long is Jennifer's shadow?**

A. Suppose Jennifer's shadow were only
0.1 m longer than Brian's shadow.
How long would her shadow be?

0.3 m

1.9 m

Brian   Jennifer

0.0 m 0.1 0.2 0.3 0.4 0.5 0.6 0.7 0.8 0.9 **1.0 m** 1.1 1.2 1.3 1.4 1.5 1.6 1.7 1.8 1.9 **2.0 m** 2.1 2.2 2.3 2.4

$$1.9 + 0.1 = \blacksquare$$

B. How much more is 0.3 than 0.1?

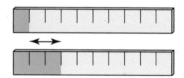

C. How can you use your answer to part B
to find the length of Jennifer's shadow?

D. Suppose the shadow of a light pole is 1.8 m
longer than Jennifer's shadow.
How long is the light pole's shadow?

2.0 m   3.0 m   4.0 m   5.0 m

Reflecting

1. How do you know your answers are reasonable?

2. How could you use decimetres to check the addition?

Checking

3. Later in the day, Jennifer's shadow is 4.4 m long.
   Brian stands at the end of her shadow.
   His shadow is 3.8 m long.
   a) Why would the length of their shadows together
      be less than 8.4 m?
   b) What is the length of their shadows together?
      Use a picture, words, or symbols to explain
      your answer.

Practising

4. Late in the day, Jennifer's shadow is 6.4 m long.
   Her shadow grows longer, first by 2.3 m and then
   by another 2.5 m. How long is Jennifer's shadow?
   Use a model or picture to find the answer.
   Show your work.

5. Add the lengths. Show your work.
   a) 4.5 m and 1.7 m   c) 3.2 cm and 3.8 cm
   b) 1.6 m and 3.7 m   d) 2.6 dm and 9.1 dm

6. Find each sum. Show your work.
   a) $1.9 + 7.2$ b) $0.4 + 5.8$ c) $6.1 + 1.9$ d) $4.5 + 2.6$

7. A shadow with a length between 1 m and 2 m grows
   to be twice as long.
   a) What is the longest the shadow could be?
   b) What is the shortest the shadow could be?

8. How many different pairs of decimal tenths add
   together to make 1.0? Show your work.

7

Subtracting Decimal Tenths

Goal Subtract decimals in tenths.

A baby boa constrictor is about 0.6 m long at birth.
An adult boa constrictor might be 2.1 m long.

? **How much does the boa constrictor grow?**

Chantal's Method

The answer will be between 1 m and 2 m.

I started with the length of the baby boa constrictor and counted on to the length of the adult.

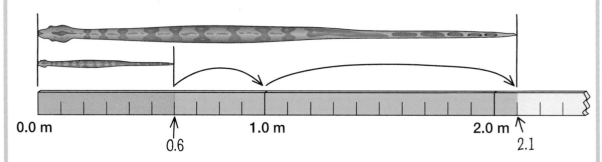

0.0 m   0.6   1.0 m   2.0 m   2.1

I counted on 0.4 m to get from 0.6 m to 1.0 m.

Then it's another 1.1 m to get from 1.0 m to 2.1 m.

$0.4 + 1.1 = 1.5$

The boa constrictor grew by 1.5 m.

Reflecting

1. Why do you think Chantal knew the answer would be between 1 m and 2 m?

2. How could you use decimetres to do the subtraction?

Checking

3. A bull snake can grow to be 1.5 m long. If a baby bull snake is about 0.4 m long, how much will it grow?

Practising

4. A giraffe's neck can be about 2.5 m long. If a giraffe is about 5.4 m tall, how tall is the rest of its body? Show your work.

5. Find the difference between these lengths.
   a) 5.5 m and 1.4 m   b) 4.3 cm and 3.4 cm

6. Find each difference.
   a) 6.6 − 5.9   b) 9.0 − 6.5   c) 22.8 − 12.5

7. a) Which difference is greatest in Question 6?
   b) How much greater is this difference than the least difference?

8. A snake grew 1.7 m over its lifetime. The snake was shorter than 1 m when it was born. What could its birth length and its final length have been? Give 2 possibilities.

1.7 m

8 Communicate About Decimal Operations

You will need
- base ten blocks

Goal Use a model to explain how to add and subtract decimals.

You can spot an American kestrel in flight because its wingspan is more than double its body length.

? **How can Vinh explain how to find the difference between the American kestrel's wingspan and its body length?**

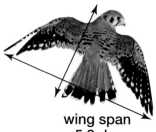

body length
2.7 dm

wing span
5.8 dm

American kestrel

Vinh's Explanation

I'll use blocks to explain.

This rod is 1 dm long.

This cube is 0.1 dm long.

First, I model the wingspan and the body length.
The wingspan is 5.8 dm.
The body length is 2.7 dm.

The difference is how much longer the wingspan is than the length.
I count the whole decimetres in the difference first.

Then I count tenths of a decimetre.
I look for 10 tenths, or 1 dm.

The difference is 2 dm + 1 dm + 0.1 dm = 3.1 dm.

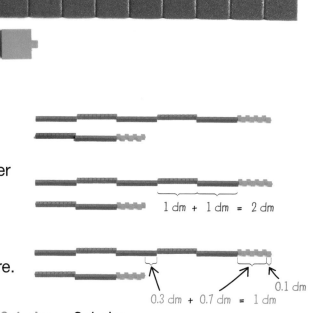

1 dm + 1 dm = 2 dm

0.3 dm + 0.7 dm = 1 dm

0.1 dm

A. How can you tell that Vinh considered all the questions in the Communication Checklist?

B. How does the block model help to make Vinh's words easier to understand?

C. Explain why Vinh could add 2.7 dm + 3.1 dm to check his answer.

D. Use blocks to explain to a classmate how you would add 2.7 dm + 3.1 dm.

Reflecting

1. Use the Communication Checklist.
   a) What strengths can you identify in the way you explained your addition steps in part D?
   b) Suggest 1 way to improve your explanation.

Checking

2. Use blocks to show how you would subtract to find the difference between the least bittern's wingspan and its body length.

least bittern
body length 3.3 dm
wingspan 4.4 dm

Practising

3. The least bittern has a wingspan of 4.4 dm. The American kestrel has a wingspan of 5.8 dm. Use blocks to explain how you would subtract to find the difference between these 2 wingspans.

4. The broad-winged hawk is 4.1 dm long. Its wingspan is 4.5 dm longer than its body length. Use blocks to explain how you would add to find its wingspan.

broad-winged hawk
body length 4.1 dm

9 Decimal Hundredths Less Than or Equal to 1

Goal Write hundredths as decimals using words and symbols.

Pedro drew a design on a 100 grid using different colours.

? **How can Pedro use decimals to describe his design?**

Pedro's Grid

My grid is divided into 100 parts.

I coloured 1 part red.

One hundredth of the grid is red.

I write the fraction $\frac{1}{100}$ as the decimal 0.01.

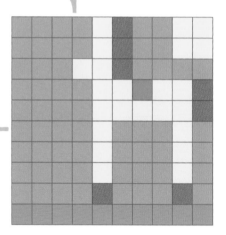

Pedro's whole grid is represented by 1 or $\frac{100}{100}$.

A. Which colour covers $\frac{23}{100}$ or 0.23 of the grid?

B. Write a fraction and a decimal in hundredths for every other colour in the grid.

C. Arrange your decimals in order from least to greatest. Explain how you know your answer is right.

Reflecting

1. Is 0.07 closer to 0 or to 1? How do you know?

2. Use a 100 grid to explain how 0.07 is different from 0.70.

Checking

3. Write a fraction and a decimal for the shaded part.

a)

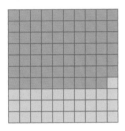

b)

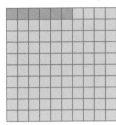

Practising

4. Write a fraction and a decimal for the shaded part.

a)

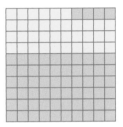

b)

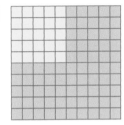

5. Write each fraction as a decimal.

   a) $\frac{89}{100}$
   b) $\frac{7}{100}$
   c) $\frac{30}{100}$
   d) $\frac{12}{100}$

6. Write each decimal as a fraction.

   a) 0.67
   b) 0.29
   c) 0.40
   d) 0.04

7. Write the decimals in Question 6 in order from least to greatest.

8. a) What fraction, in hundredths, describes half of the 100 grid?
   b) What decimal describes half of the 100 grid?
   c) Is the blue part of Pedro's design closer to $\frac{1}{2}$ or 1? Explain how you know.

9. a) Create your own design on a 100 grid. Use at least 4 colours.
   b) Describe your design using words, fractions, and decimals.
   c) Which colour is closest to half of your design? Explain how you know.

10 Add and Subtract Hundredths

You will need

• a 100 grid

• pencil crayons

• a calculator

Goal Add and subtract decimal hundredths using grids and calculators.

A city plans to develop 1 square kilometre of land.
The city will use 0.45 of a square kilometre for housing
and 0.32 of a square kilometre for a park.
The rest of the land will be used for a shopping mall.

? **How much land will be used for housing and parks?**

Carmen's Solution

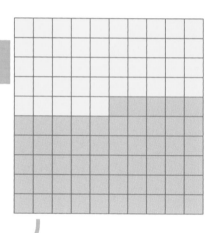

I can use a 100 grid to represent the land.

Each small square is 0.01 of a square kilometre.

I can colour 45 hundredths yellow to represent
0.45 of a square kilometre of housing.

I can colour the park green.

A. Colour the housing and the park on your grid.

B. How many small squares are coloured in all?
How much land will be used for housing and the park?

C. How can you use a calculator to check your answer?

D. How much land will be used for the mall?
Write a subtraction equation.

E. Which covers the most land: the housing, the
park, or the mall? Which covers the least land?
Show how you know.

344

Reflecting

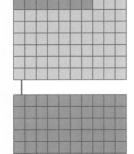

1. How can you use a 100 grid to show the addition of 2 different decimals like 0.37 + 0.54? Use a calculator to check your answer.

2. How can you use a 100 grid to show the subtraction of 2 decimals like 0.63 − 0.15? Use a calculator to check your answer.

Checking

3. Use a 100 grid.
   a) Add 0.15 over and over.
      Use a different colour for each 0.15.
      Stop when you reach the sum of 0.75.
   b) How many different colours did you use?
   c) Show the steps with a calculator.

4. Use a 100 grid.
   a) Start with 1.00 and subtract 0.09 over and over.
      Use a different colour each time.
      Stop when 0.10 of the grid is still blank.
   b) How many colours did you use?
   c) Use a calculator to check your subtraction.
      Record each answer and describe the patterns in the digits.

Practising

5. Add or subtract using a 100 grid.
   Use a calculator to check your answer.
   a) 0.43 + 0.26   c) 0.23 + 0.07   e) 0.37 − 0.16
   b) 0.35 + 0.47   d) 1.00 − 0.54   f) 0.45 − 0.09

6. a) Find 2 different pairs of decimals that add to 1.
   b) Find 2 different pairs of decimals that have a difference of 0.35. Show your work.

11 Relating Fractions and Decimals

Goal Explore, model, and calculate how fractions and decimals are related.

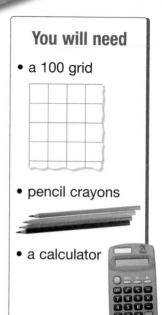

? **What fractions can you write as decimals in tenths or hundredths?**

The fraction $\frac{1}{4}$ can represent 1 out of 4 equal parts of a 100 grid.

A. What decimal in hundredths represents $\frac{1}{4}$?

B. Divide 1 by 4 on a calculator. How does your answer relate to what you see on the grid?

C. Replace the denominator in $\frac{1}{\blacksquare}$ with other numbers from 2 to 10.
Estimate the area of a 100 grid that will be covered for each fraction.
Colour and label a grid to match your estimate.

D. Use a calculator to divide 1 by each denominator from 2 to 10. Which values give you an exact number of tenths or hundredths? Compare your grids from part C to each calculator value.

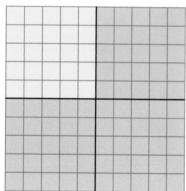

Reflecting

1. What pattern did you see in the shaded grids as the denominator increased?

2. How could you predict that $\frac{1}{3}$ would not be an exact number of tenths or hundredths?

3. How could you predict that $\frac{3}{4}$ can be written as
$0.25 + 0.25 + 0.25 = 0.75$?

Quarters and Dimes

Jon spends $0.75 for a bus ticket.
He pays with a $2 coin.
How much change will Jon receive?

Jon's Change

$0.75 is 3 quarters and $2 is 8 quarters.

8 quarters – 3 quarters = 5 quarters

I will get $1.25 in change.

A. How did Jon know that $2 is the same as 8 quarters?

B. What other way could Jon count coins to calculate his change mentally?

Try These

1. Use Jon's method to find the change.
   a) spend $0.75 from a $5 bill
   b) spend $0.30 from a $1 coin

2. Find the change.
   a) $2.00 − $0.25   c) $5.00 − $3.75
   b) $1.50 − $0.75   d) $2.00 − $0.70

3. Find the sum.
   a) $2.00 + $1.75   c) $2.75 + $1.25
   b) $1.50+ $0.75   d) $1.70 + $0.60

4. How can thinking about money help you to add decimals like 1.75 + 3.50?

Skills Bank

LESSON

1

1. Which flags show thirds?

a)

France

b)

Hungary

c)

Georgia

2. Which fraction is greater?

a) $\frac{3}{5}$ or $\frac{4}{5}$ b) $\frac{5}{7}$ or $\frac{3}{7}$ c) $\frac{7}{9}$ or $\frac{6}{9}$ d) $\frac{4}{6}$ or $\frac{5}{6}$

2

3. Think of a yellow hexagon as the whole.
What fraction of the hexagon is each number of shapes?
Write an improper fraction and a mixed number.

a) 7 **green** triangles   c) 4 **blue** rhombuses

b) 5 **red** trapezoids   d) 13 **green** triangles

4. Which is greater?

a) $3\frac{1}{3}$ or $4\frac{1}{3}$ b) $3\frac{2}{3}$ or $1\frac{1}{3}$ c) $4\frac{1}{4}$ or $3\frac{3}{4}$ d) $2\frac{1}{4}$ or $2\frac{3}{4}$

3

5. Write a mixed number for each improper fraction.

a) $\frac{9}{8}$ c) $\frac{31}{10}$ e) $\frac{16}{3}$

b) $\frac{8}{5}$ d) $\frac{8}{6}$ f) $\frac{21}{5}$

6. Write an improper fraction for each mixed number.

a) $2\frac{1}{10}$ c) $4\frac{2}{5}$ e) $2\frac{2}{3}$

b) $3\frac{1}{3}$ d) $1\frac{1}{4}$ f) $5\frac{2}{5}$

7. There are 6 pop cans in a carton.
Brady needs 15 cans of pop for a party.
How many cartons does she need?
Write your answer as a mixed number.

8. Write fractions, decimals, and words for the shaded parts of the fraction rectangles.

a)

b)

c)

d)

9. Write each as a fraction and a decimal.
a) three tenths   b) six tenths   c) five tenths

10. Tell whether each decimal is closer to 0, $\frac{1}{2}$, or 1.
a) 0.2   b) 0.3   c) 0.6   d) 0.8

11. Complete each measurement.
a) 1 m 4 dm = 1.■ m   c) 2 m 5 dm = ■.■ m
b) 27 dm = ■.7 m   d) 36 dm = ■.■ m

12. Arrange each set of measurements from shortest to longest.
a) 1.9 m, 2.5 m, 0.8 m, 2.9 m, 2.3 m
b) 2.3 m, 3.5 m, 1.9 m, 0.8 m, 4.1 m
c) 1.5 m, 3.2 m, 0.6 m, 0.1 m, 2.4 m

13. Add the lengths. Show your work.
a) 5.9 m and 3.4 m   c) 3.0 m and 5.9 m
b) 2.9 cm and 2.1 cm   d) 4.2 dm and 3.3 dm

14. Find each sum. Show your work.

a)   2.9   b)   0.3   c)   7.3   d)   5.6
   + 3.6   + 5.9   + 1.9   + 3.4

15. Brian and Karyn built Lego towers.
Brian's tower is 3.7 dm tall.
Karyn's tower is 4.8 dm taller.
How tall is Karyn's tower? Show your work.

16. Find the difference between these lengths. Show your work.

    a) 3.7 m and 2.1 m   **c)** 4.6 m and 2.2 m

    b) 6.2 cm and 4.8 cm   **d)** 6.9 cm and 3.7 cm

17. Find each difference. Show your work.

    a)   7.9   **b)**   6.3   **c)**   8.3   **d)**   4.6

       − 3.5   − 5.9   − 1.7   − 3.8

18. Kylie is running a 10 km race.
She stops for a drink at 6.5 km.
How much farther does she need to run?
Show your work.

19. Write a fraction and decimal for the shaded part.

    a) 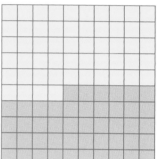   **b)** 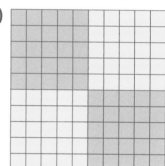   **c)**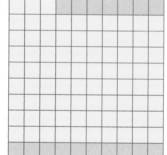

20. Write each fraction as a decimal.

    a) $\frac{50}{100}$ **b)** $\frac{9}{100}$ **c)** $\frac{63}{100}$ **d)** $\frac{90}{100}$

21. Write each decimal as a fraction.

    a) 0.67   **b)** 0.38   **c)** 0.06   **d)** 0.70

22. Add or subtract.
Use a grid or a calculator.

    a) 0.21 + 0.34   **d)** 0.62 + 0.17   **g)** 0.87 − 0.45

    b) 0.09 + 0.80   **e)** 0.99 − 0.02   **h)** 0.32 − 0.12

    c) 0.89 + 0.02   **f)** 1.00 − 0.32   **i)** 0.56 + 0.34

Problem Bank

1 1. If $\frac{3}{8}$ of a circle graph is red and the rest is green, which colour will cover more area?
Show how you know.

2. Find 6 different ways to divide a square into 4 equal areas.

2 3. If 2 yellow pattern-block hexagons are the whole, how much of the hexagons would 7 blue rhombuses cover?
Write an improper fraction and a mixed number.
Draw a picture to show how you know.

4. If a red trapezoid is the whole, how much of the trapezoid would 11 green triangles cover?
Write an improper fraction and a mixed number.
Draw a picture to show how you know.

4 5. A junk drawer has 5 pencils, 2 erasers, 1 pencil sharpener, and 2 crayons.
Write decimals and fractions that tell about the things in the junk drawer.

6 6. Which of these decimals add up to 5.0?
1.2 0.8 4.2 1.0 2.2 1.7 0.3 0.6
Find more than 1 group of decimals that add up to 5.0. Show how you know.

7 7. A baby deer leaps 1.4 m. Its mother leaps 4 m.
How much farther did the mother leap than the baby?

11 8. Susan thinks that 0.23 of the whole numbers between 1 and 100 have the digit 3 in them.
Is she correct? Show your work.

Chapter Review

LESSON

1 1. 3 friends went to the Square Pizza Shop. Show how the friends could share 1 pizza equally.

2 2. 6 green triangles cover 1 yellow hexagon. What fraction of a hexagon is 1 triangle?

3. How many hexagons are covered? Write an improper fraction and a mixed number.
   a) 7 triangles   b) 8 triangles   c) 9 triangles

4 4. This nursery rhyme has been popular for more than 2 centuries.
   Suppose the old lady had 3 rings on each hand and 2 bells on each foot.
   a) Describe the lady's rings using words, fractions, and decimals.
   b) Describe the lady's bells using words, fractions, and decimals.

Ride a cock-horse to Banbury Cross
To see an old lady get up on her horse.
Rings on her fingers and bells on her toes,
She will make music wherever she goes.

5 5. Write an improper fraction and a decimal for each mixed number.
   a) $3\frac{3}{10}$ b) $9\frac{2}{10}$ c) $6\frac{2}{10}$ d) $1\frac{1}{10}$

6. Draw a picture to show a decimal number that is between 3 and 4.

6   **7.** A rabbit hops 2.4 m to the right.
Then the rabbit hops another 1.1 m to the right.
How far is the rabbit from where it began?
Show your work.

7   **8.** What are the missing digits?

   a)   2.9   **b)**   4.■
       $\underline{+ \ ■.7}$ $\underline{- \ 3.6}$
        4.6   0.5

10   **9.** The grade 4 students at Whitney School were
surveyed about their favourite desserts.
The results are shown in the bar graph.

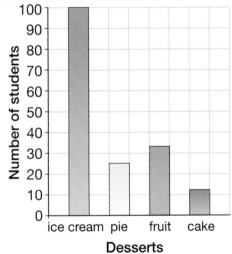

Favourite Desserts of Grade 4 Students

  a) The pie bar is about 0.25, or $\frac{1}{4}$, of the ice cream bar.
Use decimals and fractions to compare the other
desserts with ice cream.

  b) Which 2 desserts together add up to about 0.45
of the ice cream bar?

  c) The cake bar is about half of the pie bar.
How would you compare cake and fruit?

  d) How would you compare pie and fruit?

Chapter Task

Decimal Kites

Shani's Kites

I designed these 4 kites using different shapes and colours.

kite 1

kite 2

kite 3

kite 4

? **How can you design and describe a kite?**

Part 1

A. For each of Shani's kites, describe the shape and express each color as a fraction.

B. Express each colour fraction as a decimal.

Part 2

C. Draw your own kite.

D. Describe your kite completely using words and numbers.

Task Checklist

☑ Did you include a diagram?

☑ Did you describe your kite using fractions and decimals?

☑ Did you use math language?

Probability

Goals

You will be able to

- **describe the probability of events using mathematical language**

- **compare the probability of events**

- **conduct probability experiments**

- **predict the probability of events**

- **solve probability problems using tree diagrams**

Spinning

Getting Started

What's Likely?

There is a storm warning. Our field trip to the beach will be cancelled tomorrow!

Even if it rains, they will never cancel the trip.

They'll cancel the trip if there's lightning. You can't go in the water if there's lightning!

? **How can you describe the probabilities of events?**

A. Who is likely to be right? Explain your thinking.

B. Who is likely to be wrong? Explain your thinking.

C. Describe the probability of each **event**.
Use a word from 1 of the cards below.
  a) I will have a sandwich for lunch tomorrow.
  b) The teacher will be away from school next week.
  c) The sun will rise in the morning.
  d) It will get darker when the sun sets.
  e) A dinosaur will walk into the classroom soon.
  f) Every day will be pizza day in school.
  g) There will be a full moon tonight.
  h) Tomorrow will come after today.
  i) It will rain on sports day.
  j) Our school volleyball team will be the champions.

| likely | unlikely | possible | impossible | certain |

Do You Remember?

1. a) Describe 2 events that are certain to happen at school this week.
   b) Describe 2 events that are impossible to have happen at school this week.
   c) Describe 2 events that are likely to happen at school this week.

2. Describe 2 other events that might happen at school. Which of the events is more likely to happen?

3. When you toss a coin, what 2 events are equally likely to happen?

1 Probability Lines

Goal Use a probability line to compare the probability of events.

? Where do Mandy's events go on the probability line?

Mandy's Events

I made a list of events in a chart.
I described the probability of each event.
I will probably phone Rey this week, so event A is likely.

Events		Probability
A	I will use the phone this week.	likely
B	I will go to the North Pole this year.	very unlikely
C	I will stay home or go away for summer vacation.	equally likely
D	I will go to school on Monday.	very likely
E	I will have a birthday this year.	certain
F	I will sit and run at the same time.	impossible
G	I will miss the bus after school.	unlikely

I can place each event on a **probability line** between impossible and certain. Event A is likely, so I put it closer to certain than impossible.

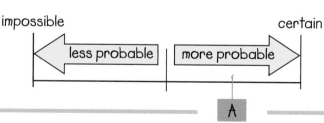

impossible   certain

less probable   more probable

A

A. Finish placing Mandy's events.

Reflecting

1. Explain your placement of each event.

2. a) Which events are closer to impossible than certain?

   b) Which events are closer to certain than impossible?

3. Look at 2 events that are beside each other. Discuss which event is more **probable**.

Checking

4. Use probability words to describe the probability of each event.
   a) I will have eggs for breakfast.
   b) I will be allowed to stay up late tonight.
   c) I will have a party this year.
   d) A tree will talk to me today.
   e) The teacher will give us homework today.
   f) I will go swimming this summer.

5. Draw a probability line. Label it with the letters of the events from Question 4.

Practising

6. a) Use these headlines or go through newspapers to find events with probability words. Write the events on strips of paper.

   b) Make a probability line with *impossible* at one end and *certain* at the other. Use chart paper. Glue the events on the probability line.

   c) Write your own headline and place it on the probability line.

City Council will probably support Olympic bid

Workers unlikely to approve deal

Possible rain showers on Friday

Movie likely to be a hit

Health bill pass is improbable

2 Experimenting with Spinners

Goal Make predictions and experiment with spinners with equal sections.

You will need
- spinners

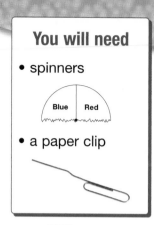

| Blue | Red |

- a paper clip

Jon got a board game
for his birthday.
The game has 2 spinners in it.
Spinning **red** wins a game.

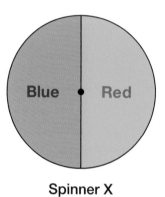

Blue · Red

Spinner X

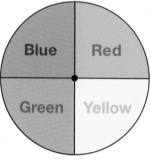

| Blue | Red |
| Green | Yellow |

Spinner Y

? **Which spinner should Jon choose?**

Jon's Experiment

I spun Spinner X 20 times.
I recorded the result of
each spin.
Then I made a tally chart.

B, R, B, B, B, R, B, R, R, R,
R, B, B, B, R, B, R, R, B, B

Red	Blue
~~HHH~~ IIII	~~HHH~~ ~~HHH~~ I

A. Jon says that **red** and **blue** are **equally probable** on Spinner X. Explain why he thinks so.

B. Spin Spinner Y 20 times.
Record the results in a tally chart.

C. Which spinner is more likely to spin **red**?
Give a reason for your answer.

Reflecting

1. Use probability words to describe the probability of spinning **green** with Spinner X.

2. Which spinner should Jon choose to win his game? Give a reason for your choice.

Checking

3. Use Spinner Z.
   a) Predict the number of times you will spin **red** in 20 spins on Spinner Z.
   b) Spin 20 times and record the results.
   c) Compare the results with your prediction.
   d) Compare the probabilities of spinning **red** and **blue**.
   e) Is spinning **red** more probable on Spinner X or Spinner Z? Give a reason for your answer.
   f) Is spinning **red** more probable on Spinner Y or Spinner Z? Give a reason for your answer.

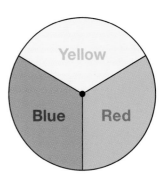

Spinner Z

Practising

4. a) Predict the number of times you will spin an even number in 20 spins on Spinner P.
   b) Spin 20 times and record the results. Compare the results with your prediction.

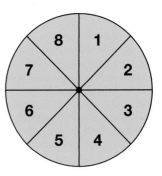

Spinner P

5. Use probability words to describe the probability of each spin on Spinner Q.
   a) spinning an even number
   b) spinning an odd number

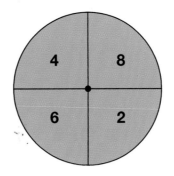

Spinner Q

3 Making Predictions

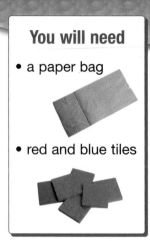
Goal Make predictions and design and carry out experiments.

Suppose you put 2 colours of tile in a paper bag.

? **What colour tile are you more likely to draw from the bag?**

Experiment 1

A. Put 5 **red** tiles and 5 **blue** tiles in a paper bag.

B. Predict the number of tiles of each colour you will pick in 20 draws.

C. Draw a tile from the paper bag. Record its colour in a tally chart like this. Replace the tile.

D. Repeat the experiment 20 times.

E. Compare the results to your prediction.

Prediction: _____ Red _____ Blue	
Red	**Blue**
Result: _____ Red _____ Blue	

Experiment 2

F. Sketch a bag that contains 10 tiles. Design the bag so that drawing a **blue** tile is more probable than drawing a **red** tile.

G. Explain your strategy for designing the bag.

H. Predict the result of 20 draws from your bag.

I. Put the tiles in the bag and draw from the bag 20 times. Replace the tile after each draw. Record your results in a tally chart.

J. Compare the results to your prediction.

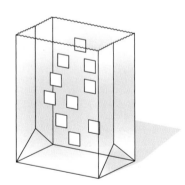

Reflecting

1. When you draw a tile from the bag, what is certain about its colour?

2. a) In which experiment is drawing a **blue** tile more probable than drawing a **red** tile?
   b) How are the probabilities related to the number of tiles of each colour in the bag?

3. Was it easy to predict the results of each experiment? Explain why or why not.

Predicting Tiles

You will need

- a paper bag
- red and blue tiles

Number of players: 2
How to play: Predict the colour of the tile you will draw.

Step 1 Put 7 **red** tiles and 3 **blue** tiles in a bag.

Step 2 Both players predict what colour tile will be drawn.

Step 3 Draw a tile from the bag.

Step 4 Score 1 point if the colour of the tile matches a prediction of **red**.
Score 2 points if the colour of the tile matches a prediction of **blue**.

Step 5 Replace the tile.

Play until a player has 10 points.

Mid-Chapter Review

LESSON

1

1. Draw a probability line and place these words along it.

   impossible   unlikely   likely
   certain   very likely

2. Use a probability word to describe each event.
   a) There will be a fire drill today.
   b) The next time I am in a car, I will wear a seat belt.
   c) A dog will come to school today.
   d) I will grow to be 3 m tall.

2

3. A board game has these 2 spinners.

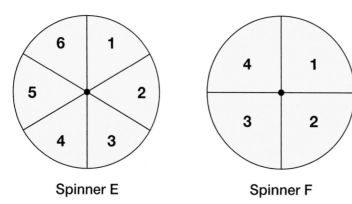

Spinner E   Spinner F

   a) Use probability words to describe the probability
      of spinning 2 on each spinner.
   b) Predict the number of times you would spin 2 in
      20 spins of each spinner. Explain your prediction.

3

4. Sketch a draw bag to match each description.
   Each bag should contain 10 tiles.
   a) Red will certainly be drawn.
   b) Black will never be drawn.
   c) 2 colours are equally likely to be drawn.
   d) 1 colour is more likely to be drawn than another
      colour.

Choose Your Spinner

Number of players: 2 to 4

How to play: Take turns spinning and moving your marker toward **Finish**.

Start	Green	Red	**Blue**	Green
Red	**Blue**	Green	Red	**Blue**
Green	Red	**Blue**	Green	Red
Blue	Green	Red	**Blue**	Green
Red	**Blue**	Green	Red	**Finish**

Step 1 All players begin by placing a marker on **Start**.

Step 2 Choose a spinner and spin it.

Step 3 Move to the next square only if you spin its colour. You can move vertically or horizontally, but not diagonally.

The first player to arrive at **Finish** wins.

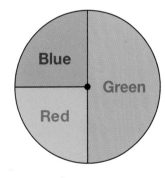

Spinner 1

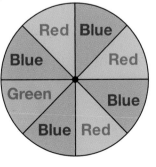

Spinner 2

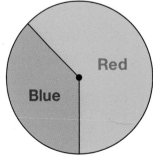

Spinner 3

4 Comparing Probabilities

Goal Make predictions and experiment with spinners with unequal sections.

You will need
- spinners

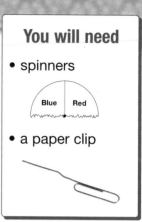

- a paper clip

Sarah can win a stuffed bear by spinning **blue** at a Playland booth.

? **How likely is it that Sarah will win with 1 spin?**

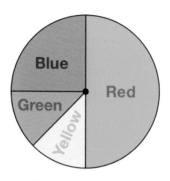

Playland Spinner

A. Predict the number of times you will spin **blue** in 40 spins on the Playland Spinner.

B. Spin 40 times. Record the results in a tally chart.

C. Compare the results with your prediction.

D. Is spinning **red** more probable than spinning **green**? Explain your thinking.

E. Is spinning **blue** more probable than spinning **green**? Explain your thinking.

F. What 2 spins are **equally probable**?

G. Place the colours (**R**, **Y**, **G**, **B**) on a probability line. Explain your placement of each colour.

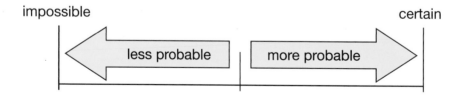

impossible   certain

less probable   more probable

Reflecting

1. When you are experimenting, why is it better to spin many times instead of spinning 1 time?

2. How likely is it that Sarah will win with 1 spin? Explain your thinking.

Checking

3. Sarah can also win a stuffed bear by spinning **blue** at a Funland booth.
   a) Make a probability line for spinning the Funland colours.
   b) Which spin is most probable?
   c) Which spins are equally probable?
   d) Which Playland colour is impossible to spin at Funland?
   e) Which spin is equally probable at both Playland and Funland?
   f) Should Sarah play the game at Playland or Funland? Explain your thinking.

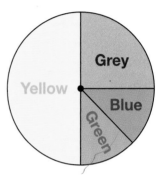

Funland Spinner

Practising

4. A game has 2 spinners, S and T. You get 1 spin. Explain your thinking for each question.
   a) Is spinning **green** more probable on Spinner S or Spinner T?
   b) On which spinner is **blue** more probable?
   c) Which colours on Spinner T are impossible to spin on Spinner S?
   d) Which colour is equally likely on Spinner S and Spinner T?

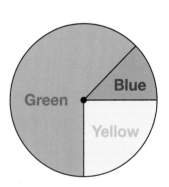

Spinner S

5. Make a probability line for Spinner S and for Spinner T. Place each colour on the line.

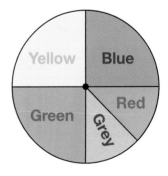

Spinner T

5 Creating Spinners

You will need
• spinners

• a paper clip

Goal Design spinners to meet given conditions and test the spinners.

? How can you design a spinner to match given probabilities?

Understand

The spinner should meet the conditions shown on 1 of the cards.

A. If 1 colour is more probable than another, what do you know about the sections?

Make a Plan

B. Choose 1 card.

C. How many colours should the spinner have? Decide on your colours.

D. Decide what size each colour section will be.

Carry Out the Plan

E. Create your spinner.

Look Back

F. Test your spinner by spinning it 20 times. Record the results in a tally chart.

G. Choose another card. Design and test another spinner.

2 colours
1 colour is more probable than the other.

3 colours
Blue is very likely.
Red is impossible.

3 colours
2 colours are equally probable. Another colour is less probable.

4 colours
All colours are equally probable.

Yellow is certain.

Reflecting

1. Could you have designed your spinners differently? Explain your thinking.

2. Can you design 1 spinner to match conditions on more than 1 card? If so, explain how.

NEL

Probability and Fractions

1 Fractions can be used to describe probability. If $\frac{1}{4}$ of a spinner is yellow, the probability of spinning yellow is $\frac{1}{4}$. Write a fraction for the probability of spinning each colour.

a) green   b) blue   c) red

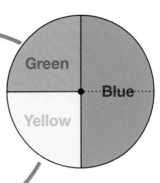

2 Sketch a spinner with a $\frac{1}{3}$ probability for spinning red, $\frac{1}{3}$ for yellow, and $\frac{1}{3}$ for blue.

3
a) Use a probability word to describe the probability of spinning red.
b) Use a number to describe the probability of spinning red.

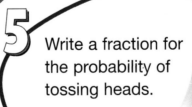
Red

4 Write a fraction for the probability of spinning each colour.

a) red   b) green   c) blue   d) yellow

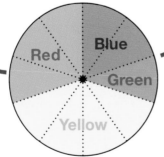

5 Write a fraction for the probability of tossing heads.

6 Solve Problems Using Tree Diagrams

Goal Use tree diagrams to find all possible combinations.

Calvin's class brought white bread and brown bread, turkey, tuna, and cheese to make sandwiches for a trip.

? How many types of sandwiches are possible?

Calvin's Tree Diagram

Understand
I assume that each sandwich is made with 1 type of bread and 1 filling.

Make a Plan
I will draw a **tree diagram** to find all the combinations of breads and fillings.

> **tree diagram**
> A way to record and count combinations of events

Carry Out the Plan
This is my diagram.

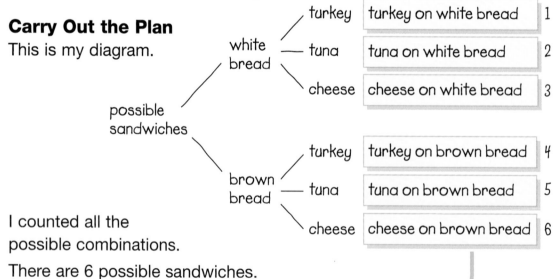

I counted all the possible combinations.

There are 6 possible sandwiches.

Reflecting

1. How did the tree diagram help Calvin solve the problem?

2. What kind of sorting do you have to do first before you draw the branches of a tree diagram?

3. Suppose Calvin ate one of the sandwiches. Is it more probable that he ate a sandwich on white bread, or a turkey sandwich on brown bread? Explain using the tree diagram.

Checking

4. The students brought muffins and icing.
   Muffins: carrot, banana
   Icing: cream cheese, chocolate, strawberry, vanilla
   a) Make a tree diagram to show all the possible combinations of muffins and icing.
   b) How many combinations are possible?
   c) A student eats a muffin with icing.
      Is it more probable that the muffin was
      • a banana muffin with any icing, or
      • a carrot muffin with cream cheese icing?
      Explain your answer.

Practising

5. The students brought chips and dips.
   Chips: corn, salted potato, plain potato
   Dips: salsa, sour cream, chick pea
   a) How many combinations are possible?
   b) A student dips and eats a chip.
      Is it more probable that the chip and dip were
      • a corn chip with salsa, or
      • any potato chip with sour cream?
      Explain your answer.

Spinning Decimals

1. **Blue** is 0.10 of this spinner.
   a) How can you tell that yellow is greater than 0.50?
   b) What is the sum of these 3 decimals?
   c) Estimate the decimals for yellow and red.

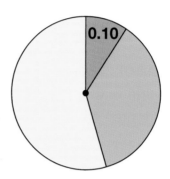

2. **Blue** is 0.50 of this spinner. Estimate the decimals for the other 2 colours.

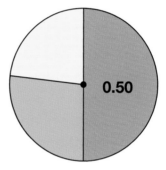

3. a) Trace this circle. Divide it into 3 or more parts.
   b) Estimate the decimal for each part of the circle.

Skills Bank

LESSON

1

1. **a)** Draw a probability line.
   Label it with the letters of these events.

   impossible   certain

   ⟵ less probable ⟶ | more probable ⟶

   A. Everyone who lives in Ottawa will ski this winter.
   B. I will eat something tomorrow.
   C. It will rain tomorrow.
   D. At least 1 teacher in Vancouver will give homework tonight.
   E. Most grade 4 students in Canada are in school today.

   b) Make up an event to match each probability word. Add the new events to the probability line from part a).
   F. very probable
   G. probable
   H. not probable

2

2. Predict the number of times you will spin a number greater than 5 in 20 spins.

   a)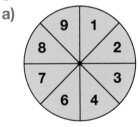

   b)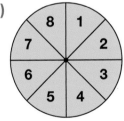

   c)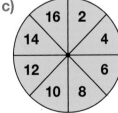

3. Use a probability word to describe the probability of each spin.
   a) a number less than 9
   b) a number less than 6
   c) 6
   d) a number greater than 9
   e) an even number

   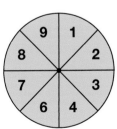

4. Predict the number of tiles of each colour you will get in 20 draws.

a)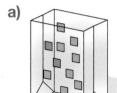

b)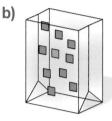

c)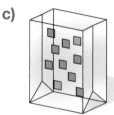

5. A game has 2 spinners, S and T.
Each player gets 1 spin.

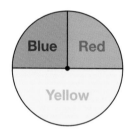

Spinner S

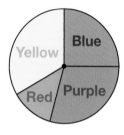

Spinner T

a) Is spinning **red** more probable on Spinner S or Spinner T?

b) On which spinner is yellow more probable?

c) Which colour on Spinner T is impossible to spin on Spinner S?

d) Make a probability line for each spinner. Place the colours (**R**, **B**, Y, **P**) on the line.

e) Which colour is equally likely on Spinner S and Spinner T?

6. Draw 4 spinners, one for each set of conditions.

a) On this spinner, **blue** is certain.

b) This spinner has 2 colours. 1 colour is less probable than the other.

c) This spinner has 3 colours. **Red**, **blue**, and **green** are equally probable.

d) This spinner has 3 colours. Yellow is impossible. **Red** is very likely. **Blue** is possible. **Green** is less likely than blue.

Problem Bank

3

1. Sketch a draw bag to match each description.
   a) The colour **green** is certain to be drawn.
   b) The colour **red** is impossible to draw.
   c) There are 3 colours. All 3 colours are equally likely to be drawn.

2. a) Is it possible to design a draw bag to satisfy all 3 descriptions in Question 1? Explain your thinking.
   b) Is it possible to design a draw bag to satisfy 2 of the descriptions in Question 1? Explain your thinking.

5

3. The planners of this year's school fun fair want to include a fish pond booth.
   The pond will have 40 fish in it.
   There will be 4 colours of fish.
   Design the pond so that 3 colours of fish are equally likely to be caught.
   The 4th colour of fish wins a big prize, and must be very unlikely.

6

4. In a 3-legged race, each team must have 1 boy and 1 girl.
   a) List all the possible teams.
   b) The names are put in 2 bags, 1 bag for boy names and 1 bag for girl names. A boy's name and a girl's name are drawn from the bags. Describe the probability that both names start with R.

Sign up for the 3-legged race!

Boys	Girls
Rob	Rose
Andrew	Emma
Ron	Mei-Fung
	Rebecca

Chapter Review

LESSON

1 1. Describe an event to match each probability.
   a) impossible   c) very likely
   b) unlikely   d) certain

2 2. A game has 2 spinners, G and H.

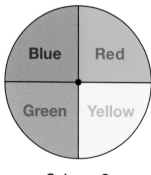

Spinner G

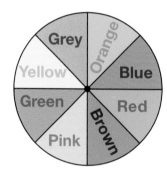

Spinner H

   a) Which colours are equally probable on Spinner G?
   b) Predict the number of times you will spin **red** in 20 spins of each spinner. Explain each prediction.
   c) If you want to spin **green**, which spinner would you choose? Explain your thinking.

3 3. A draw bag contains 7 **green** marbles and 3 **black** marbles.
   a) Is it more probable to draw a **black** marble or a **green** marble from the bag? Explain how you know.
   b) Use probability words to describe the probability of drawing a **green** marble from the bag.

   4. a) Sketch a draw bag with 2 colours of tile. It should be more probable to draw 1 colour from the bag than the other colour.
   b) Explain why there is more than 1 way to colour the tiles.

5. A game booth has 2 spinners, O and P.

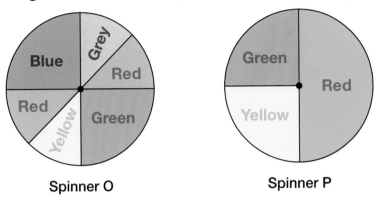

Spinner O   Spinner P

a) On which spinner is spinning **red** more probable?
b) Make a probability line for each spinner.
   Label each line with the colours of each spinner.
c) The owner of the game booth wants players
   to have the same probability of winning no
   matter which spinner they choose.
   What should be the winning colour?

6. Design a spinner to match each description.
   a) There are 3 numbers.
      All the numbers are equally probable.
   b) There are 2 colours. Spinning 1 colour is more
      probable than spinning the other colour.
   c) There are 3 colours. **Red** and **black** are equally
      probable. **Blue** is less probable.

7. Vanessa is making sundaes at her party.
   Ice cream: vanilla, chocolate
   Toppings: strawberry, pineapple, chocolate, caramel
   a) Make a tree diagram of the sundaes that can be
      made with 1 type of ice cream and 1 topping.
   b) Vanessa gives you the sundae she has just made.
      Which is more probable:
      • the sundae has chocolate ice cream and
        chocolate topping, or
      • the sundae has vanilla ice cream and
        fruit topping?

Chapter Task

Probability Prizes

Paulette wants to design a spinner
for her booth at the fun fair.

Paulette's Prizes

I want visitors to my booth to
win the prize that they spin.

I drew this probability line to
show how the prizes will be won.

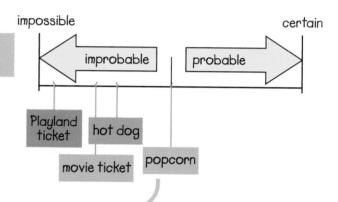

? **What spinner would you design for the booth?**

Understand

A. Which is more likely, a hot dog or a movie ticket?

Make a Plan

B. How many different sections does the spinner need?
Which section should be the biggest?

Carry Out the Plan

C. Gather the materials and make the spinner.

D. Make a prediction. If you spin 40 times, how many
times will each prize be won?

E. Conduct the experiment.
Compare the results with your prediction.

Look Back

F. Explain how your spinner shows the probabilities
on Paulette's probability line.

Task Checklist

☑ Did you include
diagrams?

☑ Did you include
the data from your
experiment?

☑ Did you explain
your thinking?

☑ Did you use
math language?

CHAPTER 14

Patterns and Motion in Geometry

Goals

You will be able to

- **extend, create, and describe geometric patterns**

- **use and describe translations, rotations, and reflections**

- **solve pattern problems using geometric transformations**

A star blanket

Getting Started

Identifying Geometric Patterns

❓ What patterns do you see in the belts?

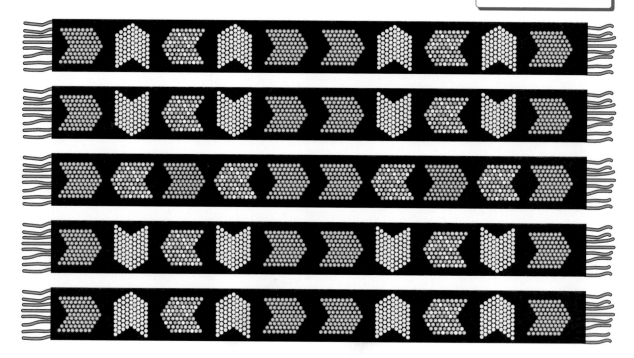

A. Describe each belt pattern.

B. Which patterns are based on the changing **attribute** of colour?

C. Which patterns are based on the changing attribute of direction?

D. Which patterns are based on a combination of changing attributes? Explain your answer.

E. Make different patterns in rows, columns, and diagonals. Use large grid paper and trapezoid pattern blocks.

F. Challenge a partner to describe as many patterns in your grid as possible.

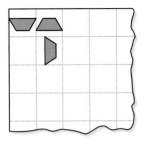

Do You Remember?

1. a) Which shapes show a slide?
   b) Which shapes show a flip?

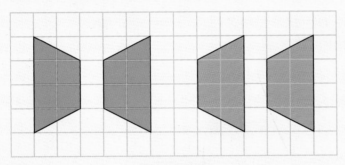

2. Copy the red triangle onto grid paper.
   a) Show a half turn about the dot.
   b) Show a quarter turn counterclockwise.

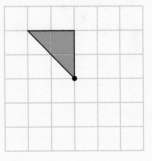

3. Sketch the next 3 shapes in this growing pattern. Describe the pattern.

1 Coordinate Grids

Goal Identify and describe locations on a grid.

? How can you locate spaces on a grid?

Manitok's Grid

I got this grid for playing BINGO.
To get BINGO, I have to cover 5 squares to complete a row, a column, or a diagonal.

The green counter is under the G and it covers the number 2. Its **coordinates** are G2.

coordinates
Numbers or letters that describe the location of a space on a grid

A. Name the coordinates of the other counters on Manitok's grid.

B. What are the coordinates of the FREE square?

C. What coordinates could be covered to get BINGO on Manitok's grid?

This grid shows another way to label coordinates. The red counter is at C4.

D. Name the coordinates of the other counters.

E. What coordinates would complete the diagonal?

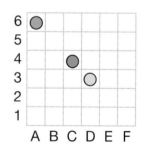

Reflecting

1. Can the same coordinates describe 2 different spaces on a grid? Explain your answer.

Checking

2. The coordinates G4, O5, B2, I3, N4, and G1 have been called. Would these coordinates make BINGO on Manitok's grid? Explain your answer.

B	I	N	G	O
5	5	5	5	5
4	4	4	4	4
3	3	FREE	3	3
2	2	2	2	2
1	1	1	1	1

3. Suppose B2, E2, D2, and A2 are covered. What other spaces could be covered to complete a row on the coordinate grid? Show your work.

Practising

4. a) What are the coordinates of the red counters on this BINGO card?
   b) What coordinates could be called to get BINGO in a row?
   c) What coordinates could be called to get BINGO in a column?

5. In this game, each rectangle covers 3 spaces on a coordinate grid.
   Players take turns guessing the coordinates of the other player's rectangles.
   The shaded spaces show correct guesses that have already been made. What coordinates would you guess to complete the rectangles?

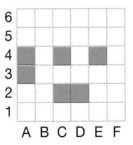

6. Use a 6 by 6 coordinate grid like the one in Question 3. Write the coordinates of 4 spaces that would make a square on this grid.

2 Translating Shapes

Goal Use and describe translations.

❓ How many squares can you cover in the translation game?

Number of players: 2
How to play: Use **translations** to place shapes on empty squares.

Step 1 Each player chooses a shape.

Step 2 Roll 1 die. Use the number to make a translation by moving up, down, left, or right from Start (D4). You can change direction once in each turn. Place your shape on the grid. Describe your translation.

Step 3 The other player takes a turn.

Step 4 On your next turn, make a translation counting from the position of your last shape. If the space you land on is empty, put a new shape on it. Otherwise, lose your turn.

The game is over when neither player can move to cover squares on the grid.

You will need

- a coordinate grid

- pattern blocks

- a die

translation
The result of a slide. The slide must be along straight lines (left or right, up or down).

Miki's Next Turn

I rolled a 4. I went 3 right and 1 down. I put a new trapezoid on E2.

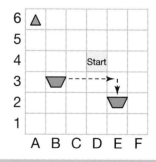

Chantal's Turn

Miki went first. She placed her trapezoid on B3. I rolled a 5. I placed my triangle 3 left and 2 up from Start.

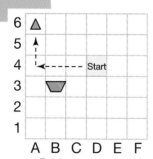

A. What did Miki roll on her 1st turn? Explain your thinking.

B. Finish the translation game.
How many squares did both players cover?

Reflecting

1. A right/left and up/down rule is normally used to describe translations.
   Is that true for the green trapezoids?

2. Is the red trapezoid on D2 a translation of the red trapezoid on B4? Explain your answer.

3. a) If you translated the trapezoid on B4 1 left and 3 down, where would you be?
   b) Describe a single translation that takes the green trapezoid on A5 to the same place as the translation in part a).

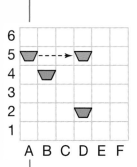

Checking

4. a) Translate the trapezoid on B2 2 right and 3 up. Name the new coordinates.
   b) What translation would move the red trapezoid onto the blue trapezoid?

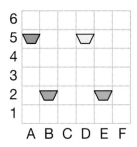

Practising

5. Name the coordinates at the end of each translation.
   a) The triangle on E5 moves 4 left and 2 down.
   b) The triangle on C2 moves 1 left and 3 up.
   c) The triangle on C2 moves 1 right and 3 up.

6. Name a translation for moving from C2 to E5.

7. Draw 3 translations in different directions on a 6 by 6 coordinate grid. Describe your translations.

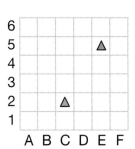

3 Rotating Shapes

You will need

- dot paper
- a protractor

- a triangle cutout

Goal Use and describe rotations.

? How can you describe a **rotation** of a shape?

Pedro's Rotations

I wanted to find out how the dark green triangles of this quilt design are related.

I cut out a triangle to match the quilt design and put it on dot paper.
Then I rotated the triangle about point O.
Point O is the **centre of rotation**.

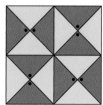

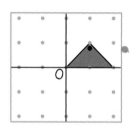

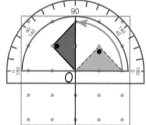

rotation
The result of a turn. The turn must keep each point in a shape the same distance from the **centre of rotation**.

The angle of rotation of the triangle was 90°.
The triangle was rotated **counterclockwise** (CCW).

I can see other rotations in the quilt.

180° counterclockwise (CCW) about point P

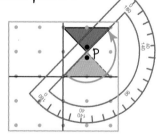

90° clockwise (CW) about point Q

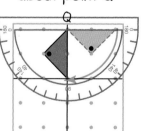

180° clockwise about point R

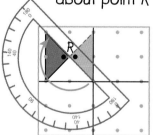

Reflecting

1. What 3 attributes do you need to describe a rotation?

2. a) How are translations and rotations different?
   b) How are translations and rotations the same?

Checking

3. Show each rotation of the red triangle on dot paper.
   a) 90° CW about point O
   b) 90° CCW about point B
   c) 90° CCW about point X
   d) 180° CW about point O
   e) 180° CCW about point O

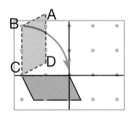

4. Which rotations in Question 3 have the same result?

Practising

5. A parallelogram was rotated as shown. Describe the angle, centre, and direction of each rotation.

a)
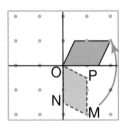

b)
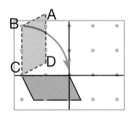

6. a) Draw the Windmill quilt square design on dot paper.
   b) Describe the rotations in the design.

7. Make your own quilt design using rotations on dot paper.
   Label the centres of rotation in your design.
   Label the angles of rotation in your design.

Windmill quilt square

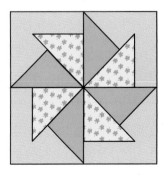

4 Reflecting Shapes

Goal Use and describe reflections.

Allison's Reflection

Chris placed half a symmetrical design on pattern block grid paper. I want to know what the whole design looks like.

I can find out by looking at a **reflection** of the design in a transparent mirror.

I place the pattern blocks on the reflection.

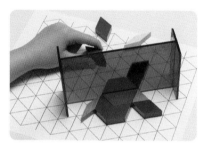

? How can you reflect designs?

A. Place pattern blocks on pattern block grid paper like Chris did.

B. Place a mirror along the edge of the design so that you can see the reflection of the design.

C. Place pattern blocks on the other side of the mirror to show the reflection.

D. Remove the mirror. Draw the line of reflection where the mirror was.

E. Remove the pattern blocks one at a time. Draw and colour the whole design.

reflection
The result of a flip of a 2-D shape. Each point is flipped to the opposite side of a line, but stays the same distance from the line.

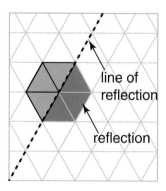

line of reflection

reflection

Reflecting

1. a) How does a 2-D shape change when it is reflected?
   b) What stays the same? Explain your answer.

2. a) How are reflections and rotations different?
   b) How are reflections and rotations the same?

Checking

3. Copy this design onto pattern block grid paper. Draw the reflection of the pattern blocks and the line of reflection.

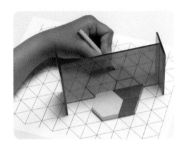

Practising

4. Copy each shape and line of reflection. Draw the reflection of each shape.

   a)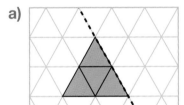

   b)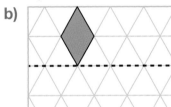

5. a) Copy this design onto pattern block grid paper. Show where to place a transparent mirror on a line of reflection to make a butterfly shape.
   b) Show where to place the mirror on a line of reflection to make a boomerang shape.
   c) Show where to place the mirror on a line of reflection to make a hexagon.

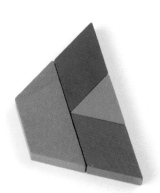

6. a) Create your own design using reflections of a set of pattern blocks. Use pattern block grid paper. Show the reflection lines.
   b) Create a problem about your design. Show how to solve your problem.

Mid-Chapter Review

LESSON

1 1. In this game, each rectangle covers 3 spaces. Terry has shaded parts of 2 rectangles on the grid.

   a) Give possible coordinates for the missing parts of Terry's rectangles.

   b) Natalie has selected the coordinates B5, D3, and E4. Has she completed any of Terry's rectangles? Explain your answer.

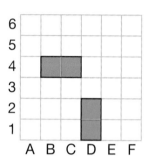

2 2. a) Name the translation that puts the blue triangle on D2.

   b) The yellow triangle was translated 3 right and 4 up. Where was the yellow triangle before the translation?

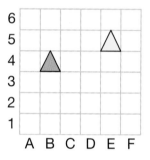

3 3. Copy each shape onto a grid and rotate it 90° CCW about the point. Draw the rotation. Label the angle of rotation.

a)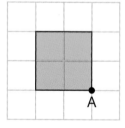

b)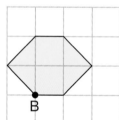

c)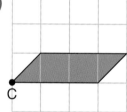

4 4. Draw a reflection of each shape. Show the line of reflection.

a)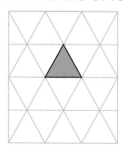

b)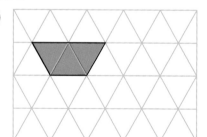

c)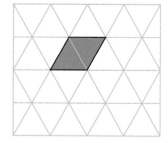

Grid Hide and Seek

Number of players: 2

How to play: Players guess the coordinates of another player's counters on a grid.

Step 1 Each player gets 1 coordinate grid and 3 counters. Set up a divider so the other player cannot see your grid.

Step 2 Place 3 counters on the spaces of your grid.

Step 3 Take turns guessing the coordinates of the other player's counters.
If a guess is correct, say "Found."
If a guess is incorrect, say "Keep looking."
If a guess is 1 space away from a counter, say "Very close."

Continue playing until a player guesses all of the other player's coordinates.

You will need

- counters

- a coordinate grid

- a divider

5 Communicate About Transformations

Goal Describe translations, rotations, and reflections.

Carmen wrote instructions for making a
Yankee Puzzle quilt block.
She read her instructions to Rey.

Yankee Puzzle quilt block

? How can Carmen improve her instructions?

Carmen's Instructions

Start with a grid that has 4 squares.

Cut out a triangle that is half the area of
a square. Trace around the triangle to
make the design.

Step 1 Put the triangle in the
bottom right square.

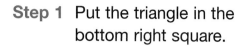

Step 2 Rotate the triangle 90°
about the point that is
in the centre of the square.

Rey's Results

Step 3 Translate the triangle
1 space up.

Step 4 Reflect the triangle across
the vertical line between
the top 2 squares.

I'm not sure what
to do next.

If I translate my
triangle 1 space up
in Step 3, it will end
up outside the grid.

Step 5 Repeat to make 4 squares.
Put them together to make
the whole design.

NEL

A. Identify some of the strengths of Carmen's instructions. Use the Communication Checklist.

B. Why did Rey have trouble after Step 2? What other parts of Carmen's instructions were unclear?

Communication Checklist
☑ Did you show all the steps?
☑ Did you put the steps in order?
☑ Did you show the right amount of detail?
☑ Did you include diagrams?
☑ Did you use math language?

Reflecting

1. Why is each of these items important when giving instructions?
   a) the order of the steps
   b) details about what happens in each step
   c) the use of mathematical language

2. Why is it a good idea to read your instructions to someone else to test?

Checking

3. Rewrite each instruction using the Communication Checklist.
   a) To get to shape B, move shape A right 5 spaces.
   b) To get to shape C, reflect shape A then move it 3 down.

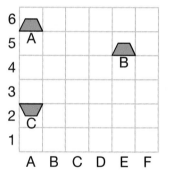

Practising

4. a) Write instructions for making this quilt block. Have someone test your instructions.

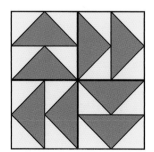

   b) Identify the strengths of your instructions.
   c) How could you improve your instructions?

6 Transformation Patterns

You will need

- computer drawing software

or
- a ruler

- pencil crayons

Goal Make patterns using transformations.

Mandy's Transformation Pattern

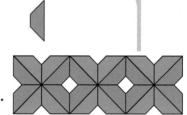

I used a computer to draw and colour a trapezoid.

Then I made this pattern using translations, reflections, and rotations.

I tried to make the pattern using the fewest steps.

? **What steps did Mandy take to make her pattern?**

Understand
A. How does Mandy's pattern repeat?

Make a Plan
B. Examine a trapezoid. How could you use reflections, translations, or rotations to match the trapezoids in Mandy's pattern?

Carry Out the Plan
C. Make Mandy's pattern on a computer. Show each step.

Reflecting

1. Are there different ways to create Mandy's pattern? Explain your answer.

2. Create your own trapezoid pattern. Explain how to make your pattern using the fewest steps.

Predicting Rotations

Picture this triangle rolling along a line to the right.

Sarah's Rotation

Point C is the centre of rotation, so it will stay in the same place. Point B will rotate clockwise and point A will follow point B.

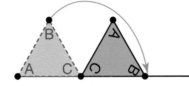

A. Imagine rolling the triangle to the right again. Describe the positions of points A and C.

B. Check by turning and drawing the triangle.

C. Predict what the triangle would look like after rolling 3 times to the right. Check by turning and drawing the triangle.

Try These

1. Predict what the square would look like after rolling 3 times to the right. Check your prediction with a drawing.

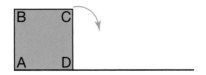

2. Draw and label the corners of a shape. Create a problem about rolling your shape. Give your problem to another student to solve.

7 Extending Transformation Patterns

You will need
• grid paper
• pencil crayons

 Goal Extend geometric patterns.

When you combine quilt blocks, the rows make geometric patterns.

❓ **What geometric patterns can you find in a quilt?**

Jon's Pattern

I copied the Flying Birds quilt block on a grid to make a pattern.

Flying Birds quilt block

row 1⟶
row 2⟶
row 3⟶

A. Extend Jon's pattern 3 more times to the right.

B. List the attributes of the pattern in each row.

C. Write a pattern rule for each row.

Reflecting

1. Compare your pattern rule with a classmate's rule.

2. Describe the strategy you used to write your pattern rule.

Checking

End of the Day quilt block

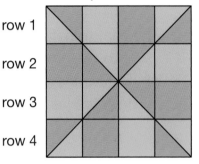

3. a) Copy the End of the Day quilt block onto a grid 3 times.
   b) Choose 1 row and describe a pattern in the row.
   c) List the attributes of the pattern.
   d) Write the pattern rule for the row. Justify your answer.

row 1

row 2

row 3

row 4

Practising

4. Choose 2 rows from this design.
   a) For each row, copy the geometric pattern onto grid paper.
   b) Extend each row to the right for 2 repetitions.
   c) Write the pattern rule for each row.

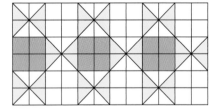

5. a) Write a rule to make a pattern with this triangle. Use 1 reflection, 1 rotation, and 1 translation in your rule.

   b) Use your rule to extend the pattern.

6. a) Create your own quilt block that has at least 2 geometric patterns in it. Use grid paper.
   b) Write a pattern rule for each geometric pattern.

Skills Bank

1 1. What are the coordinates of each trapezoid?
   a) green   b) yellow   c) red   d) blue

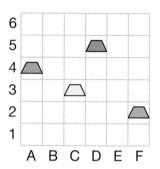

2. a) Translate the yellow trapezoid 2 left and 2 down.
      Name the new coordinates.
   b) What translation would move the red trapezoid
      onto the blue trapezoid?
   c) What translation would move the blue trapezoid
      onto the green trapezoid?
   d) What translation would move the green trapezoid
      onto the yellow trapezoid?

3. Use a 6 by 6 coordinate grid.
   Draw a red trapezoid on C4.
   Translate the red trapezoid 2 right and 3 down.
   Colour it green.
   Translate the green trapezoid 4 left and 5 up.
   Colour it blue.

3 4. Show each rotation of the
      triangle on dot paper.
   a) 90° CW about point E
   b) 90° CW about point F
   c) 90° CCW about point F
   d) 180° CW about point E

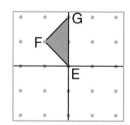

5. Describe the angle, centre, and direction of
   each rotation.
   a)

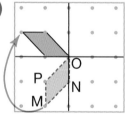

   b)

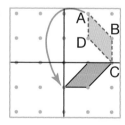

4

6. Copy each shape and line of reflection.
Draw the reflection of each shape.
Use a transparent mirror.

a)
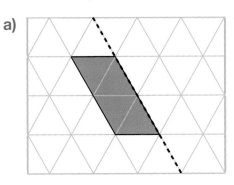

c)
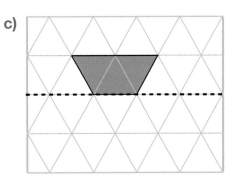

b)
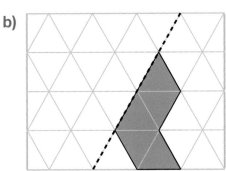

d)
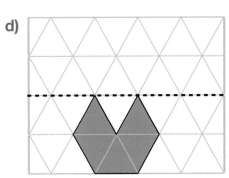

7

7. Choose a row from this design.
   a) Copy the geometric pattern on grid paper.
   b) Extend it to the right for 2 repetitions.
   c) Write the pattern rule.

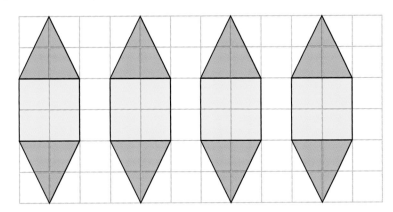

8. Repeat Question 7 for another row.
Choose a row with orange shapes.

Problem Bank

LESSON

2 1. Use this map of New Brunswick to answer the questions.
   a) What are the coordinates for Saint John?
   b) What are the coordinates for Fredericton?
   c) Which town has the coordinates B7?
   d) A plane flies from Bathurst to Moncton.
      Describe this translation.

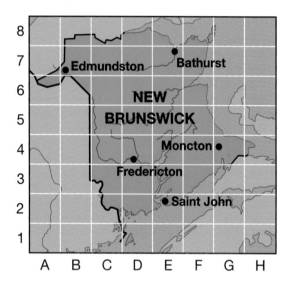

2. Brad can walk from his home to school in
   2 different ways.
   a) Describe the translations for each walking path.
   b) Which path is shorter? Explain your answer.

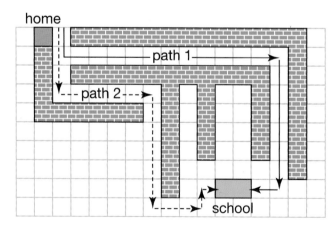

3. Describe the transformations needed to put each piece into the puzzle. Explain your answer.

a)

b)

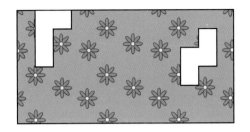

4. Move the red triangle to the position of the green triangle.
   • You can use translations up, down, left, or right.
   • You can use rotations about points A, B, and C.
   • You can use reflections in any line of the grid.
   • You must move around the obstacles.
   a) Describe the transformation you used.
   b) Justify your description using a labelled drawing.

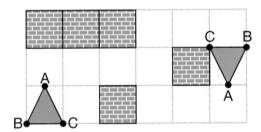

5. The Star Blanket design can be described using geometric transformations. Describe or show a place where you see each transformation in the blanket.
   a) translation
   b) rotation
   c) reflection

Star Blanket

6. a) Copy 1 row or column pattern from the Star Blanket onto grid paper.
   b) Describe the attributes of the pattern.
   c) Write the pattern rule. Justify your answer.

Chapter Review

LESSON

1. a) What are the coordinates of the counters on this grid?

   b) Where would you put new counters to complete a row? Name the coordinates.

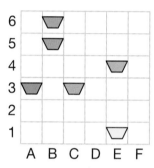

2. a) What translation will move the red trapezoid onto D3?

   b) The yellow trapezoid was moved from A1. Name the translation.

   c) Which trapezoid will be at C1 if it is translated 2 right and 2 down? Explain your answer.

3. Describe 2 rotations in this figure. Name the centre, direction, and size of each rotation.

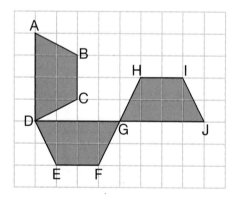

4. This design was made using reflections of hexagon A. Explain how reflections of hexagon A can create each of the other hexagons. Use a transparent mirror and a drawing.

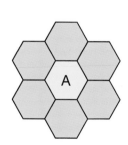

5.

Rami's Puzzle

Did I use a reflection or a translation to move the rectangle?

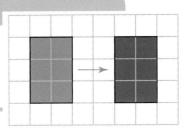

a) Can you be sure whether Rami used a reflection or a translation?
Explain your thinking using a diagram.

b) Draw another shape that looks the same whether it is translated or reflected. Show a translation and a reflection of your shape using a labelled diagram.

c) Draw a rotation of a rectangle that could have been a translation or a reflection of the shape. Show the rotation, the translation, and the reflection in separate labelled diagrams.

6. Improve each description if necessary. If the description does not need improvement, write "OK as is."

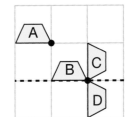

a) To get to shape B, shape A moved 1 right.

b) To get to shape C, shape B rotated 90°.

c) To get to shape D, shape C was reflected in the heavy horizontal line.

7. This design can be used to make patterns. Write a pattern rule for each pattern.

a)

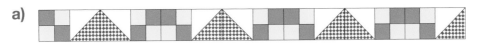

b)

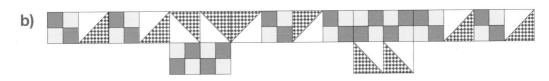

8. Draw the next shape in each pattern in Question 6.

Chapter Task

Making a Math Quilt

Quilts are a way to tell stories about ideas and events. The colours, materials, and patterns in a quilt show story ideas.

? **How can you create a math story quilt?**

A. Decide what math story you want to tell.

B. Make the quilt sections using grid paper. Show your steps.

C. Describe the patterns in your quilt.

D. Explain the math in your story quilt.

Task Checklist
☑ Did you show the right amount of detail?
☑ Did you explain your thinking?
☑ Did you include diagrams?
☑ Did you use math language?

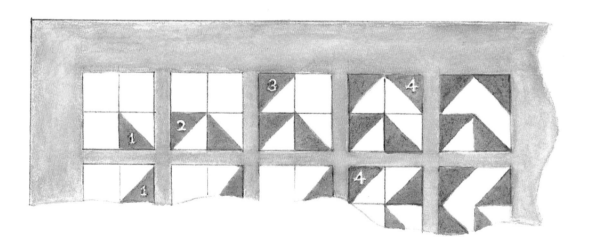

Cumulative Review

Cross-Strand Multiple Choice

1. Which pictures could you use to compare $1\frac{4}{6}$ with $\frac{9}{6}$?

   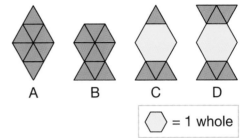

   A. D and C
   B. C and B
   C. B and D
   D. C and A

2. Which decimal set is in order from greatest to least?

   E. 0.22, 0.2, 0.21, 0.02, 0.12   G. 0.02, 0.22, 0.2, 0.21, 0.12
   F. 0.02, 0.12, 0.2, 0.21, 0.22   H. 0.22, 0.21, 0.2, 0.12, 0.02

3. Jon spun 20 times and got the results in the chart. Which spinner did he likely use?

    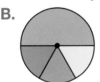 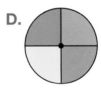

Section	Spins
blue	3
red	10
yellow	3
green	4

4. How many possible combinations are there for 1 pancake and 1 syrup flavour?
   Pancakes: plain, blueberry
   Syrup: maple, raspberry, blueberry

   E. 6   F. 5   G. 9   H. 2

5. Which red squares are not covered by white counters?

   A. B1, B4, D3   C. B1, C5, D3
   B. B1, C5, D2   D. B1, B4, D2

   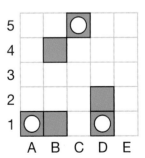

6. What shape should come next in this pattern?

   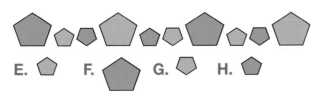

   E.   F.   G.   H.

Cross-Strand Investigation

A Butterfly Conservatory

The number of giant owl butterflies at a conservatory is the same as the number of blue morpho butterflies. There are half as many monarch butterflies.

You want to find out if visitors are more likely to see a monarch butterfly first or a blue morpho butterfly.

You will use an experiment to find out.

giant owl butterfly

blue morpho butterfly

monarch butterfly

7. a) Create a spinner with sections for each kind of butterfly. The sections should correctly describe how likely it is to see each kind of butterfly.

   b) Get ready to spin. First, predict what you will discover. Then spin 20 times and record the results. Compare the results with your prediction.

   c) Pose a different problem about comparing 2 spinner sections. Predict the solution and then spin 20 times. What happened?

This stone tile walkway is incomplete.

8. a) Copy the diagram onto a grid with 5 columns of 20 squares. Reflect the 2 left columns across the yellow area to fill in the empty columns.

   b) Describe 1 example of a translation and 1 example of a rotation from the diagram. Use mathematical words and label your diagram.

   c) Your diagram has 5 columns of 20 squares or 100 squares in all. Write a fraction and a decimal to describe each part.

   i) number of dark brown stones

   ii) number of grey stones

   iii) total number of light brown and dark brown stones

   iv) difference between the number of light brown and dark brown stones

Butterfly Exhibit

Glossary

Instructional Words

calculate: Figure out the number that answers a question; compute

clarify: Make a statement easier to understand; provide an example

classify: Put things into groups according to a rule and label the groups; organize into categories

compare: Look at 2 or more objects or numbers and identify how they are the same and how they are different (e.g., Compare the numbers 6.5 and 5.6. Compare the size of the students' feet. Compare 2 shapes.)

construct: Make or build a model; draw an accurate geometric shape (e.g., Use a ruler and a protractor to construct an angle.)

create: Make your own example

describe: Tell, draw, or write about what something is or what something looks like; tell about a process in a step-by-step way

draw: 1. Show something in picture form (e.g., Draw a diagram.)
2. Pull or select an object (e.g., Draw a card from the deck. Draw a tile from the bag.)

estimate: Use your knowledge to make a sensible decision about an amount; make a reasonable guess (e.g., Estimate how long it takes to cycle from your home to school. Estimate how many leaves are on a tree. What is your estimate of 3210 + 789?)

evaluate: Determine if something makes sense; judge

explain: Tell what you did; show your mathematical thinking at every stage; show how you know

explore: Investigate a problem by questioning, brainstorming, and trying new ideas

extend: 1. In patterning, continue the pattern
2. In problem solving, create a new problem that takes the idea of the original problem farther

justify: Give convincing reasons for a prediction, an estimate, or a solution; tell why you think your answer is correct

list: Record thoughts or things one under the other

measure: Use a tool to describe an object or determine an amount (e.g., Use a ruler to measure the height or distance around something. Use a protractor to measure an angle. Use balance scales to measure mass. Use a measuring cup to measure capacity. Use a stopwatch to measure the time in seconds or minutes.)

model: Show an idea using objects and/or pictures (e.g., Model a number using base ten blocks.)

predict: Use what you know to work out what is going to happen (e.g., Predict the next number in the pattern 1, 2, 4, 8, ….)

reason: Develop ideas and relate them to the purpose of the task and to each other; analyze relevant information to show understanding

record: Set down work in writing or pictures

relate: Show a connection between objects, drawings, ideas, or numbers

represent: Show information or an idea in a different way that makes it easier to understand (e.g., Draw a graph. Make a model. Create a rhyme.)

show (your work): Record all calculations, drawings, numbers, words, or symbols that make up the solution

sketch: Make a rough drawing (e.g., Sketch a picture of the field with dimensions.)

solve: Develop and carry out a process for finding a solution to a problem

sort: Separate a set of objects, drawings, ideas, or numbers according to an attribute (e.g., Sort 2-D shapes by the number of sides.)

validate: Check an idea by showing that it works

verify: Work out an answer or solution again, usually in another way, to show that the original answer is correct; show evidence of

visualize: Form a picture in your mind of what something is like; imagine

Glossary

Mathematical Words

 A

addend: A number that is added to another number

algorithm: A series of steps you can use to carry out a procedure (e.g., add, subtract, multiply, or divide)

analog clock: A clock that measures time using rotating hands

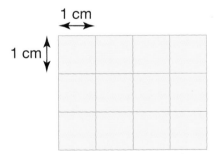

angle: An amount of turn measured in **degrees**

area: The number of square units needed to cover a surface

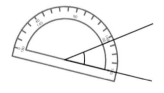

area = 12 square centimetres

array: A rectangular arrangement of items or pictures in **rows** and **columns** (e.g., An array can show why 2 × 3 and 3 × 2 have the same product.)

 This array shows 2 rows of 3 or 2 × 3.
It also shows 3 columns of 2 or 3 × 2.
In both cases, the product is 6.

attribute: A characteristic or quality, usually of a pattern or geometric shape (e.g., Some common attributes of shapes are size, colour, texture, and number of edges.)

axis (plural is **axes**): A horizontal or vertical line in a graph, labelled with words or numbers to show what the bars or pictures in the graph mean

B

bar graph: A way to show data that uses horizontal or vertical bars

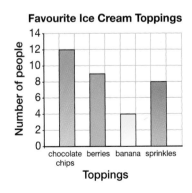

base: 1. In a 3-D shape, the **face** on which it is resting

2. In a prism, the face that determines the number of edges

3. In a 2-D shape, the **line segment** at the bottom

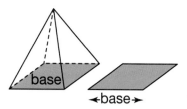

base ten blocks: Blocks that represent numbers as ones, tens, hundreds, and thousands

Thousands	Hundreds	Tens	Ones
2	3	5	4

capacity: The amount, in mL or L, that a container can hold

centimetre (cm): A unit of measurement for **length**; one hundredth of a metre (e.g., A fingertip is about 1 cm wide.) 1 cm = 10 mm, 100 cm = 1 m

centre of rotation: the point that a shape rotates around (e.g., point O is the centre of rotation for the triangle)

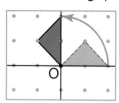

century: A unit of measurement for time; 100 years

certain outcome: A result that will always occur (e.g., If you roll a die with a 3 on every face, rolling a 3 is a certain outcome.)

circle graph: A way to show data that uses parts of a circle to represent parts of the set of data (e.g., A circle graph can be used to show how students spend their days.)

My Day

closed: A shape that has no **endpoints** (e.g., A square is a closed shape.)

column: A set of items lined up vertically (See also **row**.)

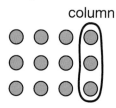

concave: Curved or pointed inward (e.g., A concave **polygon** has 1 **vertex** that points inward.)

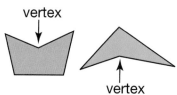

congruent: Identical in size and shape

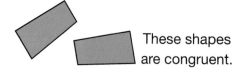

These shapes are congruent.

convex: Curved or pointed outward (e.g., A convex **polygon** has all of its **vertices** pointing outward.)

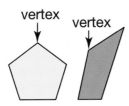

vertex   vertex

coordinates: A way of describing the location of spaces or objects (e.g., The counter is on C4.)

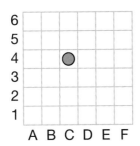

cube: A 3-D shape with 6 **congruent** square faces

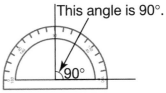

data: Information gathered in a survey, in an experiment, or by observing (e.g., Data can be in words like a list of students' names, in numbers like quiz marks, or in pictures like drawings of favourite pets.)

decade: A unit of measurement for time; 10 years

decimal: A way of writing a **fraction** or **mixed number** when the **denominator** is 10, 100, 1000, …

decimal point: A dot used to separate the whole number part from the fractional part in a decimal

decimetre (dm): A unit of measurement for **length**; one tenth of a **metre** (e.g., A tens rod from a set of **base ten blocks** is 1 dm long.); 1 dm = 10 cm, 10 dm = 1 m

degree (°): A unit of measurement for angle size

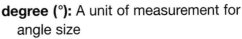

This angle is 90°.

90°

degree Celsius (°C): A unit of measurement for temperature (e.g., Water freezes at 0°C and boils at 100°C.)

denominator: The number in a fraction that tells how many are in the whole set, or how many parts the whole or set has been divided into. (See also **numerator**.) (e.g., In $\frac{3}{4}$ the fractional unit is fourths.)

$$\frac{3}{4} \longleftarrow \text{denominator}$$

diagonal: In a 2-D shape, a diagonal can join any 2 **vertices** that are not next to each other. In a 3-D shape, a diagonal can join any 2 vertices that are not on the same **face**.

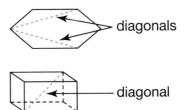

diagonals

diagonal

difference: The result when you subtract; the amount by which one number is greater than or less than another number

$$\begin{array}{r} 93 \\ -45 \\ \hline 48 \end{array} \longleftarrow \text{difference}$$

dimension: A way to describe how an object can be measured (e.g., A line has only length, so it is 1-dimensional. Area is 2-dimensional (2-D). Volume is 3-dimensional (3-D).)

dividend: The number that is divided into equal parts in a division operation

$$9 \div 3 = 3$$

dividend

divisible: Can be divided with no remainder (e.g., 30 is divisible by 6 because you can make exactly 5 groups of 6 from 30.)

divisor: The number you divide by in a division operation

$$24 \div 3 = 8$$

divisor

double: To multiply a number by 2

 E

edge: The **line segment** formed where 2 **faces** meet on a 3-D shape

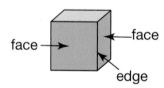

face → ← face

edge

endpoint: The point at which a **line segment** begins or ends

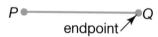

P •————————• Q

endpoint

equally likely outcomes: Results that have an equal chance of occurring (e.g., In flipping a coin, heads and tails are equally likely outcomes.)

equation: A number sentence in which the left side is equal to the right side (e.g., $4 + 2 = 6$, $5 + 3 = 4 + 4$)

estimate: A reasoned guess about a measurement or answer

even number: A number that is **divisible** by 2 (e.g., 12 is even because $12 \div 2 = 6$.)

event: 1 **possible outcome** of a **probability** experiment (e.g., When rolling a die, you could decide that rolling an even number, such as 2, 4, or 6, is an event.)

expanded form: A way to write a number that shows the value of each digit (e.g., In expanded form, 2365 is $2000 + 300 + 60 + 5$ or 2 thousands + 3 hundreds + 6 tens + 5 ones.)

 F

face: A 2-D shape that forms a flat surface of a 3-D shape

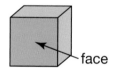

face

fact: An addition, subtraction, multiplication, or division **equation** (e.g., In grade 4, we learn multiplication facts to $9 \times 9 = 81$.)

fact

fact family: A set of addition and subtraction or multiplication and division facts; each fact uses the same numbers

$$3 \times 2 = 6 \qquad 6 \div 3 = 2$$
$$2 \times 3 = 6 \qquad 6 \div 2 = 3$$

factor: One of the numbers you multiply in a multiplication operation

$$2 \times 6 = 12$$

factor   factor

flip: A reflection of a shape across a line

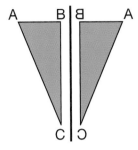

fraction: Numbers used to name part of a whole or part of a set
(e.g., $\frac{3}{4}$ is a **proper fraction**;

$\frac{4}{3}$ is an **improper fraction**;

0.2 is a **decimal** fraction;

$5\frac{1}{2}$ is a **mixed number**.

See also **numerator** and **denominator**.)

gram (g): A unit of measurement for **mass** (e.g., 1 mL of water has a mass of 1 g.); 1000 g = 1 kg

graph: A way of showing information so it is more easily understood. A graph can be concrete (e.g., boys in one line and girls in another), pictorial (e.g., pictures of boys in 1 row and girls in another), or abstract (e.g., 2 bars on a bar graph to show how many students are boys and how many are girls)

greater than (>): A sign used when comparing 2 numbers (e.g., 10 is greater than 5, or 10 > 5.)

halve: To divide a number by 2

heptagon: A polygon with 7 straight sides and 7 angles

hexagon: A **polygon** with 6 straight sides and 6 angles

horizontal line: A line across a page that is **parallel** to the bottom edge, or a line that is level with the floor

impossible outcome: A result that cannot occur (e.g., If you roll a die with a 3 on every face, rolling a 5 is an impossible outcome.)

improper fraction: A fraction in which the **numerator** is greater than the **denominator** (e.g., $\frac{4}{3}$)

interval: The distance between 2 endpoints on a graph scale; intervals in a graph should be equal (e.g., If the scale axis is numbered 0, 5, 10, 15, …, then the intervals are 5.)

kilogram (kg): A unit of measurement for **mass** (e.g., A math textbook has a mass of about 1 kg.); 1 kg = 1000 g

kilometre (km): A unit of measurement for **length**; one thousand metres; 1 km = 1000 m

kite: A quadrilateral that has 2 pairs of equal sides with no sides parallel

L

legend: A feature on a map or graph that explains what colours or symbols mean

length: The distance from one end of a **line segment** to the other end

The length of this line segment is 2 cm.

less than (<): A sign used when comparing 2 numbers (e.g., 5 is less than 10, or 5 < 10.)

like denominators: When the parts of 2 or more fractions are the same size (e.g., $\frac{3}{8}$ and $\frac{7}{8}$ have like denominators, eighths.)

likely outcome: A result that can easily occur (e.g., If you roll a die with a 3 on all the faces but one, rolling a 3 is a likely outcome.)

line of symmetry: The fold line that divides a 2-D shape into matching halves

line of
symmetry

linear pattern: A pattern in which the difference between each item and the next is always the same (e.g., 2, 4, 6, 8, 10, ... is linear because it always increases by 2.
98, 96, 94, 92, 90, ... is linear because it always decreases by 2.)

line segment: A piece of a line that has 2 **endpoints**

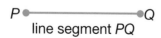

line segment *PQ*

litre (L): A unit of measurement for **capacity**; 1L = 1000 mL

M

mass: The amount of matter in an object (e.g., Common units of measurement are grams (g) and kilograms (kg).)

metre (m): A unit of measurement for **length** (e.g., 1 m is about the distance from a doorknob to the floor.);
1000 mm = 1 m; 100 cm = 1 m;
1000 m = 1 km

millennium: A unit of measurement for time; 1000 years

millilitre (mL): A unit of measurement for **capacity**; 1000 mL = 1 L

millimetre (mm): A unit of measurement for **length** (e.g., A dime is about 1 mm thick.);
10 mm = 1 cm, 1000 mm = 1 m

mixed number: A number made up of a **whole number** and a **fraction** (e.g., $3\frac{1}{2}$)

multiples: The products of a whole number when multiplied by any other whole numbers (e.g., When you multiply 10 by the whole numbers 0 to 4, you get the multiples 0, 10, 20, 30, and 40.)

N

net: A 2-D pattern you can fold to create a 3-D shape

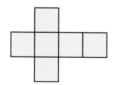

This is a net for a cube.

414

nonlinear pattern: A pattern in which the difference between each term and the next does not stay the same (e.g., 1, 3, 6, 10, 15, ... is nonlinear because the differences are 2, 3, 4, and so on.)

nonstandard unit: A unit of measurement that is not part of a customary system (e.g., A desk is about 5 juice cans wide.)

number line: A diagram that shows ordered numbers or points on a line

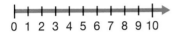

0 1 2 3 4 5 6 7 8 9 10

number sentence: A mathematical statement that shows how 2 quantities are related (e.g., 3 × 8 = 24; 3 < 8; See also **equation**.)

numeral: The written symbol for a number (e.g., 148, $\frac{3}{4}$, and 2.8)

numerator: The number in a **fraction** that shows how many parts of a given size the fraction represents. (See also **denominator**.)

$\frac{3}{4}$ ◀— numerator

octagon: A **polygon** with 8 straight sides and 8 angles

odd number: A number that has a remainder of 1 when it is divided by 2 (e.g., 15 is odd because 15 ÷ 2 = 7 R1.)

open sentence: A number sentence containing at least 1 unknown number (e.g., 2 × ■ = 8)

ordinal number: A way of describing an item's place in a numbered sequence (e.g., 1st, third, 15th)

organized list: The problem-solving strategy of following an order to find all possibilities

outcome: A single result (e.g., If you roll a die, the possible outcomes are 1, 2, 3, 4, 5, and 6; 7 is an impossible outcome.)

parallel: Always the same distance apart

parallelogram: A **quadrilateral** with equal and **parallel** opposite sides (e.g., A **rhombus**, a **rectangle**, and a **square** are all types of parallelograms.)

pattern: Something that follows a rule while repeating or changing

pattern rule: A description of how a pattern starts and how it can be extended

pentagon: A **polygon** with 5 straight sides and 5 angles

perimeter: The total length of the sides of a shape

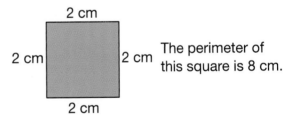

The perimeter of this square is 8 cm.

pictograph: A **graph** that uses pictures or symbols to represent quantities

How Old Are You?

7 ☺ ☺ ☺ ☺
8 ☺ ☺ ☺ ☺ ☺ ☺ ☺ ☺
9 ☺ ☺ ☺ ☺ ☺ ☺ ☺
10 ☺ ☺ ☺

Each ☺ means 5 people.

place value: The value given to a digit based on its position in a multi-digit number (e.g., The 3 in the number 237 represents 3 tens, while in the number 5.03 it represents 3 hundredths.)

polygon: A closed 2-D shape with sides made from straight lines

possible outcome: Any result that can occur (e.g., If you roll a die, the possible outcomes are 1, 2, 3, 4, 5, and 6.)

precision: A way to compare tools and measurements (e.g., A measurement made with a ruler divided in millimetres is more precise than a measurement made with a ruler divided in centimetres.)

prism: A 3-D shape with opposite **congruent bases**; the other faces are parallelograms (e.g., a triangle-based prism)

triangle base

triangle base

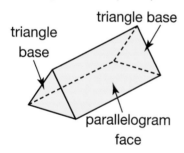

parallelogram face

probability: How likely it is that a particular result will occur

probability line: A way to show probabilities of several outcomes

impossible   certain

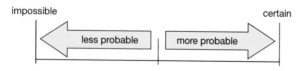

less probable   more probable

product: The result when you multiply

$$2 \times 6 = 12$$

product

proper fraction: A fraction in which the **denominator** is greater than the **numerator** $\left(\text{e.g., } \frac{1}{2}, \frac{5}{6}, \frac{2}{7}\right)$

protractor: A tool used to measure **angles**

pyramid: A 3-D shape with a polygon for a base; the other faces are triangles that meet at a single **vertex** (e.g., a rectangle-based pyramid)

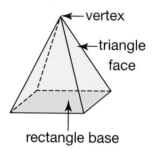

vertex

triangle face

rectangle base

quadrilateral: A closed shape with 4 straight sides and 4 angles (See also **kite**, **parallelogram**, **rectangle**, **rhombus**, **square**, **trapezoid**.)

quotient: The result when you divide, not including the **remainder**

$$12 \div 5 = 2 \text{ R2}$$

quotient

R

range: The **difference** between the greatest and least values in a set of data (e.g., For the numbers 1, 2, 5, 7, 9, 11, 12, the range is 12 − 1 or 11.)

rectangle: A **parallelogram** with 4 square corners

reflection: The result of a flip of a 2-D shape; each point in a 2-D shape flips to the opposite side of the line of reflection, but stays the same distance from the line (See also **transformation**.)

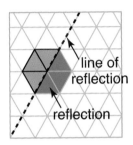

regroup: Trade 10 smaller units for 1 larger unit, or 1 larger unit for 10 smaller units

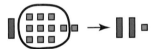

regular polygon: A closed, straight-sided 2-D shape with equal sides

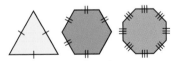

remainder: The number of items left over after division

$$14 \div 4 = 3 \text{ R2}$$

remainder

rhombus: A **parallelogram** with 4 equal sides

rotation: The result of turning a shape; each point in the shape must stay an equal distance from the **centre of rotation** (See also **transformation**.)

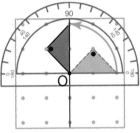

This is a 90° counterclockwise rotation about point O.

round: To approximate a number to a given place (e.g., 8327 rounded to the nearest hundred is 8300.)

row: A set of items lined up horizontally (See also **column**.)

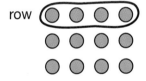

S

scale: Numbers and marks arranged at regular intervals that are used for measurement or to establish position (e.g., the markings on the side of a measuring cup or on the **axis** of a graph)

set: A collection of items or numbers; Each item in the set is called a "member" of the set

shape: 1. A geometric object (e.g., A square is a 2-D shape. A cube is a 3-D shape.) 2. The **attribute** that describes the form of a geometric object (e.g., Circles and spheres both have a round shape.)

side: One of the line segments that forms a polygon

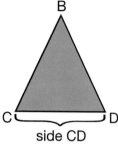

side CD

similar: Identical in shape, but not necessarily the same size (See also **congruent**.)

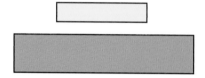

These are similar rectangles.

skeleton: A 3-D shape that has only edges and vertices

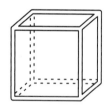

skip count: To count without using every number, but according to a set pattern or rule (e.g., counting to 100 by 5s)

slide: To move a shape left or right, up or down, without turning or flipping (See also **transformation** and **translation**.)

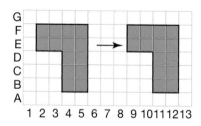

square: A **parallelogram** with 4 equal sides and 4 square corners

square centimetre: A unit of measurement for **area**; the area covered by a square with sides that are 1 cm long

square corner: A vertex of a shape that forms an angle of 90° (e.g., Squares and rectangles have 4 square corners.)

square metre: A unit of measurement for **area**; the area covered by a square with sides that are 1 m long

square unit: A nonstandard unit of measurement for **area**

standard form: The usual way in which we write numbers (e.g., 2365 is written in standard form. See also **expanded form** and **written form**.)

standard unit: A unit of measurement that is part of an accepted measurement system (e.g., metres, kilograms, litres, and square metres are all standard units.) (See also **nonstandard unit**.)

stem-and-leaf plot: A way to organize data in groups according to place value; The stem shows the beginning of a number and the leaf shows the rest of the number (e.g., The circled leaf in this stem-and-leaf plot represents the number 258.)

Stem	Leaves
24	1 5 8
25	2 2 3 4 7 ⑧ 9
26	0 3
27	
28	8

sum: The result when you add

$$14 + 37 = 51$$

↑
sum

survey: 1. A set of questions designed to obtain information directly from people 2. To ask a group of people a set of questions

2-D shape: A shape that has the dimensions of length and width

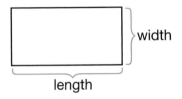

3-D shape: A shape that has the dimensions of length, width, and height

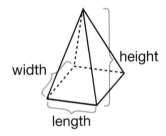

tally: A way to keep track of data using marks

~~HHt~~ ~~HHt~~ /

tally chart: A way to record tallies (e.g., If you are surveying students about favourite flavours of ice cream you could use a tally chart like this one.)

Favourite Ice Cream Flavours	
vanilla	~~HHt~~ ~~HHt~~ /
chocolate	~~HHt~~ ~~HHt~~ ~~HHt~~ ~~HHt~~ ///
strawberry	~~HHt~~

t-chart: A way to organize information; both sides of the T are labelled

Weeks	Days
1	7
2	14
3	21

tetrahedron: A 3-D shape with 4 **faces** that are **polygons**

transformation: The result of moving a shape according to a rule; transformations include **translations**, **rotations**, and **reflections**

translation: The result of a slide; the slide must be along straight lines, left or right, up or down (See also **transformation**.)

trapezoid: A **quadrilateral** with only 1 pair of **parallel** sides

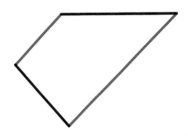

tree diagram: A way to record and count all combinations of **events** (e.g., This tree diagram shows all the 3-digit numbers that can be made from the digits 1, 2, and 3, if 1 must be the first digit and each digit is used only once.)

1 <2–3 (123)
3
2 (132)

triangle: A closed 2-D shape with 3 straight sides and 3 angles

turn: To move a shape around a turn centre (See also **transformation**.)

unlikely outcome: A result that has little chance of occurring (e.g., If you roll a die with a 3 on all the faces but one, rolling a number other than 3 is an unlikely outcome.)

Venn diagram: A way of showing the relationship(s) between collections of objects or numbers

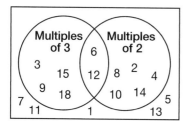

This Venn diagram shows that 6 and 12 are both **multiples** of 2 and multiples of 3.

vertex (plural is vertices): The point at the corner of an angle or a shape (e.g., A cube has 8 vertices. A cone has 1 vertex. An angle has 1 vertex.)

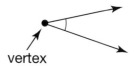

vertex

vertical line: A line that goes up and down a page parallel to the side edge, or straight up and down from the floor

volume: The amount of space occupied by an object

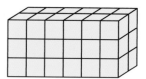

The volume of this box is 36 cubes.

whole numbers: The counting numbers that begin at 0 and continue forever; 0, 1, 2, 3, …

written form: The way a number is presented in words (e.g., In written form, 2365 is two thousand three hundred sixty-five.)

Index

0. *See* zero

100 charts. *See* hundred charts

Abbreviations, length units, 123

Acting out of problems, 196–197

Adding
and calculators, 10–11, 13, 90–91, 92–93
curious math, 21, 107
decimal hundredths, 112–113, 243, 344–345, 347
decimal tenths, 336–337, 341
and estimating, 90–91, 92–93
hidden digits (puzzles), 107
math game, 97, 103
mental math (decimals, money), 87, 110–111, 112–113, 243, 347
mental math (no decimals), 21, 37, 88–89, 167, 265
with middle number, 167
and multiplying by repeated addition, 148–149
and number lines, 88–89, 90–91
Pascal's triangle, 21
with place value charts, 94–96
sum-and-product puzzle, 237

Adding on
in making multiplication table, 164–166
in mental-math subtracting, 99

Angles
definition (by picture), 192
math game, 201
measuring, 192–193
in rotations, 386–387

Area
fractions of, 322–323, 324–325
math game, 217
measuring, 210–221
of pentomino, 225
of rectangle, from side lengths, 222–224
of rectangle, from square blocks, 226–227
units of measurement, 212, 214–215, 218–219

Arrays
chapter task, 178
definition, 154
and fact families, 154–155, 178, 263
models for (blocks, tiles), 158–159, 234–235
and multiplication, division facts, 154–155, 234–235
and simplification of multiplying, 238–239

Average, 283

Bar graphs
interpreting, 56–57, 68–69
interval for, 66–67
math game, 75
mistakes in, 68–69
scale for, 62–63

Base ten blocks
for adding, subtracting decimal tenths, 340–341
chapter task, 54
for division of whole numbers, 270–271, 280–281

for multiplying whole numbers, 236, 240–241, 246–247, 248–250
and number patterns, 18–19
and place value charts, 30–38
puzzle, 36, 54
for representing whole numbers, 28–38

Bead patterns, 2–3, 4–5, 380

Belt patterns, 380

Blocks and tiles. *See* base ten blocks; linking blocks; pattern blocks; probabilities

Calculators
adding, 10–11, 13, 90–91, 92–93
division-by-0 error, 161
and estimating, 90–91, 92–93
finding persistence of numbers, 237
math game based on, 13
multiplying, 252–253
and number patterns, 10, 13

Capacity
definition, 306
measuring, 306, 308–309

Centimetre. *See also* square centimetre (definition)
abbreviation, 123

Centre of rotation, 386

Century, 136–137

Certain, likely, ... events. *See* probabilities

Chains of numbers, 16–17

Change (money), 110–111, 112–113

Charts. *See* hundred charts; place value charts; tally (sorting) charts; t-charts

Regrouping. *See also* grouping
in adding, 88, 94–96
definition, 95
in division, 270–271,
280–281
in subtracting, 104–106,
108–109

Remainder
definition, 266
interpreting, 268
math game, 275

Representing numbers. *See*
base ten blocks

Rhombus
attributes of, 181
definition, 183
line of symmetry, 199
in puzzle pieces, 180–181
rotations, 387

Rotations
attributes of, 386–387
centre, 386
communicating clearly
about, 392–393
compared with reflections,
389
compared with
translations, 387
with computer, 394
definition, 386
of rhombus, 387
of square, 395
of triangle, 386–387,
392–393, 395

Rounding
and estimating, 87, 90–91
and measuring, 124–125
to nearest ten, hundred, ...,
42–43
and number line, 90–91

Rows. *See* arrays

Rulers. *See* measuring

Scale
for bar graphs, 62–63
for pictographs, 59

Set, fractions of, 328–329

Shadows of 3-D shapes, 299

Shape patterns. *See*
patterns, shape

Shapes, 2-D. *See* area;
congruent shapes (2-D);
heptagon (math game);
hexagon; kite; mental
imagery; models; octagon
(triangle pattern blocks);
parallelogram; pattern blocks;
pentomino; perimeter;
quadrilateral; rectangle;
reflections; rhombus;
rotations; similar shapes
(2-D); sorting; square;
symmetry, line of; tangram
quadrilateral; translations;
trapezoid; triangle

Shapes, 3-D. *See* capacity;
cross-sections; cube; edges
(3-D shapes); faces; mass;
mental imagery; prism;
pyramid; skeleton models;
solid models (3-D shapes);
tetrahedron; vertices; volume

Sharing. *See* grouping

Similar shapes (2-D). *See
also* congruent shapes (2-D)
definition, 188
examples, 188–189
testing (rectangles,
triangles), 190

Simplifying of problems
division, 278–279
multiplying, 238–239

**Skeleton models of 3-D
shapes,** 298–299

Software. *See* computers

Solid models (3-D shapes),
294, 297, 310–311

Sorting
of 2-D shapes, 181,
182–183, 200
to make a pattern, 2–3
and tally charts, 56–57, 64

Sorting charts. *See* tally
(sorting) charts

Spinners and probabilities
chapter task, 378
math game, 365
with sections equal,
360–361
with sections unequal,
365, 366–367, 368, 369,
372, 378

**Spreadsheets and
graphing,** 71

Square
area of, compared with
parallelogram, 213
definition, 183
in dot-paper diagram,
61, 198
as face in 3-D shapes, 296
on geoboard, 221
line of symmetry, 198
as part of 2-D shapes, 225,
226–227
rotations, 395

**Square centimetre
(definition),** 214

Square metre (definition), 218

Standard form, for writing
numbers. *See also* expanded
form, for writing numbers
definition, 32

Stem-and-leaf plots
definition (curious math), 65

**Stem-and-leaf plots
(curious math),** 65

**Straws, in modelling of
quadrilaterals,** 184

Subtracting
curious math, 107
decimal hundredths,
344–345
decimal tenths, 338–339,
341
division by repeated
subtraction, 266–267
and estimating, 102–103
hidden digits (puzzles), 107
math game, 103
mental math, 100–101,
112–113, 347

with place value charts, 104–106
and regrouping, 104–106, 108–109

Sum-and-product puzzle, 237

Sums. *See* adding

Surveys
chapter task, 82
communicating clearly about, 72–73
planning and conducting of, 74

Symmetry, line of
definition, 198
hexagon, 199
and Mira, 185, 198–199, 388–389
in tangram quadrilaterals, 185
in triangle, square, rectangle, ..., 198–199

Tables. *See also* multiplication table
tally (sorting) charts, 56–57

Tally (sorting) charts
and bar graphs, 56–57, 62–63
ranges in data, 64

Tangram quadrilateral, 185

T-charts and number patterns, 8, 10

Technology. *See* calculators; computers

Tenths. *See* decimal tenths

Tetrahedron, 302–303

Tiles and blocks. *See* base ten blocks; linking blocks; pattern blocks; probabilities

Time
on clocks, 123, 138–139
measuring, 123, 136–139
patterns with, 10, 123, 260

Time line, 137

Transformations. *See* reflections; rotations; translations

Translations
attributes of, 384–385
communicating clearly about, 392–393
compared with rotations, 387
with computer, 394
definition, 384
of trapezoid, 384–385
of triangle, 392–393

Trapezoid
definition, 183
and models with straws, 184
pattern blocks, 196–197, 381, 384–385
reflections, 388, 394
rotations, 394
translations, 384–385, 394

Travel. *See* distances

Tree diagrams
definition, 370
for probabilities, 370–371

Triangle
as face in 3-D shapes, 296
as part of hexagon, 195
as part of parallelogram, 195
perimeter of, 122–123
reflections, 389, 392–393
rotations, 386–387, 392–393, 395
similarity, through computer graphics, 188
translations, 392–393

Triangle, Pascal's, 21

Trips. *See* distances

Units of measurement
area, 212, 214–215, 218–219
capacity, 306–307, 308–309
length, 123–129, 133
mass, 305, 308–309
time, 136–139

Unlikely, likely events. *See* probabilities

Venn diagrams
interpreting, 57
and sorting of quadrilaterals, 183

Vertices
of 3-D shapes from squares, triangles, 296
of prism, pyramid,..., 293, 294, 295, 298–299

Volume
communicating clearly about, 318
definition, 310
estimating, 311
in models of 3-D shapes, 310–311

Years and days (patterns), 10, 260

Zero, multiplying and division, 161

428

Credits

Cover Image © Corbis/Magma

Chapter 2 Opener Page 27: © Gabriel Jecan/Corbis/Magma; Page 30: © Ken Wilson; Papilio/Corbis/Magma; Page 31: First Light; Page 33 top: © Jerry Cooke/Corbis/Magma, bottom: David Madison/Stone/Getty Images; Page 34: © AFP/Corbis/Magma; Page 40: Mike Johnson; Page 53: © Reuters New Media Inc./Corbis/Magma

Chapter 3 Page 58: Gotta Find a Footprint excerpted from BONE POEMS. Text copyright © 1997 by Jeff Moss. Used by permission of Workman Publishing Co., Inc., New York. All Rights Reserved; Page 71: Corbis/Magma

Chapter 4 Opener Page 85: © Kevin Fleming/Corbis/Magma; Page 86: © Michael Newman/Photo Edit; Page 93: First Light

Chapter 5 Page 136; Corel

Chapter 6 Opener Page 145: Eyewire/Getty Images; Page 166: Ryan McVay/PhotoDisc/Getty Images; Page 169: Corbis/Magma

Chapter 7 Opener Page 179: Gary Conner/Index Stock; Page 180: Corbis/Magma

Chapter 8 Opener Page 209: © David Zimmerman/Corbis/Magma

Chapter 9 Opener Page 233: © Canadian Museum of Civilization, photographer Harry Foster, 1988, image no. S89-1873; Page 239: © David Lees/Corbis/Magma; Page 244: Corbis/Magma; Page 246: Infocus International/Image Bank/Getty Images; Page 247 top: Corel, bottom: © Jim Winkley; Ecoscene/Corbis/Magma

Chapter 10 Page 278: Viktor Pivovarov/CP Picture Archive; Page 280: © Kevin R. Morris/Corbis/Magma; Page 286: Jules Frazier/PhotoDisc/Getty Images; Page 287: Russell Illiq/PhotoDisc; Page 288: David Young-Wolff/Photo Edit

Chapter 11 Opener Page 291: Courtesy of Levitt Architect Limited; Page 296: © James Davis; Eye Ubiquitous/Corbis/Magma; Page 298: First Light; Page 300: © Tony Freeman/Photo Edit; Page 303 both: Courtesy of Levitt Architect Limited; Page 305 left: Ryan McVay/PhotoDisc/Getty Images right: © David Young-Wolf Photo Edit; Page 309 1st row (i): Evan Sklar/Foodpix/Getty Images, right: © David Young-Wolff/Photo Edit; (ii): © Owaki-Kulla/Corbis/Magma, (iii): Nelson photo, 2nd row (i): PhotoDisc/Getty Images; (ii): C-Squared Studios/PhotoDisc/Getty Images, (iii): PhotoLink/PhotoDisc/Getty Images, 3rd row (i): Nelson photo, (ii): © Kevin R. Morris/Corbis/Magma, (iii): Corbis/Magma, 4th row (i): Great American Stock/IndexStock, (ii): First Light, (iii) Corel; Page 317: HIRB/Index Stock

Chapter 12 Opener Page 321: © Ron Watts/Corbis/Magma; Page 334: First Light; Page 338: Oxford Scientific Films; Page 339 top: W. Perry Conway/Corbis/Magma, bottom: Digital Vision/Getty Images; Page 340: © W. Perry Conway/Corbis/Magma; Page 341 top: S. Charles Brown, Frank Lane Picture Agency/ Corbis/Magma, bottom: © Ron Austing; Frank Lane Picture Agency/Corbis/Magma; Page 344: © John B. Boykin/Corbis/Magma

Chapter 14 Page 379: © Bonnie Kamin/Photo Edit; Page 406 top: © Buddy Mays/Corbis/Magma, centre: Gail Shumway/Taxi/Getty Images, bottom: First Light

fon Home work
foor Home wort